PHR®/SPHR®
Exam
FOR
DUMMIES®
A Wiley Brand

by
Sandra M. Reed, SPHR, PHR

PHR®/SPHR® Exam For Dummies®

Published by
John Wiley & Sons, Inc.,
111 River Street,
Hoboken, NJ 07030-5774,
www.wiley.com

Copyright © 2016 by John Wiley & Sons, Inc., Hoboken, New Jersey

Published simultaneously in Canada

For general information on our other products and services, please contact our Customer Care Department within the U.S. at 877-762-2974, outside the U.S. at 317-572-3993, or fax 317-572-4002. For technical support, please visit www.wiley.com/techsupport.

Wiley publishes in a variety of print and electronic formats and by print-on-demand. Some material included with standard print versions of this book may not be included in e-books or in print-on-demand. If this book refers to media such as a CD or DVD that is not included in the version you purchased, you may download this material at http://booksupport.wiley.com. For more information about Wiley products, visit www.wiley.com.

Library of Congress Control Number: 2015938260

ISBN 978-1-118-60362-8 (pbk); ISBN 978-1-118-72291-8 (ebk); ISBN 978-1-118-72290-1 (ebk)

Manufactured in the United States of America

10 9 8 7 6 5 4 3 2 1

Contents at a Glance

Table of Contents

Introduction

I wrote this book for the all HR professionals who are intent on leaving no stone unturned on their quest for the PHR or SPHR designation. It rounds out the edges of the preparation process, seeking to keep you on track and focused on the steps necessary to pass.

PHR/SPHR Exam For Dummies also is a reminder that it's not about what you know at this stage in the process, but rather what you don't know that requires your full attention.

This book is for the tenacious and the curious and the self-deprecating, possibly because I find humility an attractive trait in individuals getting ready for a tough test. Those traits can keep your mind open and eyes alert. Resolute curiosity can force you to grab a thread and follow it all the way to the end, which is the absolute best way to master and apply the information that you're about to discover while getting ready for these exams.

About This Book

The focus of *PHR/SPHR Exam For Dummies* is to orient you, the experienced HR professional to the task at hand: getting ready to become professionally certified. With pass rates low and nerves high, this guidebook takes you on your preparation journey, serving as a resource to get you organized and introduce you to key elements of these tests. In no other preparation resource will you find

- An advanced discussion of the exam bodies of knowledge (BOK) and their importance
- A review of how the knowledge and objectives work together
- Information on how to use the Internet to enhance your efforts
- A study of the HR Certification Institute's (HRCI) website (www.hrci.org) and the exam BOK for content markers

Furthermore, adult learners tend to do better when they understand how information applies to them. In this case, taking a 50,000-foot view of key exam concepts and exam preparation activities allows you to take control of the exam prep process. As with anything worth doing, a haphazard, unstructured approach to preparation won't serve a positive outcome. Just as a true career isn't an accident, neither is successful certification — it takes both planning and strategic execution.

The primary purpose of your exam preparation activities is to successfully pass a fairly difficult test. For this reason, I include two sample tests in this book — one for the PHR and one for the SPHR. Similar to the exam that you'll see on test day, 175 questions and content are directly related to the content of the exams. Although I provide bubble sheets for easy use, consider also putting your answers on a blank piece of paper so you can use the tests again.

Foolish Assumptions

Assumptions are simply things that I think I already know about you, my dear reader, that guided my decisions on what to include in this book. For the PHR and SPHR exams, they are as follows:

- ✔ You're an experienced HR professional. Because exam eligibility is based on years of practical experience, even with a bit of education, I know that you know the basics of HR.

- ✔ You're preparing for an exam, not looking for *HR in a jar*. This book is about what you need to do to prepare to take a test about HR. It doesn't teach you all you need to know about the field of human resources. In fact, the purpose of this book is to guide you to multiple resources for exam preparation.

- ✔ You have a baseline knowledge of business and management principles. Corporate America, small businesses, and nonprofits all have shared HR and business needs. I assume that you're a working professional in one of these categories and understand business terms such as *strategy* and *organizational structure*.

- ✔ You know how to conduct an Internet research. So much of what you need to pass the tests can be found online, and I encourage you throughout the book to do so.

Probably the most impressive assumption I make about you is that you're self-motivated, driven, and determined. Successful performers aren't generally satisfied with the status quo. If you're reaching out to take one of these tests, you're among those individuals that demand more out of themselves and by extension, your preparation resources. For this reason in this book, I recommend adding study time, admonish you to take an expanded view of a topic, and encourage you to create other dimensions to the content. You must find it and touch it and interpret it yourself to fully grasp the nuances of the exam content. This process requires that you take control of your study time and resources. Leaving it to a single author or only your past work experience isn't enough to get you through. I need you to tap into that drive and commit to doing what it takes to pass the first time around, or at least be a heck of a lot better for it after the process.

Icons Used in This Book

Consistent with the *For Dummies* series are the use of special icons. They serve as markers for information that may be of increased importance or interesting. I incorporate the following icons:

In general, I use this icon when you have a special opportunity to apply a behavior in its easiest form. In most cases, a tip can save you both time and energy, building upon the experience of those individuals who have gone before you.

I use this icon to reinforce an important principle. Pay attention to this information because it's important.

This icon directs you to some examples of the types of questions that appear on the PHR and SPHR exams. It also gives you examples of how the content may be represented in the workplace.

Beyond This Book

In addition to the content of this book, you can access some related material online. You can access a free Cheat Sheet at www.dummies.com/cheatsheet/phrsphrexam that contains additional information about the exam. You can also access some additional helpful bits of information at www.dummies.com/extras/phrsphrexam. For example, you can read an online Part of Tens to whet your appetite. Find excellent information on the first ten days of your preparation activities or the top ten smartphone apps to help you prepare. Access the online articles giving you the perspectives of an exam prep author, or tips to selecting the right exam. Doing so helps you choose your starting place.

An added feature to the online content are two additional exams to support your learning. Taking multiple practice exams is an absolute must as you get ready for several reasons:

- ✔ The exam level of difficulty requires that you're familiar with question phrasing and multiple choice setup. Keep in mind that these questions, also called *items*, can be highly situational. Taking practice exams can remove that element of surprise.

- ✔ Answer distractors are common obstacles to a passing score. My online practice exams help condition your brain to recognize and eliminate the obvious wrong answers, increasing your chance of making a correct selection.

- ✔ The online practice tests include a description of the right and wrong answers, which makes the practice exams extremely valuable, because they're much more than another bank of questions. Taking these exams also helps you master content.

The general recommendation is that you can't take too many practice assessments, and this book plus the online content is an excellent place to start. You can find the practice exams at www.dummies.com/go/phrsprhexam.

To gain access to additional tests and practice online, all you have to do is register. Just follow these simple steps:

1. **Find your PIN access code:**

   - **Print-book users:** If you purchased a print copy of this book, turn to the inside front cover of the book to find your access code.

   - **E-book users:** If you purchased this book as an e-book, you can get your access code by registering your e-book at www.dummies.com/go/getaccess. Go to this website, find your book and click it, and answer the security questions to verify your purchase. You'll receive an email with your access code.

2. **Go to Dummies.com and click Activate Now.**

3. **Find your product (*PHR/SPHR Exam For Dummies*) and then follow the on-screen prompts to activate your PIN.**

Now you're ready to go! You can come back to the program as often as you want — simply log on with the username and password you created during your initial login. No need to enter the access code a second time.

For Technical Support, please visit http://wiley.custhelp.com or call Wiley at 800-762-2974 (U.S.), 317-572-3994 (international).

Where to Go from Here

One of the reasons why preparing for this exam has been reported to be difficult is because of the sheer volume of reading that is required. This book can help a bit with all that reading. This book is modular in that you don't have to read it in order from cover to cover. Feel free to pick and choose the bits that you think will serve you best.

I wrote it so that you can pick any chapter and begin reading. To the ordered mind, doing so may be an unusual prospect, so go ahead and proceed in chapter order — the content will bear up to the pressure. For those of you who are only interested in certain exam elements, you have come to the right place. Feel free to bounce around or even begin with the end by starting with a practice exam and simply see how you fare. That may highlight for you a correct starting point for your unique preparation needs.

If you need some help in finding somewhere to begin, scan the table of contents or the index, find a few topics that interest you, and jump in.

Regardless of where you begin, the absolute *first* and most important step is to build a study plan. This book is full of useful tips and information to fill in the blanks of a plan, so maximize your investment by taking heed and writing down your plans. What gets measured gets done, so strengthen your odds by getting organized.

Part I
Getting Started with the PHR/SPHR Exam

getting started
with

PHR/SPHR

Exam

Visit www.dummies.com/cheatsheet/phrsphrexam for a free Cheat Sheet that provides more important reminders and tips about signing up for the PHR or SPHR.

In this part . . .

✔ Get a firm grasp of the structure for the PHR and SPHR so that you can begin to prepare a plan of attack to study for the exam.

✔ Figure out the exam eligibility to ensure that you're qualified to take the right exam.

✔ Know how to talk to your boss about taking the test and how you may persuade her to pay for the test.

✔ Select proper resources so you maximize your study efforts and have access to what you need to know in preparing for a passing score.

✔ Identify the different types of questions on the PHR and SPHR in order to be able to figure out the best way to answer them.

✔ Familiarize yourself with the ins and outs of test day to make sure that you show up ready to go.

Chapter 1

Introducing the PHR/SPHR Exam: Just the Basics, Please

Preparing to sit for either the PHR or SPHR exam means that you're investing in yourself through professional certification to differentiate your talent from the rest of the pack. It indicates a professional curiosity and commitment to excellence that characterizes the HR profession. In fact, the PHR and the SPHR remain two of the most sought-after designations in the HR industry.

The reasons to become certified are many. Personally, you may be seeking validation of your knowledge and competencies. Professionally, you may desire more job responsibilities or pay increases. Regardless of your reasons, earning the initials to place next to your name is the mark of a skilled and competent professional. This chapter serves as your launch pad to the rest of the book and your journey toward the title.

PHR or SPHR: Which Exam Is Right for You

One of the first decisions you'll have to make is which exam to take. The Human Resource Certification Institute (HRCI) offers six accredited designations in the field of human resources. The institute's generalist certificates are the Professional in Human Resources (PHR) and the Senior Professional in Human Resources (SPHR).

The PHR exam is recommend for individuals with a broad knowledge of the operational side of the HR house whereas the SPHR exam is more suited toward individuals with a background in strategic HR management. Possibly the most common eliminator is that you must have a minimum years of *exempt-level* experience in order to qualify to take the tests, which means that your HR roles have been qualified by job duties to be paid as a professional (non-hourly).

You don't need a college degree in human resources to be exam eligible to take the PHR and SPHR.

HRCI's Certification Handbook identifies the ideal profile of a PHR and SPHR candidate, which is definitely worth a review while you're making your decision. Table 1-1 gives you a sample of that information.

Table 1-1	Ideal Traits for PHR and SPHR Candidates
PHR	**SPHR**
The candidate reports to another HR professional.	The candidate is responsible for the HR function at the company, either independently or with staff.
The candidate's job responsibilities impact the function of HR rather than the company as a whole.	The candidate manages the relationships necessary to achieve organizational outcomes, including with employees and within departments.
The candidate doesn't have progressive HR experience due to length of time in the industry.	The candidate understands both general business principles and industry specific conventions (both HR and their company industries).

The Cheat Sheet at www.dummies.com/cheatsheet/phrsphrexam is your go-to resource to help you pick the right test. It includes information related to all the exam eligibility requirements and assessing the amount of time you have available to study.

Comparing the two exams

Taking the right exam has an effect on more than simply making the preparation process less stressful. Choosing the appropriate test also can impact your future job and earnings potential. Think about applying for an upper level HR job that requires exposure, experience, and problem-solving in business management and strategy that may be validated by the SPHR credential. Suppose that you squeak by the SPHR exam and are successfully certified. If you get the job based on an SPHR credential but don't have the depth and breadth of practical experience that goes along with it, more than likely you'll struggle in the role. Taking the right exam also allows you to engage in the proper recertification activities.

The professional certification process is an investment in your career, not a one-time shot at a credential. Starting with the PHR is perfectly reasonable. You can get the baseline under your belt and then chase after the SPHR in the following year or two over another period of 12 to 14 weeks of studying. The knowledge gained by studying has served many HR professionals well time and time again, opening doors that would have never opened without the credentials.

Each exam has its own eligibility requirements. Take a look at Table 1-2 to make sure you meet the minimum requirements for your exam of choice.

Just because you can doesn't mean that you should. For example, just because you have 20 years of experience as a recruiter doesn't necessarily mean that you're ready to take the SPHR exam.

A general rule: Use the HRCI's years of experience qualifier and apply it to the top three areas of exam content, which looks something like this:

Table 1-2	Figuring Out Which Exam Is Right
PHR	**SPHR**
A minimum of one year of experience in a professional-level HR position with a master's degree or higher.	A minimum of four years of experience in a professional-level HR position with a master's degree or higher.
or	or
A minimum of two years of experience in a professional-level HR position with a bachelor's degree.	A minimum of five years of experience in a professional-level HR position with a bachelor's degree
or	or
A minimum of four years of experience in a professional-level HR position with less than a bachelor's degree.	A minimum of seven years of experience in a professional-level HR position with less than a bachelor's degree.

Check out HRCI's Guide to Professional Level Experience to further assess your exam readiness.

✔ **PHR:** For the PHR, 63 percent of the exam content for the PHR is in the areas of Workforce Planning and Employment (24 percent), Employee Labor Relations (20 percent), and Compensation and Benefits (19 percent). Aim for the minimum years of experience requirements in *each* of these top three areas. For example, if you have a master's degree, you should be fine if you have one year of experience in workforce planning and employment, labor relations, and compensation and benefits.

✔ **SPHR:** For the SPHR, 66 percent of the exam content is in the areas of Business Management and Strategy (30 percent), HR Development (19 percent), and Workforce Planning and Employment (17 percent). This information translates for someone without a bachelor's degree as seven years of experience in each of these top functional areas. Yes, it's 21 years, and yes, the exam content will demand it of you.

If this information seems to be excessive, at minimum, aim for the number one area of content in the minimum experience requirements.

Don't quickly dismiss these percentages as overkill. Take a moment and look at the exam pass rates or read the online forums of failed exam takers condemning HRCI for exam level difficulty. Consider just for a moment that *diluting the exam value* by making it easier is less effective than individuals simply *choosing the right exam* the first time. It's also worth noting that professional exams for attorneys and accountants share similar levels of difficulty. Do you take your profession seriously?

Head to www.dummies.com/extras/phrsphrexam for additional information about why people seek PHR or SPHR certification.

Making your decision: Certification is a journey, not an event

Many individuals believe that if they meet the SPHR exam eligibility requirements, then they should start there. However, this assumption is both important and dangerous for three reasons:

✔ If you take the SPHR and fail it the first time around, you'll have to pay a second exam fee to take it again. Starting with the PHR makes more sense. You gather your baseline knowledge in your brain and then can go round two with the SPHR on firm ground.

Passing the PHR first and then taking the SPHR is a much better use of two exam fees, and most importantly, it spreads your learning out over an extended period of time, which impacts long-term retention for career application. At the end of the day, career progression really is the point of putting you through the process.

✔ Depending on the amount of time that you have available to study, reaching for the SPHR first may make for an unnecessarily stressful exam preparation process. Unless you have unlimited time to study and very few other obligations such as work and family, spreading your certification over two exam windows is perfectly reasonable.

✔ Rome wasn't built in a day, and neither is your career. Both exams require recertification credits with a goal of lifelong learning. Instead of recertifying your PHR exam with webinars and classes, take the time to study and successfully pass the SPHR exam. Renewal, refreshment, and most importantly, *relevance* are the keys to a successful career in HR, and this path allows for all three.

If you want more information about the recertification process after you pass the PHR or SPHR Exam, check out www.dummies.com/extras/phrsphrexam.

Still undecided? Taking practice tests

The best way to know where you stand is to invest in a couple of practice exams, which are designed to assess your level of knowledge before any studying or preparation has occurred. Don't worry if you don't completely pass the practice test; passing on your first or second time isn't the goal. The purpose is to measure where you are at so you can anticipate what it will take to get you to a passing score for either exam and what subject materials you need to spend time studying.

If you're truly undecided, take both a PHR and an SPHR practice test and compare scores. This investment is worthwhile and may very well have the answer that you're searching for. At the very least, you'll now be ready to create a study plan that targets your low scores.

You can find a practice PHR test in Chapter 13 and an SPHR test in Chapter 15. (Chapter 14 provides the answer explanations for the practice PHR test and the SPHR answer explanations in Chapter 16.) You can also find PHR and SPHR practice tests online at www.dummies.com/go/phrsphrexam.

Knowing What to Expect on the Exams

Anticipation is often worse than the actual experience, which seems to hold particularly true for both the PHR and SPHR exam day. The chapters in Part I are all about sharing with you what to expect on the big day. These sections give you a quick overview.

Looking at the exams' structure and types of questions

Both exams have questions that are written by certified HR professionals, not academics. HRCI correlates exam scores to the years of experience that are required for the tests, which is in part to justify the need for practical work experience for a successful test. Furthermore, as part of the accreditation process, the exam content is validated to the exam bodies of knowledge (BOK). The exam's BOK are based on an analysis of the HR field as a whole. Test questions are written to the exam specifications to validate the relevance of each question.

Chapter 3 discusses the exam structure, including a review of the different types of test questions. Although all test items are multiple choice with four possible options, each question may be worded differently. The exams include scenario, direct, and fill-in-the-blank questions.

Grasping how the exams are scored

Many test takers are really only concerned with passing or failing, which is fine. Students must have a total scaled score of 500 to pass these exams.

However, the exams have two types of scores that affect what you need to pass:

- ✔ **Raw:** The *raw score* is the actual number of items answered correctly on your test.

- ✔ **Scaled:** The *scaled score* represents the difficulty level of the random exam you received.

There are thousands of PHR and SPHR test questions. You only have to answer 175 of them. You may receive 175 of the questions that are rated as difficult whereas the person next to you may receive 175 of the fairly easy ones. That means that you'll be allowed some wiggle room while still needing to achieve the scaled score of 500 in order to pass. It's an exercise in fairness.

Don't leave a question unanswered. Scoring is based on the number of correct answers, so leaving an item blank — even if it's an educated guess — eliminates the possibility of that item counting in your scaled score. Refer to Chapter 3 for some strategies about guessing on the PHR and SPHR exams.

Preparing to Tackle the Exam

Very few individuals take this test with no preparation. The degree to which you prepare is based on your unique work experience and education. They include the following (Chapter 2 discusses these factors in greater detail):

- ✔ **Study plans:** A study plan is a tool that you design. It's a written plan of attack that addresses the things that make you unique — your specific strengths and weaknesses and the amount of time you have available to study — which means that you'll need to have a general idea of your exam date and assessment scores. I'm not a fan of absolute statements, but I make an exception here: Successful test takers *must* have a written plan of attack. Get organized and stay organized to ensure that you don't miss studying critical exam content.

- ✔ **Practice exams:** You can't possibly know the extent of your strengths and weaknesses without taking a sample test. You may be as knowledgeable as any other successful candidate, but applying that knowledge takes preparation. The practice tests are the tool that you can use to accomplish it.

- ✔ **Study groups:** Another option for getting ready for the exam is by joining a study group. You can join a study group, either through a college campus or independently. Chapter 2 discusses the pros and cons of this support option.

HRCI generally recommends that you use multiple preparation resources to study for the exam. For this reason, have a preparation resource specific to your exam and then surround yourself with other resources that can take you deeper into the content. In each of the Part III chapters, I suggest numerous websites that can help you begin your research.

Tackling the 24 Hours before, during, and after the Exam

Regardless of how long you prepare for the exam, nothing is quite like the trio — the day before, the day of, and the day after the exam day.

✔ **Before the test:** You'll need to be make many decisions in advance of the 24 hours before test day. For example, some individuals prefer to book a hotel room near the exam facility, which minimizes the possibility of heavy traffic and allows for a quiet evening before to review. Regardless of your decision, in the 24 hours before your test, turn off the cell phone, TV, and other distractions, and concentrate on a relaxed state of mind. Make sure that you get a good night's rest.

✔ **On exam day:** Exam day basics should focus on stamina. Sitting in a small room for a few hours while your brain is drained isn't an easy task. Distractors such as fatigue and hunger are real threats to success. For this reason having a plan of attack before you're faced with the conditions is helpful. Chapter 4 discusses more strategies on taking breaks and eating snacks to keep you focused.

✔ **After the test:** I'm confident that you'll feel a sense of relief as you answer the last question. In some cases, you may have marked questions for review and will need to go back and finish them before you cross the finish line. If you fail the exam, a more detailed score report will be mailed to you so you can see how close you were and in what functional areas you didn't pass. Regardless of a pass or fail score, you have just spent several weeks immersing yourself in the world of HR. Refer to Chapter 5 information on how to apply your knowledge on the job.

At the end of the day, you are a unique individual with individual needs, and no one-size-fits-all solution exists to how well you manage before, during, and after the test. Some students swear by cramming the night before whereas others say doing so confused them. Eating a large meal before the test was impossible for some, whereas others knew that low blood sugar during the exam would sink them. Knowing your needs and extracting advice that meets those needs is the purpose of these discussions so that you can be at maximum performance level when it counts.

On exam day, you don't need a calculator. Most math-related questions are written to be easily calculated. Don't worry though. If you prefer a calculator, one is available on the desktop computer from which you take your exam.

Examining the Core Subject Areas on the Exam

Both exams share functional areas in terms of content, but you need to know what to do with this information in order for it to serve you. Similar to the test questions, you must be able to apply the knowledge to be successful. The exams have six functional areas, in addition to the core knowledge requirements. These sections provide a brief overview of what you can expect about the core knowledge and functional areas of the PHR and SPHR exams. I include chapter references to help you apply them.

SPHR test questions are highly scenario-based and require the ability to integrate information from *all* of these functional areas in your analysis.

Functional area 01 — Business Management and Strategy

If you're taking the SPHR exam, your main focus should be Business Management and Strategy. If you're a PHR candidate, don't ignore this subject. Study this functional area from the perspective of strategy. For example, explore how operations can contribute to an organization's strategic plan or how industry changes affect a company's ability to compete. Chapter 7 breaks down these concepts and more, giving you the keys to unlock this important function.

Functional area 02 — Workforce Planning and Employment

The functional area of Workforce Planning and Employment carries quite the punch on both exams, making up more than 30 questions on both tests. Although heavily oriented toward recruiting, selection, and labor law compliance, it also delves into the application of "employees are assets" business practice. Be prepared to discover about recruitment strategies, job descriptions, and more as you navigate this exam area. Chapter 8 explains the ins and outs of this subject area.

Functional area 03 — Human Resource Development

Human Resource Development is about more than just training workers. Tied closely to organizational development, it expands upon the idea that training and performance management will help organizations meet both current and future needs. Among the exam objectives expect to see HR behaviors such as executive coaching, career development, and organizational theories/application. You can read more about this subject area in Chapter 9.

Functional area 04 — Compensation and Benefits

Labor costs are often the top expense for organizations, so executing this function well is the focus of Compensation and Benefits. Successful exam takers must be able to develop, implement, and evaluate the effectiveness of employer compensation and benefits plans while staying compliant with the vast area of labor law related to this topic. Studying this exam area can teach you about cash and noncash compensation methods, budgeting and accounting practices for payroll, and for SPHR candidates, a good dose of executive compensation plans and challenges. Check out Chapter 10 to get a good feel for what you need to know about this subject area for the PHR and SPHR exams.

Functional area 05 — Employee and Labor Relations

Not just union management anymore, this functional area has evolved to the management of all relationships in the workplace. Coming at the content from that perspective can enable to you to identify factors that determine whether a relationship is good or bad, which includes gathering feedback from workers and addressing their complaints when necessary. The flip side of that coin is embracing their hard work through recognition and special events, keeping them involved and harnessing their talent for maximum effect. Head to Chapter 11 for more information about this subject area.

Functional area 06 — Risk Management

Knowing that this functional area long ago was titled Workplace Safety and Health should help you understand what is at the core of Risk Management. This exam content is highly oriented toward identifying and addressing risks to the human, physical, and financial assets of a business. With workplace violence, cyber attacks, and a global customer base, this exam content is filled with the need for plans and policies to address 21st-century issues. Chapter 12 gives you the lowdown of this subject area.

Remembering the Core Knowledge Requirements

No discussion of exam content would be complete without a snapshot of the core knowledge requirements (CKR). Chapter 6 provides you with a complete list of these requirements and goes into more detail about how to utilize this roadmap to the exam content. It's important to note two things about the CKR:

- ✔ You can read and organize it as a stand-alone document for studying, which is why it's numbered consecutively.
- ✔ HRCI's BOK document sorts them by functional area to support your studying of the exam objectives.

The CKR is an excellent place to begin to organize your study plan and launch your preparation efforts.

Understanding That You Can't Be Taught the Exam

HRCI makes no secret that these exams can't be taught. Yet individuals who fail the exams gnash their teeth and wail loudly, wondering how they're supposed to prepare for an exam that has no precise preparation resource. Thinking this way is unfair and unrealistic perspective, because of the following reasons:

- ✔ **The exam is deeply experience based.** Writing a study guide that gauges every exam taker's level of experience and breaks down the content into the right size piece for everyman's palette is impossible. It comes down to quantity versus quality. Having the right number of years of experience doesn't guarantee that you'll pass. The quality, depth, and breadth of the experience get you an invitation to the certified members' lounge.
- ✔ **The exam isn't about rote memorization and to suggest that it must become so is diluting the value for those professionals who are certified and the profession as a whole.** Dumbing it down into memorizable pieces mocks the profession, because it doesn't translate into practice. Imagine binding HR professionals to textbook answers

and one-size-fits-all strategies. C-suite executives would take one cross-eyed look at that approach and go rogue, exposing businesses to risk and devaluing an HR professional's role. Talk about why executives avoid HR! This approach damages HR's credibility and effectiveness.

✔ **The homework, research, and creative studying methods make you a better HR practitioner.** You'll come out of the preparation trial-by-fire well-seasoned and tempered to be the business partner that your enterprise needs. Unless you hope to go back to party planning and payroll, jump on the bandwagon and dig deep. These exams aren't for the faint at heart.

✔ **Just because you fail doesn't mean that you aren't good at your job.** You may not be a good test taker. The testing room may have been too hot. Perhaps you aced one area, but you need more rounding out in others. Toughen up and try again. As an HR professional, you need to be the model of perseverance for those impacted by your talent, and inflating your ability or transferring blame serves no one. Having a do-over is okay. Review how far you came in terms of knowledge before you began preparing compared to test day. Growth is happening, so believe that with another few months of studying those initials shall be by your name as well. And guess what — you'll have earned the certification.

My exam journey

Making the decision to become professionally certified certainly helps your career, but the decision is also highly personal. Fear of failure, fear of success, and worry about the exam level difficulty are a host of pitfalls that may keep you from being successful. I hope my own journey can help you in your journey.

I left the world of full-time HR the day my son was born and began teaching classes at night. I realized that to be credible, I needed to at minimum get my PHR certification. Back in the days of the pencil and paper test, I self-studied with a group, sat for the exam, and passed after waiting six weeks for the results.

Fast forward four years, pregnant with my daughter, I found out that I was being laid off from my teaching position. I worried a bit at the time because I didn't have any sort of college degree, and I felt that I wouldn't be a competitive candidate in the market. I remembered that the process of getting certified the first time renewed my interest and taught me so much more about HR, so I decided to go the SPHR route while my final students were finishing their program. I self-studied again, this time with the Internet. My exam date was right around Christmas, and I remember how nervous I was while listening to my audio recordings as I drove to the hotel in the city where my testing center was located. I crammed the night before and remember sitting on the bed surrounded by my books, papers, and flashcards.

I felt guilty for being away from home and completely unprepared, despite my studying efforts over the last 12 weeks. I had my "ah-ha" moment right then and there, when suddenly the processes began to make sense. The common denominators declared themselves, and the information linking functional area to functional area took shape. I sat for the SPHR exam the next morning, finishing an hour early and passed on the first try. Now I just needed to do something with the credential.

Although I had a strong desire to stay home with my kids, I wanted and needed to put my newfound knowledge to use. So when I found that the Society for Human Resource Management (SHRM) accepted proposals for case studies and learning modules, I jumped on it, having three projects accepted and published. I began HR consulting as a sideline and soon started writing test-prep books about the exams.

The PHR and SPHR certifications allowed me to pursue my passion while still living the life that I loved with my children who are now 9 and 13 years old. Certification has validated my talent and opened doors that would have firmly remained closed without it. So, you can worry about the pass rates and the time commitment and continue to put you and career second to all of the other important things in your life or you can seize the tiger by the tail and go for it.

Chapter 2

Preparing for the Exam

. . . .

In This Chapter

▶ Anticipating the content of the PHR and SPHR exams

▶ Benefitting from practice exams

▶ Putting together a study plan

▶ Making the decision to participate in a study group

▶ Asking your employer to pay for certification

. . . .

All exams aren't created equal nor all exam takers the same. Hence, you must consider both the exam selection and your individual skill set when preparing for the PHR or the SPHR.

"Pass it ugly" is a term I use to remind overachievers that they don't need to ace this exam. All they have to do is pass it. Having a comprehensive study plan is critical when preparing for the exam because it ensures that you focus on the right things, not necessarily on all things.

Focusing on the right things begins by anticipating exam content, comparing the content to your individual assessment results, and accessing resources that are uniquely suited to your exam readiness.

This chapter discusses tips, tricks, and best practices that take into account your unique ability and resource availability and how you can get organized for maximum effect. As with all things HR, proper planning is the first activity leading to ultimate success.

Considering Exam Weights by Functional Area

Weighting the exam content allows the test builders to rank information in the order of importance. Exam weights are expressed as percentages — the higher the percentage, the more important the information. The following sections take a closer look at how much the different functional areas are worth on the two exams.

For example, the functional area of Business Management and Strategy weighs in at approximately 30 percent of the content of the SPHR exam, making it a top priority for SPHR exam takers. PHR candidates should pay special attention to the category of Workforce Planning and Employment, which is 24 percent of that exam.

Ignore this critical exam feature at your peril, because the weights tell you exactly where you should spend the bulk of your study time, regardless of your test selection.

Both the PHR and the SPHR exams have the same body of knowledge (BOK) with identical exam objectives. That means that you must be prepared to see similar content on both exams. Although both exams have 175 questions, they each place different emphasis on the exam objectives. See Table 2-1 for the exam weights sorted by functional area for the two exams. For example, the PHR exam has 24 percent of its questions devoted to Workforce Planning and Employment, which is approximately 42 questions.

Table 2-1	PHR and SPHR Exam Weights			
Functional Area	*Exam Weight — SPHR*	*Number of Questions SPHR*	*Exam Weight — PHR*	*Number of Questions PHR*
Business Management and Strategy	30 percent	53	11 percent	19
Workforce Planning and Employment	17 percent	30	24 percent	42
Human Resource Development	19 percent	33	18 percent	32
Compensation and Benefits	13 percent	23	19 percent	33
Employee and Labor Relations	14 percent	25	20 percent	35
Risk Management	7 percent	12	8 percent	14

Note: The core knowledge requirements are the seventh studying area. These concepts exist and apply throughout all of the preceding objectives, but they aren't necessarily stand-alone.

If you're on an accelerated study schedule or just want to brush up on the salient points, take a look at Table 2-2 that shows you the three functional areas that make up more than 50 percent of the PHR and the SPHR exam.

Table 2-2	The Top Three Functional Areas		
PHR	*Functional Area*	*Exam Weight*	*Number of Questions*
	Workforce Planning and Employment	24 percent	42
	Employee and Labor Relations	20 percent	35
	Compensation and Benefits	19 percent	33
Total		63 percent	110/175 questions
SPHR	*Functional Area*	*Exam Weight*	*Number of Questions*
	Business Management and Strategy	30 percent	53
	Workforce Planning and Employment	17 percent	30
	Human Resources Development	19 percent	33
Total		66 percent	116/175 questions

The two exams differ in two ways. The Human Resource Certification Institute (HRCI) specifies these differences in the following ways:

✔ Some of the exam objectives are marked as SPHR or PHR only, which means that only the designated exam will carry questions about that specific objective.

✔ The exams questions are worded differently. The easiest way to describe the differences is by using the terms operational versus strategic:

- The PHR, being operational in nature, words questions in ways that ask for how you would do something on the job or what the impact a decision may have on other departments.

- SPHR questions are more subjective, requiring you to call upon your knowledge and experience base to correctly answer the question.

✔ For example, even though both exams may have questions related to recruiting, the PHR exam will deal with operational specificity, whereas the SPHR exam will be more focused on oversight and strategic implications. Here are two sample questions asking a very similar question with a different correct answer to illustrate this significant difference.

First the PHR question:

A position has just opened for a quality technician in the Research and Development department of the company you work for. The position is part time, requires some education, and could have a flexible schedule for the right talent. Which of the following recruiting sources would BEST result in qualified applicants?

(A) School-to-work programs

(B) College or trade school recruiting

(C) Online sources, such as recruiting sites and social media

(D) Daycares and elementary schools

Although all of the answers have potential to result in a qualified individual, the correct answer is (B). College or trade schools is a targeted resource and most likely to have candidates who are interested in part-time work while having some education in the field. (A) requires a more significant relationship investment in a partnership with local schools, and (D) doesn't target the labor pool adequately. Answer (C) is a broader scope than may be necessary for this job opening.

Compare it to this am SPHR question:

ABC Manufacturing has launched a total quality management program in order to be eligible to service international clientele. As a result, the company will need to regularly add quality inspectors to its R & D department over the next three to five years, with newly trained employees being deployed to the logistic center in need. The position will be part time, require some technical aptitude, and have nontraditional hours. Which of the following recruitment sources would BEST result in a steady flow of qualified candidates?

(E) School-to-work programs

(F) College or trade school recruiting

(G) Online sources, such as recruiting sites and social media

(H) Daycares and elementary schools

In this example, answer (A) is best. A school-to-work program is a community partnership that works with local high school campuses to both train and funnel qualified individuals for job openings. Answers (B) and (C) are quite useful for short-term recruiting needs rather than a long-term sustained effort. (D) isn't targeted at all toward the position.

Being armed with information about the exams, such as assessment results and question formatting, can feel a bit overwhelming. The exam content is already cumbersome and tricky, and tracking and managing information *about* the exams rather than what is *on* the exams may seem unnecessary. However doing the legwork before you dive into the exam content is worth it. It can reduce anxiety and ensure that you have adequate time to prepare for both the exam content and the pitfalls to avoid.

Practicing for Results

The old statement really is true: Practice makes perfect. Simply studying content and expecting to apply it successfully in an exam setting isn't enough. Your goal should be to be an accomplished test taker by test day (the day of judgment) arrives.

Use practice exams to focus on one of two things:

- **Content review:** In content review, the goal is to get you to dive into the exam objectives to test your knowledge. Use the tests to study different concepts and reinforce what you know and don't know. It includes chapter review tests and focal review quizzes.

- **Exam simulations:** They measure your knowledge, but they also simulate testing conditions. You may not have sat for a professional exam, so more than likely you're unfamiliar with protocols and format. In order to simulate exam day conditions, be sure to take practice tests that are at least 175 questions and that give you only three hours to complete. When you take the test, be sure and watch the time so you properly pace yourself and get used to answering each question in just over a minute. Practice marking questions for review and changing your answers to see if your first choice was correct. If yes, alter your technique to *not* change answers and see if that works better. Doing so can help you decide how to handle the unknown when you're faced with the real deal.

I'm sorry, but no shortcuts are worth your time. In order to benefit from practice exams, you just need to take as many as possible. Doing so takes planning and a clear understanding of what you're trying to measure. (Refer to the section, "Building a Study Plan Strategy" later in this chapter to help you create a plan.) These sections focus on how practice exams can help you and what you can to reach maximum results from them.

Reaping the benefits from practice exams

In order to get the most out of taking practice exams, you need to use your time wisely. You want to practice with as many as you can before you take the actual exam. These tips can help you maximize your results.

When you're practicing with content review in mind, consider the following:

- **Take the practice tests open book.** Practice exams can serve many masters, one of which is to teach you exam content. The assessments included in this book include a comprehensive answer review that explains both the correct and the incorrect answers. Taking the tests open book can align your studying efforts with the application to the test, the most effective way to master this material.

✔ **Look for the answers online and see what reading material or videos are related to that question.** If you have time, studying the test questions this way creates a depth of knowledge that is transferable to the exam. The exams are designed to measure not only knowledge, but experience as well. Real-world examples of the concepts surface online, giving you an experience-based perspective for future recall. Take the concept of a balanced scorecard for example. When you type this phrase into your search engine, one of the top results will be the Balanced Scorecard Institute. Here you can find case studies related to companies who have used this measurement tool to great effect. Many of the exam objectives start with "design, develop, implement, and measure. . .." So, when reading your case study, highlight the activities related to the design, development, implementation, and measurements of this tool.

When going online to study, stay away from lawyer websites or generic databases. Search for sites that end in *.org* or *.gov* to ensure that you're applying the right material. Credible journal sites are also a good place for free to low cost information, giving you insight into trends and current practices in the field of HR. Popular ones include `www.forbes.com` and `www.bloomberg.com`. Check out `www.dummies.com/extras/phrsphrexam` for a list of ten apps that are good resources.

✔ **While taking a practice exam, check your answers as you go.** Doing so can ensure that you're learning the information correctly and not storing incorrect information. Focus on the content of the questions and the right answers (and why they're correct). Then take another test, trust your gut, and wait until you're finished to check your answers.

When you're focusing on exam simulation when taking practice exams, keep these tips in mind:

✔ **Practice using similar tools to what will be available at the professional testing site.** For example, use an online calculator for the math questions. Use noise-cancelling headphones or ear buds to gauge comfort level with the tools provided onsite. Most importantly, time yourself to approximately 1 minute per question to train your mind to the pace of the exam. These conditioning strategies will serve to minimize your anxiety and give you insights into your individual preferences.

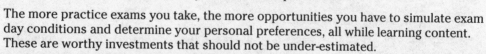

The more practice exams you take, the more opportunities you have to simulate exam day conditions and determine your personal preferences, all while learning content. These are worthy investments that should not be under-estimated.

✔ **Mimic the conditions of test day as close as possible.** Doing so is just an important exam preparation activity as is learning the content, because it minimizes the likelihood of unpleasant surprises on test day. Set aside three hours with no distractions (no crying kids, no needy pets, and no demanding co-workers). Your goal is to answer all 175 questions in three hours. For example, practice at the same time of day your exam is scheduled for. Be aware of other common distractions that happen during those conditions, such as hunger or fatigue. Know before exam day how you're going to handle these common distractors so that you don't inadvertently sabotage your success by being unprepared for the unexpected.

Measure to see if you can sit for three hours without using the restroom, which may seem somewhat silly, but you want to make sure that you're comfortable with the exact conditions that you'll face at the testing center. Plan ahead at home during a practice test rather than on game day. (If you can't sit that long without using the restroom, then you should avoid drinking anything several hours before taking the test, or account for a quick bathroom break in the amount of time that you'll have to answer each question.)

Making the right selection

Several options for practice exams are available, and they range from online tests to paper and pencil. I recommend the online solutions because you'll be taking the exam online. This book has both types of tests — written ones in the book and online versions at www.dummies.com/go/phrsphrexam — for you to practice.

When assessing your options, look for resources that have multiple practice exams available with answer explanations. The exam developers, www.hrci.org, offer short practice exams that use actual retired test questions from past exams for a very reasonable fee. This service when combined with other resources is a well-rounded approach to leveraging the benefits of practice exams.

Building a Study Plan Strategy

Having a study plan in place is a smart strategy for preparing for the PHR and SPHR exams. A study plan can direct your efforts and keep you focused on meeting your goal of passing so that you can achieve the three or four initials after your name. These exams aren't for the faint of heart, which is why an organized commitment is essential. A little planning goes a long way, and these sections describe the ins and outs of writing your plan.

Planning before you prepare your study plan

A study plan is a tool that you can use to prepare for the exam. Hence, you want your study plan to be specific to your needs. Needs to consider include the date of your exam, the amount of time you have available to dedicate to studying, and your specific strengths and weaknesses.

Prior to writing your plan, complete the following activities:

1. **Select the right exam.**

   Choose which exam you're going to take prior to building a study plan. Several resources can help you. Check out www.hrci.org under the "exam eligibility" tab. I also include some helpful information on the Cheat Sheet at www.dummies.com/cheatsheet/prhsphrexam. Feel free to refer to this information on a regular basis.

   Deciding on the proper exam for your skill level increases the odds of success and can reduce the level of preparation necessary for a passing score. Selecting the right exam prior to creating your study plan also allows you to take the right assessment test and compare your individual strengths and weaknesses to the correct exam content so you know where you need to study.

   Make sure that you choose the exam that is most reflective of your regular job responsibilities. For example, if your work is operational in nature and you report to an HR manager, then the PHR is the right test for you. If your position requires the use of independent judgment and you help set executive strategy, then the SPHR is more appropriate.

2. **Determine how much time on a daily or weekly basis you realistically have available for study activities.**

   Resist the temptation to underestimate how much time you need for planning. Training and studying may be inconvenient to the active professional, but they're a necessary evil in order to perform well on the exam. Depending on your skill set and assessment results, plan to dedicate between six to eight hours per week on exam preparation.

3. **Take an assessment to identify your strengths and weaknesses.**

An *assessment exam* helps you discover your specific strengths and weaknesses. You can then create your study plan based on those areas. Haphazardly reviewing topics that you've already mastered doesn't serve you. Conversely, not spending enough time in areas of knowledge deficiencies leaves you woefully unprepared for the contextual element of these exams.

I recommend that you purchase the assessments from www.hrci.org. They consist of retired exam questions, which can give you a realistic preview of what to expect of the question format on the exam and help you gauge your current skill level. They can be purchased for $45 per exam or a discounted rate of $70 if you purchase two.

Keep in mind that the actual exam is weighted based on level of difficulty, so there is no true passing score to use as a benchmark. As a general rule, however, you want to be at or above the 80 percent mark in each of the functional areas set for the exam.

It is unlikely that you'll pass your *practice* exam the first time, mainly because you have had little to no preparation. Don't be discouraged; that is to be expected. Not passing is actually useful because you need to know where you're deficient in order to build a meaningful study plan that focuses your study effort on the right topics. Consider giving yourself more time to study in the areas with your lowest scores.

You need to take at minimum two assessment exams: one prior to building your study plan and one at least two weeks prior to your exam date to see where you have improved and where you need to bone up.

Being organized keeps you focused

Taking the time to prepare your plan and get organized holds you accountable. You know what your expectations are and what you need to accomplish on a daily basis. (If your approach is less structured, you may be tempted to study when you can, which can create anxiety on test day and decrease your chances of success.)

You can use different tools to create your study plan, depending on your preference. Three options include

- ✔ **Calendar:** A calendar allows you to create a bird's-eye view of your preparations. Working backward from your test date, block out a specific time each week in which you'll study. One strategy is to allocate at least two weeks per functional area. Another strategy is to allocate three weeks for the top three areas in content. For example, more than 100 PHR test questions will be in the area of Workforce Planning and Employment, Employee and Labor Relations, and Compensation and Benefits.

- ✔ **To-do checklist:** A to-do list is a great way to capture your study activities. You can create a simple checklist by functional area that includes a reminder to use the exam preparation resources that you have selected. Head to www.dummies.com/extras/phrsphrexam for a sample checklist that you can use to get you started. You can use it to give you ideas on how to create your own to-do list, or you can print it and use it verbatim, whichever works best for you. You can use a checklist for each functional area of the exam. It directs you to specific studying activities, such as reading your textbook and answering the chapter review questions. You'll find it is a helpful way to ensure that you're leaving no resource unexplored as you study the material.

Get creative as you approach the material. Rote memorization is not only boring, but it may not lead to long-term retention. A good checklist takes you beyond flashcards and reminds you to tap into multiple ways of learning for maximum effectiveness.

✔ **An assessment worksheet:** For those of you that have already taken an assessment test, there is another available resource online. You'll be able to enter in your first assessment score and compare it to the exam weights to see how you fare against your test's top three content areas. It includes a column for your second assessment test that you should take a couple of weeks prior to your test date so you can see how far you've come and where you still need to spend some study time. Find it under the "course tools" heading at `http://epochresources.com/phrsphr-tools/instructor-resources/`.

Writing a study plan: The how-to

You may not have sat for an exam in a long period of time, so the prospect of writing a study plan may be daunting. The good news is that there isn't a single best practice in preparing for this exam. It's the collection of multiple efforts that will help you perform well and reach your goal. This section highlights some of the best ways to get your plan started to have maximum effect on your studying effort. Get started here and expand as you see fit.

To create your own study plan, follow these easy steps:

1. **Select your practice exam resources.**

   Align your preparation with HRCI's exam objectives. I recommend that you focus on resources that are content driven, such as a textbook or a website. Often a textbook resource also includes functional review questions, flashcards, quizzes, and other study activities that serve you. HRCI recommends that you select multiple resources to prepare for these tests.

   Many adults prefer to learn online, and many options for self-paced study are available. Several major universities offer self-paced courses, as do individual authors such as myself. In the chapters in Part III, I recommend a plethora of websites that can serve you in your study plan. Take the time to make a master list of all of the government websites related to employment. Visit them one by one to print out fact sheets on relevant topics. See Chapter 6 to find a list of other HRCI recommended authors and websites to visit as you create your study plan.

2. **Identify the areas that you'll study after taking the assessment exams based on the exam weights.**

   Take one or two assessments *prior* to beginning your studying efforts to get a baseline of your current readiness. Focus on the data in Table 2-1 to know what content areas to study. If you scored low on your assessment in an area that carries a heavier content weight on your exam, you should build extra time into your study plan to assure preparedness come exam day. (Refer to the earlier section for the advantages of assessment exams.)

   Study the areas that have the most impact first. For example, consider that the functional area of Risk Management makes up 7–8 percent of the exams, which translates to 12 questions on the SPHR and 14 questions on the PHR — a significantly small area of the exam. Depending on your assessment results, you may want to transfer some of your study time from Risk Management to areas with a denser concentration, such as Business Management and Strategy.

3. **Decide how much time you'll study per week.**

   Because these exams have seven areas to address (the six functional areas and the core knowledge requirements), you should plan for at least two weeks per functional area, or 14 weeks, depending on your assessment scores. (Check out the later section, "Making a 90-day commitment" for more specifics about the time to devote to your plan.) Hence, focus on the content areas that you scored lower on and that have more questions on the exam. (Refer to the "Considering Exam Weights by Functional Area" section earlier in this chapter to see how the exams are weighted so you know where to focus your attention.)

As you study, include practice exams to your overall study calendar. Add at least another three practice exams for review, preferably one per week. And approximately two weeks prior to your exam date, take at least two more exam simulations. Remember that no single preparation resource has all of the content of the PHR and SPHR exams; authors don't have special access to the exams, and out of thousands of possible questions, your exam will be made of just 175. Immersing yourself in practice exams from multiple resources acclimates you to the question wording, but also exposes you to broader exam content, increasing your odds of seeing something familiar on the test.

4. **Select how many weeks you'll study.**

   HRCI gives you an eight-week and a 12-week sample schedule in its certification handbook, available for purchase on its website. I highly recommend that you part with the $25 to purchase it, because it's an excellent resource for building your study plan to the exam content. Many preparers prefer a 14-week schedule because it gives you enough time to allocate two weeks per functional area, plus two weeks to review the core knowledge requirements.

   Eight, 12, or 14 weeks refers to the number of weeks until your exam date. So if your exam date is May 1 and you have a 14-week study schedule, you should begin preparing toward the end of January.

   Don't forget the exam weights. By two weeks before the exam date, you should be highly interested in your scores in the top three functional areas that make up your selected exam (refer to Table 2-2 earlier in this chapter). If you don't have passing scores in those three areas, you have a lot of work to do to be prepared for exam day.

Everyone has different preferences and needs as they prepare for this test, and so there really is no wrong way to study. Do your best to incorporate studying into your everyday activities. For example, if you exercise on a regular basis, make an audio recording using your phone and play it back while on the treadmill. If you're a parent that reads to your infant at night, read aloud from your textbook instead of from the regular bookshelf; your baby won't mind what you read as long as he hears your voice. Or, ask your tween to quiz you with a flashcard deck, showing her how hard you're willing to work to prepare for something you want.

Making a 90-day commitment

When planning your exam preparations, 14 weeks is your goal. Fourteen weeks of studying and immersion. In the big scheme of things, 14 weeks isn't a long time for a successful exam experience. You clearly have a baseline of knowledge that marks you eligible to sit for the exam, so your goal in the 90 or so prep days is to expand your knowledge of the areas that you already are comfortable with and expand your familiarity with the areas in which you may be less familiar. You also need to become aware with the exam experience because you may have not sat for a test in several years. (Refer to the earlier section, "Reaping the benefits from practice exams" for more information.)

If you have less than 90 days to study, accelerate your plan. You can make some of these adjustments to your plan:

- ✔ Consider one week per functional area rather than two.
- ✔ Focus on the areas with higher exam concentration.

✔ Wake up earlier or stay up later if necessary.

✔ Study at unconventional times, such as listening to audio resources while driving or reviewing flashcards during meals.

Regardless of your availability to study, dedicating yourself to performing well on this exam is an investment that you make in yourself.

Making outlines when you study

The Internet is also the perfect place to download fact sheets from government websites on labor laws such as the Fair Labor Standards Act (FLSA), Americans with Disabilities Act, and Title VII of the Civil Rights Act of 1964. Use the knowledge requirements for each functional area to make sure that you're hitting the main points of each law as it applies in an employment context.

Be sure and do something other than just print the fact sheets or the entire body of law. Your mind may be saturated with written content at this point, and labor law is especially tough to chew through. Think about creating a mind map or Venn diagram, looking for relationships and common threads as these labor laws apply to the functional area of choice. For example, Title VII of the

Civil Rights Act of 1964 applies to multiple functional areas, as the following figure shows a useful diagram. There is no wrong way to do this so modify these tools to best suit the information.

I like binders to keep all of this online material organized (refer to Chapter 18 for more information about how to use binders when you study). You can print out your diagrams and make notes while you work, then store them in the proper section for later review. Doing so is especially helpful if you take an assessment test closer to exam day when you can narrow your studying efforts to sections in which you didn't perform well, and your binder will be just the place to start.

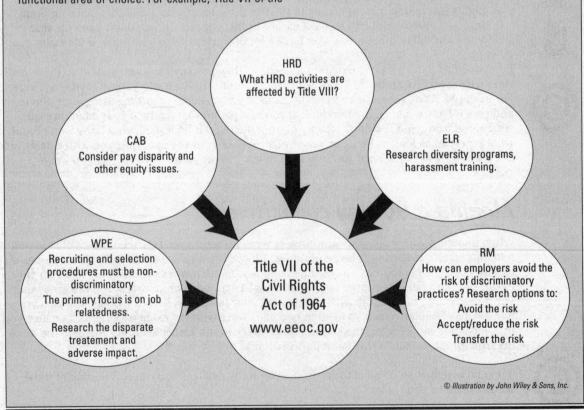

© Illustration by John Wiley & Sons, Inc.

Considering a Study Group: Yes or No?

A study group puts you in touch with other individuals like you and creates a level of accountability that may be the difference between a pass or fail score. According to HRCI, between 2012 and 2014, more than 69,000 human resource professionals applied to take either the PHR or the SPHR exam. The following sections identify the pros and cons to joining a study group to help you decide if one is right for you.

Noting the benefits of a study group

When preparing to take the PHR or SPHR, you may want to join a study group, which has these advantages, the same that Abraham Maslow wrote about in *Hierarchy of Needs:*

- **Belonging:** Adults are motivated when they belong to a group of peers, those with similar needs and desires. Aligning yourself with others in a study group creates a sense of camaraderie while reiterating the fact that you aren't, in fact, alone on this journey.

- **Self-esteem:** Most people want to contribute and believe that they have the knowledge and experience necessary to pass this exam. HR professionals have varying degrees of knowledge and experience that can only be shared in a study group. You'll bring knowledge to the table that others may not have, increasing your self-esteem and your confidence. For example, I have never worked in a union environment. Having someone in my study group who did gave me an in-depth look at how the exam content applied in the workplace, thereby increasing my understanding and exam application.

- **Self-actualization:** The top level of Maslow's hierarchy speaks to the need for individuals to realize their full potential. Sitting alone in a dark corner at a coffee shop trying to jam facts into your head doesn't inspire confidence or motivation to achieve your full potential, in this case, passing the exam. Coming together in a group motivates you to reach up and out with others beyond everyone's current capabilities and knowledge.

Note that adults' internal needs drive many of these benefits, yet you can obtain the solutions from external sources. Take yourself and this investment seriously enough to do whatever it takes to get you to a passing score.

Setting goals

Similar to the other theories of motivation that you'll study during this process, goal setting is one way to gain momentum toward success. It's not enough to simply say, "I will pass this test." Your goals must be much more specific and measurable if you're going to achieve them. Thus, "I will spend ten hours this week studying. I will read two chapters of the book and take all practice exams associated with those chapters " is a better goal than "I will study this week".

Writing your goals down is another visualization technique that will increase your odds of a passing score. This process requires that you're thoughtful about what you want and what you plan to do to achieve it. Refer to the section, "Writing a study plan: The how-to" and apply goal setting to your study checklist. It's a great way to keep you on track to help you achieve your goals.

Finally, create a level of accountability by publicly declaring your intent. At our house, we review at Sunday night dinner what needs to get done in the upcoming week. It allows us to share what we plan to achieve while coordinating and marshaling the resources necessary to do so. Making it a family affair also makes it more personal, which is an excellent motivator.

Identifying the challenges of a study group

Challenges to participating in a study group are uniquely personal. A variety of issues may revolve around inconvenient meeting times or dates, incompatibility with other group members, or other special group needs that are difficult to accommodate. Other challenges may be the lack of group knowledge diversity to add value to your specific areas of weakness.

Keep in mind, however, the old adage "the best way to learn something is to teach it." If you find yourself the strongest person in the group, take advantage by teaching a concept in which you have extensive knowledge/experience, or one in which you need a crash course.

Selecting the right group or exam prep class

If you decide to join a study group (or an exam prep class), I recommend that you reach out to your local professional networking group to identify individuals who are seeking certification during the same exam window as you. Doing so can ensure that the timing is conducive to your study plan and that you have access to support when needed. When looking to find the right study group, ask yourself these questions:

- ✔ How long does the group plan to study? How often do they intend to meet? Is it too long or too short for your needs?

- ✔ Is the group facilitated or not? What do you need? Are the other members or the facilitator experts or novices? Will the group add depth to your existing knowledge or teach you new things?

- ✔ Do the other group members have work experience and application that you lack?

- ✔ How much of the class is self-paced rather than face-to-face? Can they fit the activities around your schedule?

Finding the right study group takes effort. You may prefer to join an online forum where information is exchanged or join a group that meets face-to-face on a regular schedule to maximize accountability factors. Your goal in getting answers to these questions is to identify the deal breakers, not the excuses.

Keeping your group on task

If you decide to go with a group, note that the participants of the group that you join can be the difference between productive and nonproductive time. If you attend the first few sessions and realize that the participants have simply banded together out of fear or have shifted the responsibility of their success to a group leader, you may want to intervene. Establish the goals of the weekly meeting together and encourage others to actively participate in their own success. The last thing you want is to waste your precious study time on unrelated topics. Here are a few suggestions on keeping your study group on task:

- ✔ **Assign PowerPoint tests:** Have each participant create a PowerPoint presentation in the early weeks. Post a full question on one slide followed by the answer on the next slide. Ask the question and then discuss together what the correct answer may be. Then show the answer. If your group has it right, move on. If wrong, all should search through the study material to find the right answer.

- ✔ **Have individual members present a short lesson to the others.** Assign an area where a member is weak. Evidence is solid that you remember for many years something that you teach to others. Thus, by assigning an area of weakness you convert it to a strength.

✔ **Agree to create 100 digital flashcards and share with each other.** You can use a resource such as Quizlet (www.quizlet.com) or GoConq (www.goconq.com). This way you gain the efforts of all group members and make your own study time more efficient.

✔ **Assign a video scavenger hunt in which members troll the Internet for relevant videos in each functional area.** End your group meetings with a video segment in which the group watches and discusses the videos.

Make these sessions as productive as possible to ensure the most effective use of your time. Apply your natural leadership skills to drive the efforts, and you won't be disappointed by the amount of learning you all will gain as a result.

Getting Your Employer To Pay For Certification

Asking your employer to foot all or part of the certification is reasonable. Success is all in the approach. Here are a few helpful tips:

✔ **Collect information regarding the exact costs, including study material and the cost of a study group.** Consult your company handbook to see if your company offers a tuition reimbursement or professional development program. Be sure to research the value of certification and why you'll be a better employee.

✔ **Research your current job description and the job description of the position that you eventually want.** How will certification add to your current job responsibilities? How will certification prepare you for the next step? Will certification allow you to mentor others down the same path? Having these answers prior to making a request will help you answer the *only* question your boss will have, which is "what's in it for us?"

✔ **Schedule a face-to-face meeting with your boss to present the information, make the request, and convey your dedication to this journey.** If you try to make your request informally or by email, he may not have the time to give your request the proper consideration. Ask for a special meeting, so you can present the information professionally, and be sure to focus on the increased benefits that your certification will have for the company. Keep the focus on what this certification can do for your organization or department.

✔ **If full reimbursement is not an option, ask your manager if she is willing to pay for half or perhaps cover the exam fee.** A "no" answer may also be a timing issue, especially if your manager has a training budget that has to be considered. Giving her plenty of time to plan for the request may lead to a successful outcome, even if you have to postpone your exam date to coincide with the budget.

Even if you walk away empty-handed, you have notified your manager that you're a committed professional, ready and willing to take on new challenges and create depth in your career.

Talk to your accountant about the option of writing the expense off as professional development education to maintain skills. The cost may be a tax deduction.

Chapter 3

Identifying the Question Types and Strategizing to Answer Them

In This Chapter

▶ Knowing the best way to answer questions

▶ Understanding the question forms

▶ Navigating the multiple choice answers

▶ Dealing with the unknown

You may be aware that the questions on both the PHR and SPHR exams are tricky and that first-time test takers have low pass rates. Because you're reading this book, you are clearly taking your test preparation seriously and are doing everything you can to be successful.

With 175 questions and three hours to complete the exam, you have approximately one minute to answer each question. Some questions may take you longer to interpret, while others will be smooth sailing.

You don't have time to dillydally, so allow me to stop wasting your time. This chapter explains the types of questions that you'll encounter on the test and how to tackle them on test day.

Having a Plan to Answer the Questions

Preparing for the test and answering the questions can be similar to the way a golfer approaches a shot. If you're not a golf fan, stick with me. Approaching a shot references how the golfer goes through a few phases of preparation before actually swinging the club. He selects the right club, stands back to view the landscape, tees up the ball, and squares up to the shot. This all happens before he ever makes contact with the ball. Addressing this exam requires the same mind-set. You can follow this list to break down the tactical approach to the PHR and SPHR exam questions.

1. **Read the question thoroughly.**

   Doing so helps you figure out what knowledge you must access to select the right answer. Determine what part of your studying will best serve you.

2. **Look for clues in the question.**

   These clues can pinpoint precisely the direction toward what the question is asking.

3. **Answer the question in your mind before you look at the answer choices.**

   Most questions have answer distractors that are designed to, well, *distract* you from the correct answer. By answering the question before you see the multiple choice options, you may recognize the correct answer more easily and avoid being confused by options that also appear to be correct. Ask yourself what you would do at work. Refer to the later section, "Spotting the Correct Target" for strategies about narrowing down the answer.

4. **Select the best answer.**

   Apply the answer to the question to ensure that it's correct and then make the selection on your monitor. If you're still unsure, mark that questions for later review, but do not leave the answer blank.

Interpreting the Content While Conquering the Form

Many of your study resources may focus your attention on the exam content, which is good. What is missing however, is the need for you to conquer the format of the exam because it can be challenging. Both the PHR and SPHR exams have thousands of questions in the test bank, of which 175 will be randomly assigned to your exam. The PHR and SPHR exams have weighted questions, with difficulty levels in three ranges — easy, medium, and hard — interspersed throughout the entire exam.

What you can't predict is the precise exam objectives from which you'll see questions. No clear map lays out how the exams present the problems. You may get the more difficult questions earlier, whereas the easier ones come later. Or the exam may get progressively more difficult. What will be consistent is the weight of exam content by functional area.

No matter, being prepared for the different types of questions can help you better navigate the exam so that you don't panic when you encounter questions that are more difficult. The following sections break down the questions and answer options on the exams so that you know what to expect.

The great news about this type of variety in question stems is that you may find answers to other questions in the questions themselves, which is how marking for review can come in very handy. Refer to Chapter 17 for more information how to review.

Understanding how the questions are formed

Both exams are multiple choice with four possible options. The *stems*, or premise of the question, are phrased in a few different ways, which I discuss here. These sections focus on the questions (so I don't focus on providing answer explanations).

Direct questions

These types of items ask a specific question, usually offering background information or a summary. Here is an example of a direct question.

What type of interview bias is the result of the interviewer applying a widely held but not necessarily true characteristic to an applicant, often based on a protected class characteristic?

(A) Similar to me

(B) Stereotype

(C) Discrimination

(D) Horn effect

The correct answer is (B).

Incomplete statements

Traditionally recognized as a fill-in-the-blank style, these types of questions ask you to finish a thought or statement. The following example illustrates this type of question.

A stereotype is an example of interview_____?

(A) Bias

(B) Discrimination

(C) Judgment

(D) Error

The correct answer is (A).

Scenario questions

Scenario questions are phrased to mirror typical HR situations. They're designed to measure how well you're able to apply your knowledge to a work simulation. Especially on the SPHR exam, you may be given one scenario in which two or three questions follow. You should be able to apply facts from multiple functional areas. When you encounter these questions, be prepared to first take a broad view and then strip it down to what the question is really asking.

Kendall is a recruiter interviewing several candidates for an accounting clerk position. He rates Iris, an Asian female candidate very highly qualified, mainly because he has heard that Asian people are highly intelligent and good at math. This is an example of what kind of interviewer bias?

(A) Unlawful discrimination

(B) Bias

(C) Stereotype

(D) The halo effect

The correct answer is (C).

Spotting the target: The correct answer

Each question has four multiple choice options, of which two seem highly possible but only one is correct. When faced with this choice, think about how you would answer this question at work. Consider both answers from a federal versus a state perspective and remind yourself that these exams are based on federal law. Re-read the question and make sure that you understand what it's asking before making your answer choice. For example, a question asking you to implement a plan may have answer options related to design, implementation, and measurement of said plan. All answers are vital to the planning process, but only one is directly related to implementation, which would be the correct answer.

One of my favorite strategies to recommend for selecting the right answer is to anticipate it before you even read the answer choices. This strategy requires knowledge about the core subjects and the ability to predict what the answer choices may be. This strategy isn't a guessing technique. It's a technique designed to focus your thinking on what the question is asking so that you recognize the most likely answer when you read the options.

To use this strategy, stick to these steps:

1. **Read the questions twice.**

2. **Before looking at the available answers, identify the correct answer in your mind.**

3. **After you're confident that you know the answer, scan the multiple choice options for the most similar choice to your conclusion.**

   When you allow yourself to find the answer naturally, you're less likely to be swayed by the options and the distractors.

These tips can help you apply this strategy:

- ✔ **Properly prepare.** Make sure that you spend the time to study the material. If you're unprepared, this strategy won't work, simply because you won't have the information stored in your brain to arrive at the conclusion without assistance.

- ✔ **Read the question twice.** The first time that you read the question, you're getting the general sense and absorbing the gist of the concept being measured. The second pass involves looking for the keywords that get at what the question is truly asking. You can figure out whether it asks for action or design, questions, interpretation, or application, or if it measures knowledge or references best practices. Remember that the PHR exam will use keywords related to operational activities that focus on *performing* the work of an HR generalist. The SPHR focuses keywords on *strategizing* the role of all HR activities in a company.

- ✔ **Be confident.** Being confident that you have properly prepared and having the discipline to stick to your answer can help keep you from vacillating after you're presented with the four options.

The best way to determine whether this strategy works for you is to take a practice exam where you can try it. Measure your comfort level and confidence, not just the final score. Refer to Chapter 2 for more information about the importance of taking practice exams.

In addition to predicting the correct answer, other effective ways can help you narrow your choices. They include the following:

- ✔ **Eliminate the obvious.** Writing wrong answers is more difficult than you may think for the exam preparers. Look for slight variations in wording or partially correct answers. Search for clues such as synonyms or phrases in the answer that mirror that of the question. Find the *distractors* (extraneous information included as an answer or in the question stem that isn't relevant; refer to the next section for more help on how to locate distractors) that include correct information, but don't actually answer the question. If you know these techniques ahead of time, you can practice spotting them on exam simulations. Make it a challenge when you take practice exams.

✔ **Apply your knowledge.** An incorrect answer choice may answer part of the question, but not all of it. Incorrect choices serve to confuse you, because you know part of the answer choice is correct, so you think that perhaps it may be right. Think about how you would accomplish the activity on the job. Ask yourself important questions: What information do you need and what actions would you take? What resources would be necessary, and most importantly, what is the desired outcome? From this process, you should be able to spot the answer option that best reflects the answers to your workforce application.

With this example question, I illustrate this strategy at work. Go ahead and use this strategy and then read the answer explanation to see how you did.

Where would be the best place to find information about local labor market trends?

(A) Your city's chamber of commerce

(B) The state's workforce development agency

(C) The Department of Labor

(D) The Bureau of Labor Statistics

The correct answer is (B). Although all choices may offer you variations of labor market trends, applying the preceding techniques can help you arrive at the best answer. Rereading the question can help you identify a key word — *local*. You can eliminate choices (C) and (D) because they're national resources. Both (A) and (B) address the locality issue, so apply your working knowledge of this practice. An experienced HR professional knows that chambers of commerce don't actively collect labor market data and serve more in the capacity of employer lobbyists. Therefore, (B) is the best answer.

Half of your brain is focused on the structure of the question and interpreting the stem, whereas the other half is engaged in applying your knowledge to find the answer. Both of these functions are important to arriving at the correct conclusion. Compartmentalizing these activities during practice trains your brain to acknowledge each half during the test, minimizing anxiety because you're prepared for successful analysis.

Navigating the answer distractors

In addition to the two good answer choices, an exam question usually also has distractors. Distractors can show up in a couple of different places:

✔ **In the question stem:** This extraneous information isn't relevant to the correct answer.

✔ **In one of the four answer choices:** Some distractors are answers based on common misconceptions. Others aren't relevant to the question (such as a state requirement rather than a federal one). Some distractors are true statements that don't answer the actual question. Worse yet are the distractors that are close to the actual correct answer, but with a slight variation that renders it second best.

The difference between a distractor and a clearly wrong answer is that the distractors are plausible.

Dealing with the distractions isn't quite as difficult as you may think. Take at least one practice test with the specific intent to work through these steps:

1. **Eliminate the obviously wrong answers, which leaves the correct answers and the distractors.**

   Select one to apply.

2. **Reread the question while applying your chosen solution.**

   Determine whether the answer still seems right. If not, eliminate it and repeat with the remaining viable answer choices.

3. **After you have made your choice, decide on the correct answer and move on.**

   If you're still not sure, mark it for later review.

Practicing this approach may take a bit of time at first. The clock eventually will matter for these practice exams, but during your practice sessions, your focus should be on training your brain to think critically through each exam item.

Here is an example of a question with distractors.

Which of the following is an HR implication of the *Griggs vs. Duke Power Company* Supreme Court case?

(A) Punitive damages for sexual harassment may now be tied to organizational size.

(B) All tests used for employment selection should be job related.

(C) Employment discrimination now include categories of age, gender, and military status.

(D) Labor unions must now keep records of financial dealings in accordance with both state and federal laws.

The correct answer is (B). All statements sound true, but the court case deals with employment selection tests. To answer this question, you need to know the basics of the court case. If you knew that *Griggs vs. Duke Power* is considered the benchmark case that established the need for employment tests to be job related, you could eliminate (A), because the case isn't related to claims of sexual harassment; eliminate (C), because it didn't address protected categories; and eliminate (D) because the case didn't involve labor unions.

Recognizing Special Circumstances

Just relying on your experience and education alone isn't enough when answering questions on the exams. The exam body of knowledge (BOK) is built upon industry best practices that are examined each year through the use of subject matter experts, peer-reviewed journals, and the use of certified HR professionals to write the exam items. These sections point you in the right direction when it comes to mastering the nuances that exist on both exams.

Test takers will only be tested on subject matter included in the exam BOK. Study these exam objectives to find clues to HR best practices. Refer to each chapter for the specific objectives, or find them online at www.hrci.org/exam-preparation/bodies-of-knowledge.

Maneuvering through the best pitfall

Both the PHR and SPHR exams rely heavily on the concept of the *best* answer. It means that in a group of experts, all would agree that the answer is the best answer to a given premise. The exams use these types of questions to measure how well you're able to apply your work experience to an exam item.

To tackle these types of questions, keep in mind that you're looking for the answer that serves the exam objectives and the industry as a whole. It may not be the choice that is true all of the time, and it certainly won't be an absolute statement with terms, such as *never* or *always*. Here are a few strategies to help you get to the correct answer:

- ✔ **Find the most ethical answer.** Ethics is a huge consideration of the profession and often must serve as the final element to your decision-making. Let it serve you with these types of questions.

- ✔ **Select the choice that best serves the employee.** Erring on the side of the employee is rarely the wrong thing to do at work and often is the best choice for managing risk. This strategy reduces your risk of selecting the wrong answer. Be sure when employing this strategy that the question doesn't specify an advantage for the employer.

- ✔ **Look for similarities and differences in the answer options.** If two answers seem to be correct, compare them against each other to identify the difference and similarity, and then reread the question. Apply both answers while considering the difference/similarity and choose what makes most sense.

- ✔ **Picture the response scrutinized in court.** You're the expert at work, and you have the responsibility to give solid advice. Look for the answer that would hold up best if you had to publish your response or defend an employment action in court.

- ✔ **Select the choice that is an industry best practice.** For this strategy to work, you must have mastered the exam BOK. Although you may answer differently for your own employer, these questions are measuring what best reflects the HR industry best practices.

The practice exams will help familiarize you with these types of questions, so invest in as many credible resources as your budget allows. Refer to Chapter 2 for more information about taking practice exams.

Here is an example of a *best* question. Use these strategies and review the answer explanation to see how you did.

The BEST reason to conduct a labor market analysis is increased:

(A) Knowledge of local trends

(B) Assessment of workforce skill sets

(C) Brand awareness of your organization

(D) Identification of workforce requirements

The correct answer is (A). In many *best* questions, all the answers appear to be appropriate, so it's up to you to apply critical-thinking skills to the choices. In (B), a labor market analysis collects trends that impact the workforce skill sets, but it's only one component of the information gathered. Brand awareness (C) could certainly be a byproduct of trolling the market for information, but it isn't a directly related goal of the effort. Answer (D) is an internal activity, not an external effort.

Working with extremes — always, never, most, least

Answer choices that contain absolutes such as *never, none, all,* or *always* are virtually never correct. Absolutes must apply to all circumstances, and HR professionals know that very few things in day-to-day activities are universal. For this reason, eliminating these answers as incorrect is a safe bet.

A bit more difficult to navigate are the *most* and *least* questions. These types of questions tell you right away that all four answers apply in some fashion, and your job is to apply independent judgment and work experience to rate them in order of importance or likelihood of occurrence.

To solve these *most* and *least* problems, keep these points in mind:

- ✔ Think about what you would do if the situation were presented to you on the job.

- ✔ Consider the facts that you would gather or what resources you would employ.

- ✔ Address the legal issues that may or may not be associated with the question presented.

Consider the following example of a *most/least* problem.

OSHA discovered at your place of work that noise levels exceed the maximum levels allowed. Which of the following choices is LEAST likely to result in hazard abatement?

(A) Introduce a policy requiring employees to wear ear protection.

(B) Re-instate the manufacturing guards that control the volume of the machinery.

(C) Call out an expert to measure and confirm the original decibel findings.

(D) Discipline the employees for failing to wear their ear muffs.

The correct answer is (D). Disciplining employees for failing to wear ear protection won't solve the root cause, which is the goal of hazard abatement efforts. A policy (A) won't result in compliance although it certainly launches the process. Calling in the experts (C) is a better answer, because it seeks to find the root cause of the issue. (B) is a critical component to compliance, because the machines guards for noise protection had been bypassed.

Note in this example question that you had to infer information from the other answers. Answer (A) used the term *introduce,* from which you can deduct that there wasn't an existing policy. (B) used the term *re-instate,* implying that the guards were there but had been removed. Successful navigation of these types of questions requires a keen sense of awareness and an eye for the detail.

Dealing with the unknown

You'll inevitably run into a question (or a few) where you simply won't know the answer. Don't be surprised when you encounter one. Stay calm and don't panic. Here are some strategies to deal with the unknown:

- ✔ **Trust your first instinct.** Try not to overthink the question. If you really don't know the answer, trust your first instinct and move on, marking it for review if time permits.

✔ **Make an educated guess.** Making a guess is better than leaving an answer blank. You had to qualify by experience and education to take the exam, and you have dedicated the time in advance to prepare, so you can make a pretty good guess at what might be correct.

Guessing is actually an extremely important test-taking strategy. You start with a score of zero and build up points for every correct answer. If you leave an answer blank, you guarantee that you'll get zero points for the question. Guessing incorrectly doesn't hurt you; you simply won't get the points for the question.

✔ **Skip it and go back.** Marking questions for review is a good way to address the unknown. Other questions may actually help you answer the headache questions. You may however want to at least take an educated guess, just in case you run out of review time at the end of the exam.

Changing your answer

Some test takers choose to stick with their first answer, whereas others use the review process to make changes. The only way to know which approach works for you is to try them both. Remember that you probably haven't sat for an exam in a while, so what used to work for you may no longer be effective.

Take a practice exam in which you don't go back and change your answers and compare it to a practice exam where you allow yourself to make adjustments.

Or you can take a single exam and practice changing some answers, but not others. During the exam, write down the question numbers of those answers that you changed and the questions to which you wanted to change the answer but didn't. Measure which technique worked best for you. Try this approach a couple of times to make sure that you're confident in your approach on test day. Refer to Chapter 2 for more advice on how you can prepare for the exam.

Chapter 4

Surviving Test Day

Taking the PHR or SPHR exam can be downright nerve wracking. Those nerves can make you stop eating, eat too much, or lose sleep leading up to test day. They can show up in physical ways like shallow breathing, rashes, stomachaches, or headaches. Yet nerves also have the power to motivate you, sharpening your focus and strengthening your resolve. What you do in the week immediately preceding test day and on the day of the test can help you harness the positive energy to apply toward exam success.

Read Chapter 2 and take my advice to give yourself plenty of time to study, review, and take exam simulations. Regardless of your preparation activities however, test anxiety is a very real phenomenon that you should consider in your preparation. Knowing what to expect can help reduce the anxiety, eliminate distractors, and focus on what you came to do. This chapter examines what you can do to ease your nerves and perform well the days before and on test day.

Leading Up: The Days before the Test

Planning ahead allows you to make arrangements to tour the testing facility or get a good deal on a hotel room if you want to stay over the night before. Making decisions about cramming and packing your bag for the testing hours alleviates possible missteps or worse, forgetting the government-approved ID that gets you in the door. These are just examples of what the following section examines. I also offer tips, tricks, and strategies for you to incorporate into your preparation activities.

Avoid alcoholic beverages the night before the exam. They can lead to dehydration, causing you to overload on water the day of your test. Too many bathroom breaks in the three-hour timeframe will be a waste of your allotted time.

Cramming: Yes or no?

Some popular theorists say that cramming for your exam or putting off studying until the last moment — the week or the night before the test — is useless. Short-term memory gains are often at the expense of lost information elsewhere, which is especially true if your late-night studying breaches your normal sleep patterns, because a well rested exam taker is more successful then one who just pulled an all-nighter.

Allow me to propose a compromise. Although a panicky study session the night before isn't the best way to spend your evening hours, a well-planned, systematic review of difficult-to-understand concepts may be just the sedate activity that is a natural extension of your regular study patterns.

To do so, keep notes during your weekly study sessions of topics that you've struggled with or that you need to understand more clearly. Then during the week before your exam, engage in one or more of these activities:

- **Watch videos.** Most of your studying has probably been of the reading sort, fighting your way through the language of academia and a hodgepodge of MBA terms like *paradigms* and *deltas*. In the week before your exam, engage in watching videos produced by credible experts, such as authors or professional associations regarding the muddier concepts. You can find many of these types of videos on free websites such as www.youtube.com. You can locate others via news outlets such as CNBC and Bloomberg Business Week online. Consider subscribing to these sources so that you're notified whenever a new video is posted.

- **Stick to your review schedule.** Accelerating the amount of time you spend reviewing is fine; however, be aware of your limits. The week before the exam isn't the time to learn new concepts. Focus then on reviewing the familiar or go deeper in the more difficult. Chapter 2 helps you put together your study plan.

- **Write exam questions or create a presentation.** Doing so is harder than you think. The best way to learn something is to teach it, so writing exam questions or preparing a PowerPoint presentation as though you're getting ready to train on a difficult topic forces you to look at the material in an objective way. Strip the concept down to its core, seeking out information to teach rather than to learn. Doing so gives you greater control and less fear over the concept that has eluded retention in your information-overloaded mind.

You alone need to decide if a modified cramming schedule works for you. Abandoning all preparation activity the night before may be unrealistic for some individuals, yet quite a relief for others. Don't judge yourself after you have made a decision either way; just trust your instincts and do what feels right for you. Chapter 18 offers some additional helpful study techniques.

Eyeing the lay of the land: The testing facilities

HRCI has contracted with Prometric to administer the exams. The company has hundreds of computer-based facilities around the United States (and internationally). After you have been approved to sit for the exam, you'll be directed to the Prometric's website to schedule your exam. At this time, you'll be able to select the facility where you'll test and take note of the address and phone number.

To ensure that you don't run late, in the week before the test, take the route to the testing facility so you know how long it will take you. Then consider doubling the amount of time that you think you'll need to get there. Construction, detours, and other traffic-related delays are real possibilities when you travel to your destination, so establish a timeline that *completely eliminates the possibility* that you'll have to set a frantic pace on exam day. Arriving early and having to wait and listen to meditation recordings is better than frantically being late. For more on this relaxing technique, see the later section "Remembering the ABCs of Test Day".

Familiarizing yourself with the testing environment

When taking the test, you'll be in a room filled with workstations and computer monitors. Prometric administers many different exams, not just the PHR and SPHR. As a result, test takers have different start times, so on test day, you'll have people coming in and going out. Your goal is to stay focused and not worry about other test takers who are working more quickly than you. They may have started before you or have a shorter test, so be aware of this fact so you can ignore the movement as best as you can.

When checking in, you'll need to present proper identification (refer to the later section, "Knowing what to bring to the testing facility" for specifics). When you check in, Prometric also takes your photo and a biometric fingerprint scan.

Everyone receives a tutorial on how to use the program before the start of the exam and a survey at the end of the exam while the results are calculated. The three-hour time window doesn't start until you begin your first question.

Prometric's website (www.prometric.com) has a great video that discusses what you can expect at the testing site. Click on the "Prepare for Test Day" link for more information on what to expect.

If you're extra nervous, you can schedule a simulation check-in. If available at your site, for $30, you're allowed to go through a simulation of the check-in procedures, tutorial, and a sample test (not a PHR or SPHR though) so you can be sure you know how to get to the facility, that your ID is acceptable, and that you're prepared for the format of the exam. The best way to ensure that you can take advantage of this feature is to contact the testing site *before* you schedule your exam day. Prometric can confirm that the site you wish to choose has the exam simulation feature available and answer any questions you may have such as what to expect and processing payment for the service.

The Time Is Here: Exam Day

The day of the exam has finally arrived. All of your effort and preparedness is literally about to be put to the test. But your preparations aren't finished yet. A few important pieces of advice that I cover in these sections can increase your chances of success over the next few hours.

Regardless of how you feel when you wake up, be sure and eat a decent meal. Focus on proteins such as eggs, cheese, or nuts to fill you up and fuel your brain. Avoid sugary foods, such as donuts or candy bars, that may result in a energy crash halfway through the exam. Keep in mind that carb-heavy foods may make you feel heavy and sleepy, affecting your performance. Resist the urge to avoid food altogether, because you'll need the energy it provides for the mental marathon that you're about to begin.

On the day of the exam, stop studying. Give yourself a pep talk and picture yourself succeeding. Refer to the later section, "Remembering the ABCs of Test Day" for more information.

These sections take a closer look at what you need to bring and not bring to the testing facility.

Knowing what to bring to the testing facility

Prometric is meticulous for security on exam day to ensure the integrity of the exams aren't breached and that you are who you say you are on exam day. Make sure that you arrive at least 30 minutes prior to your scheduled time to allow for security procedures. You must present an unexpired government-issued ID when registering, when entering the test room, and when returning from a break. Acceptable ID include a valid

- ✔ Drivers license or state ID card
- ✔ Military identification card
- ✔ Passport
- ✔ National identification card

Make sure the identification you use matches the name on your application exactly, including the use of middle initials or hyphenated names. The two items shouldn't have any discrepancies. Furthermore, your primary ID must have your photo and signature. If you present an ID without either, you'll need a backup form of ID that has the missing element. Keep in mind that the backup ID must match your name on the application exactly as well. You won't be permitted to test if they don't match.

If you aren't sure what forms of ID will be accepted at your test center or just want to double-check, don't wait until exam day. Call your testing facility or contact HRCI toll free at 866-898-4724 to verify that your ID will be accepted. You want to avoid any potential issues before the morning of test day.

Knowing what you can't take into the exam room

Prometric is strict about what you can't take into the testing room. Prometric requires that you place all items — outerwear, hats, watches, purses, cell phones, food, drink — everything except your ID — into a locker to which you're given a key. Prior to entering the testing room, someone wands you with a metal detector, and you're required to turn out your pockets.

Keep in mind these restrictions during the test:

- ✔ No food or drinks, although you may leave the room and notify the test center administrator that you need to access your locker. This procedure must be followed, even to access medicine.

  The clock is still ticking for the three-hour limit, so return to the test quickly to maximize the time. If you do take a break, consider a peppermint candy because studies show that it stimulates the brain.

- ✔ No reviewing study material or accessing your mobile device during a break. Test center administrators and cameras are everywhere, so if you're caught, your test may be invalidated.

- ✔ No smoke breaks after you have started the exam.

You may wear Prometric-issued, noise-reducing headphones, or you may bring your own disposable ear plugs that are in a sealed package. If you bring your own, they'll be inspected prior to being allowed.

Remembering the ABCs of Exam Day

A few common factors can contribute to success on test day, no matter your education or experience. Here are three important tips that can help you get in the right frame of mind.

Attitude: Believe that you can succeed

To prove my point, conduct a web search on the term "the power of positive thinking" and you may be surprised at the amount of material that is available on the impact of how a person's attitude affects successful outcomes. From peer-reviewed research to bestselling books, you can find a ton of information about the impact of the positive perception of your life, knowledge, skills, and abilities.

However, having a good attitude on test day isn't enough. Your attitude toward your study time, the materials that you use, and the choices that you make can substantially influence how prepared you feel going into exam day.

The reality is that you may not pass this exam on the first try. Accepting the real fact that these tests are difficult positions so be prepared to *do your best*. Certification is truly about the journey. You're guaranteed to come out more informed and competent in your job, making this exercise well worth every second of preparation, regardless of a pass or fail score.

Breathing: It matters more than you may think

Regulating your breathing is important to clearing your mind and sharpening your focus. In through your nose, out through your mouth may feel silly, but your body needs regulated oxygen to perform optimally. In fact, taking too many shallow breaths can actually increase anxiety and even cause you to hyperventilate in the worst case.

When you're in your deepest point of sleep, your breathing is even, causing your heart rate to steady and your body to remain calm. Focusing on your breathing while you're awake can manifest those same benefits. Become conscious of your breathing while you're taking exam simulations or during your preparation activities so that you train your body to shift automatically into this calm state when you encounter the material. Conscious regulation of your breathing sends messages to your brain, impacting clarity and eliminating fuzzy thinking.

Knowing how to breathe better has many benefits to overall health. For purposes of exam preparation, proper breathing calms the fight-or-flight instinct that everyone has when faced with high stress or perceived dangerous situations. Symptoms that you're anxious include rapid heart beat, sweaty palms, and temperature changes such as flushing or feeling cold. Proper breathing requires that you take in air through your nose and then push it out from your stomach through your mouth. Here are a few training tips to help you master this technique:

- Put one hand on your stomach and the other hand on your chest. When you breathe in, your stomach should rise more than your chest, which means the air is being drawn all the way to the base of your lungs.

- Exhale slowly through your mouth. As a general rule, your exhale should be twice as long as the inhale.

- Repeat four or five times until you feel the calming results of a slower heartbeat or normalized temperature.

Meditation is another technique that you may help you enter a calmer state, which is especially useful if you suffer from test-taking or performance anxiety. Although many methods are available, look for one that addresses the basics of concentration or focuses your mind on one thought at a time. Concentrating on a simple word or phrase clears the mind of negative talk and other distractions that elevate your nerves. Effective meditation relies on breathing. Combine the two techniques by finding a calming word or phrase that you can repeat in your mind during the previous breathing exercise. Favorites may be "I am calm," "I am relaxed," or "I am peaceful or "I am thankful." If you're more serious about tackling meditation in your study plan, check out the latest edition of *Meditation For Dummies* by Stephan Bodian (John Wiley & Sons, Inc.).

Confidence: Expect success

True confidence requires that you're *honest* about your capabilities and effort up to test day. Believe in yourself, knowing that you've prepared for the test and done what you need to succeed. However if you go into your exam day expecting to fail, you may not be as motivated to perform because in your mind, the outcome is already set.

Getting to a true confident state requires that you ask yourself these questions:

- **Are you taking the right test?** Too often, exam takers reach for the SPHR before they're truly ready. Make sure and pay attention to your assessment scores and be willing to change exams if they aren't up to par. (Refer to Chapter 2 for more information about assessment tests.) It's better to pay the fee to change the test than to sit for an exam that you aren't ready for and fail.

- **Did you respect your studying time?** Be honest. You know what you did to prepare. Are you being too hard on yourself and minimizing your efforts, or are you being too generous, according effort where it really doesn't belong? The good news is that you don't have to share this answer with anyone — it's just between you and your psyche, so don't be afraid to explore at will. If you know you didn't do as much as you should have done to prepare, don't let it derail you. What matters is that you focus on the task at hand and systematically do your best to answer the questions.

  Be sure to read each question thoroughly before answering to ensure that you know what the question is asking. Eliminate the obviously wrong answers first so you can concentrate on comparing the remaining options. Go through the test and answer only the ones you're certain of first, marking the others for review. Doing so allows you to use the remaining time to puzzle through the more difficult ones that require extra concentration. For more test-taking strategies, flip to Chapter 3.

- **What stereotypes or negative self-talk has crossed your mind?** Negative self-talk erodes confidence. Thinking things like "I can't do this" or "I knew this test was going to be too hard for me" keeps you from doing your best. Focusing on what you *don't* know is at the expense of what you *do* know. Getting control of those thoughts before they change your behavior is key. If, during the test you begin to think negative thoughts, stifle them by taking a deep breath and changing the statement. For example "I should have studied harder" can be converted to "I am going to apply what I know." Or "I'm not good at taking tests" can be changed to "I'm putting myself out there and am going to get this done."

  A note of encouragement: Many people hold onto negative thoughts that they've had or negative experiences that they've survived as a kid about their knowledge or abilities. But I have good news for you: Being an excellent HR professional doesn't always require a formal college degree nor is it dominated by one race or gender. Human resources is relevant in all industries and important in all of the major countries where the work of business is getting done. You'll be successfully certified based solely on your talent and performance, and taking this step in your career signals your dedication. Be proud of yourself, regardless of the outcome on test day.

After the Test: What to Expect

Congratulations. You clicked the finish button and completed a strenuous experience. However before you can leave, you have a few small tasks to do — most importantly receiving your score. These sections explain what you need to do after you finish.

Completing the survey

Before you find out how you performed, you'll be asked to complete a short survey, conducted by HRCI. The survey asks a few general questions, such as how you prepared for the exam. Don't worry though because the answers aren't scored. HRCI uses this information to help make recommendations to other students on the studying habits of successful exam takers, so be as honest and thoughtful as possible.

Getting your results

After the timer wheel stops spinning, your preliminary results report will tell you if you passed or failed. The screen will show "congratulations, you passed" or "did not pass." You'll receive a printout of the result while your official results will be sent via email or mail. You need a scaled score of at least 500 to pass either the PHR or SPHR exams.

- ✔ **If you passed:** The official results that you'll receive via email or mail shows a snapshot of how you did in each of the functional areas for use in future development activities. These reports won't show your overall score. The reason that it doesn't is because HRCI doesn't want the score reports being misused. For example, if I scored 510 points and another candidate scored 520 points, those additional points don't necessarily mean she is a better HR candidate than me.

    You should wait to use the initials after your name or communicate your exam results until you receive the formal score report from HRCI within four to six weeks of your test date. At that point, you can search the directory of certified professionals for your name at www.hrci.org.

- ✔ **If you didn't pass:** Your official score report will compare your individual result with the score you needed to pass. You'll also see your overall performance, so that you know what areas need to be improved upon prior to retaking the test. If you didn't pass, you must wait until the next exam window to test again.

Contesting your results

If you encountered a problem during your exam, such as a computer not working properly, you need to notify Prometric. A test administrator may be able to help you on-site, although you must report any escalated issues to Prometric within 72 hours of your test date.

If you fail the exam, you can contest the results with HRCI and ask for an exam review for a fee a $50. Doing so may be worthwhile if you failed the test only by a few points. You have up to two months after your test date to submit the review request and fees.

Considering other fees

You may be interested in other services that HRCI offers. Here is a list of the other fees that you may want to consider:

✔ Reschedule after exam window opens: $85

✔ Switch the exam type: $50

✔ Cancel the exam: $75

✔ Receive a duplicate results report: $50

Part II
Managing the Basics: Pre-Test Fundamentals

Five significant insights to certification

- Justify the value of certification in a day in the life.
- Apply knowledge on the job.
- Stay relevant post-certification.
- Figure out how to use the core knowledge requirements.
- Identify credible business authors and websites to build a study plan.

With the abundance of exam prep materials available on the market today, knowing who to trust to get you prepared for the big exam can be tough. Go to www.dummies.com/extras/phrsphrexam for helpful advice.

In this part . . .

✔ Find ways that human resources can become a long-term career before you retire rather than bouncing from job to job.

✔ Explore how HR professionals are required to be business partners, not just support staff, serving as both the employer and employee advocate while companies navigate change.

✔ Examine how to positively leverage successful certification for increased job satisfaction and salary growth.

✔ Understand that the core knowledge requirements are paramount to building a study plan that serves your unique preparation needs.

Chapter 5

Career Day: Life of a Certified HR Professional

• •

In This Chapter

▶ Following tendencies in human resources

▶ Taking a closer look at the numbers

▶ Using your knowledge on the job

• •

The history of what is currently known as the PHR and SPHR exams is really quite interesting. Under its earlier name, the Society for Human Resources (SHRM) commissioned a taskforce based on a study of industrial relations in the 1960s. The focus was on whether or not the field of human resources was a true profession, similar to that of a lawyer, doctor, or accountant. This study and other studies identified characteristics that must exist in order for a body of work to be defined as a profession. Because these other industries weren't a perfect fit for the practice of HR, the discussion evolved until it was decided that the HR profession must

✔ **Be a full-time responsibility.** In human resources, the tasks, duties, and responsibilities are performed on a full-time basis in many functional areas. Examples include training, compensation, and safety.

✔ **Have a body of knowledge (BOK) from which schools could teach.** The HR body of knowledge is used for the PHR and SPHR exams, and there is a process for updating and certifying the BOK approximately every five years.

✔ **Have a professional association, along with competency and knowledge certifications.** The Society for Human Resource Management (SHRM) is perhaps the most well known HR association. In 1976, the Human Resource Certification Institute (HRCI) began offering the HR exams known today as the PHR and SPHR. Several other related professional associations have been linked to the business of HR, including World at Work (total rewards) and the Association for Talent Development (training and organizational development). Both of these associations have certifications for HR professionals.

✔ **Be governed by a code of ethics.** Although SHRM and other groups have codes of ethics, the exam-relevant code of ethics is published by HRCI. It includes standards for professional responsibility, professional development, ethical leadership, fairness and integrity, conflict of interest management, as well as how you should use that information.

Since the 1960s, a pattern has emerged. Agencies have changed names, exams have changed names, and content has developed and evolved; it has certainly been a work in progress. The same can be said of your career. An HR professional must continue to evolve to keep pace with this ever-changing profession. Although your choice to pursue certification is a strategic career move, it also serves a larger goal that brings everyone to the same table. The preparation process teaches all one language and helps everyone apply best practices to their workplaces while mentoring a new generation of talent. Your effort demonstrates a commitment to professional excellence and fits perfectly within the spirit that guides the evolution of our industry.

This chapter explores a day in the life of a certified HR professional that takes into account current trends for which you must prepare, the emerging role and responsibilities of your position of trust within the company that you serve, and how to best apply your knowledge on the job.

Tracking Trends in Human Resources

Like any business function, HR has lots of data that can be tracked and measured. In fact, much of HR's history runs parallel to the evolution of business as a whole. For this reason, it's not enough to only seek education in HR. You must commit to being a business resource for the industry in which you practice. Although HR can support industries from mining to medical billing, these industries have completely different needs from an organizational perspective. So bouncing from industry to industry on your HR career path isn't wise; find your enterprise and begin to specialize.

Trends in human resources allow you to keep pace both with your profession and best business practices. These exams update every five years for that very reason. HRCI recognizes that how people do in their jobs changes based on several factors, including the role of education in the field, technology advances, global consumer markets, and the ebb and flow of the supply and demand of talent. I discuss these factors in more detail in the following sections.

Understanding educational trends

These exams support a baseline of knowledge that you must have in order to best serve the multiple industries where you work. In fact, the process of preparing for these exams may make you feel like you're in graduate school. In addition, these exams require recertification, which means those individuals certified must engage in development activities that support the variety of exam objectives based on best practices. The great news is that getting and staying educated has truly never been easier in the HR field.

Emerging trends in HR education must begin with a discussion of the virtual playing field. The traditional classroom is no longer the only place to go to learn, and options are available for every budget. If you have some money to invest, consider an online master's degree in HR from universities such as Cornell or Penn State. These programs are often a *hybrid* — a blend of online, virtual learning, and a few weeks of the year spent on campus.

If your budget or time has constraints, other options are available for you as well. The website www.humanresourcewebinars.com offers an archive of previously recorded HR topics at no charge to participants. At www.bookboon.com, you can download and read books on just about anything (HR, project management, self confidence), also at no cost. And the trend of open universities such as the one offered at MIT offers an education without the degree, also at no cost.

Although having a formal education is helpful in HR, it isn't always required, and certification is a great alternative place to start and get you up to speed.

 When you're researching educational opportunities for your HR career or studying for either the PHR or SPHR exam, make sure the sources that you're using for your informal or formal online HR education are reputable. Just because something is on the Internet doesn't make it true. Look for clues such as websites ending in *.org, .gov,* or *.edu.* Don't rely on websites that are written by the general public or driven by opinions. Stay away from online groups that have political agendas or other bits that may render them biased advisors.

Clarifying the role of HR

The role of HR had continued to evolve alongside the needs of the employers that they support. The stereotype of a party planners has been replaced with a vision of business partners, participating in strategic planning and supporting the core competencies. You can easily view the role of an HR professional through the lens of a PEST analysis — the political, economic, social, and technological changes in the industry:

- **Political:** The most obvious way that the political climate impacts how the role of an HR professional has changed is the abundance of labor law. Changes to healthcare and immigration reform are highly visible examples of why you must stay up-to-date every year. These exams test you not only on labor law, but also on the role of HR in lobbying efforts to affect change.

- **Economic:** Like many other industries, HR hunkers down to weather out tough economies. HR is different from other jobs however in that HR professionals also help organizations create solutions when things get tight. Recent examples include managing work furloughs, controlling benefits costs, and retaining key people. Demonstrating the value of HR through leadership and excellence will likely pop up on the exams.

- **Social:** Several social indicators are likely to be on the exams that have impacted how the HR role has evolved. They include the need for employees to find balance in their work and family lives, the management of a multigenerational workforce, and the global landscape from which many companies now compete.

- **Technological:** The need for cell phone policies and the popularity of learning management systems (LMS) are just two examples of the broad impact technology has had on how HR does business. Other examples include the use of technology for employee self-service, virtual interviewing, and the need to manage and protect employee and customer confidential information.

The term *business partner (BP)* is a good way to understand what companies need from their HR people. A good BP understands the business, not just his job. A BP comprehends the finances, seeking ways to respond to threats while maintaining a competitive advantage in the competitive market. Because HR doesn't generate direct revenue, the department must find other ways to demonstrate value by continuing to evolve right alongside the business that are supported.

Social media is an exam-relevant example of how a PEST analysis can help you go deeper into content. For example,

The *political* climate is being shaken up by the National Labor Relations Board, claiming that employees' right to post complaints online about their working conditions or pay is a protected activity.

The *economic* climate has driven an increase in the use of social media to find both jobs and workers.

Socially, the employer brand is often communicated via social media websites through videos and employee testimonials.

Although *technology* has improved efficiencies, many of today's workers report surfing personal social media sites while on the job, which certainly has an impact on productivity.

Use the PEST analysis to interpret a muddy exam objective as part of your studying efforts. Suggestions include HR needs such as substance abuse, union organizing, and hiring veterans.

Using the Statistics

Understanding who is currently certified and what is most valuable to employers will help you set the course for a successful career in HR. Even if you fail the PHR or the SPHR exam on your first attempt, the information you have gained while studying has already made you a more valuable business partner and hirable candidate. Don't give up! You're already living this day in the life of HR, so reaching higher is simply an extension of what you already know. The stats in these sections show you that you're in great company.

Identifying who is certified and why this information is important

HRCI offers a wide range of exams, with more than 135,000 professionals certified in 100 countries. The HRCI exams have evolved along with the profession, adding tests in HR disciplines that are broad in scope, yet address the global diversity that the industry represents. The HRCI reports some important numbers to give you some perspective:

- **PHR:** 77,408 certified professionals
- **SPHR:** 53,577 certified professionals
- Of those certified, 38 percent serve in specialist roles, whereas 33 percent are managers.
- More than 13,000 applicants applied for the exam in the spring 2014.
- Approximately 43 percent of test takers choose to self-study in preparation for the exam.
- Similar to other professional exams in degree of difficulty, both the PHR and SPHR exams have pass rates that can run between 55 to 60 percent on average.
- Texas leads the number of certified by state with approximately 10,833, followed closely by California at 10,778.

This information is useful for you to determine how competitive your market is for human resource jobs and validates that passing this exam will set you apart from the rest.

Leveraging the impact of certification on salary

The choice to become certified is often quite personal. Although directly related to your professional development, it's a personal achievement that distinguishes you in your industrial community. The feeling of pride and accomplishment that successful certification will bring is legitimate — you worked hard! The impact of certification reaches beyond just the documentation of your talent though. In a survey of top organizations, HRCI discovered that

- Fifty percent of the companies use certification status to decide whom to interview for open HR positions.
- Forty-eight percent of the companies believed that having certified HR talent within their ranks gave them an edge over the competition.
- Fifty percent said that certified HR professionals are more knowledgeable and motivated, and they perform better than their uncertified peers.

This information is quite important for you when it comes time to leverage your new credentials to impact your salary, because it demonstrates the *value* of your certification to businesses.

Communicating your success is the first step on the path to leveraging your success. In fact, if you're anything like the thousands of other exam takers, more than likely everyone at work knew you were preparing for this exam — reading prep books at lunch, searching online for unfamiliar terms, and sharing new information as you discovered it. In short, you geeked out on all things HR for an period of time, which is excellent news. It gives you the opportunity to triumphantly enter the workplace the day after the exam and announce that your effort paid off. Here are some tips on how to get a raise post-certification:

✔ **Do more prep work.** Ask your boss before the exam what your options will be for career growth after you're successfully certified. Establishing the expectations early on aligns your boss with your goals and allows her to gain any approvals before the big day. You may still need to be groomed for that next promotion, but at least you'll know what to expect.

✔ **Ask directly.** Take yourself seriously. You'll just have passed a difficult exam, and that effort should be recognized. Depending on the culture of your work environment, that recognition may come in different forms.

✔ **Establish a plan.** Receiving increased pay, a title change, or a promotion is *not* unreasonable for the newly certified HR professional, but it may take some time. If you've already done the legwork pre-test, then you know that the plan is to increase your pay. If the company you work for isn't able to financially reward your professional success, perhaps the company can offer other ways for you to benefit, such as gaining a senior title. A title is nothing to scoff at, because it demonstrates professional growth on your resume.

You chose to go down the road of certification for some reason, and it certainly wasn't the path of least resistance. You must have your own career plan to help you decide whether you should stay with your current company or look elsewhere for opportunities. Where possible, job changes should serve your resume, not just your pocketbook.

Applying Your Knowledge on the Job

At the end of the day, whether you're able to get a pay increase or not, your role at work is going to change. It's not just because you now have initials next to your name. The preparation process taught you new things, and as the consummate professional that you are, you'll begin to seek change in your workgroup.

These changes will apply in two areas:

✔ **In your department:** Depending on the size of your HR department, you may suddenly become a go-to person for input and advice. If so, consider mentoring a co-worker and coaching him down the certification path. Make it a goal for everyone in the department to become certified so that you're all speaking the same HR language. In another scenario, you may be an HR department of one. If so, I'm sure that you'll have identified areas for increased efficiencies within your workspace all throughout the exam prep process. Proper planning and staying organized will keep you from becoming overwhelmed.

Focus on one or two projects at a time, like auditing Form I-9s or researching employee benefit plans (sooner than the month before open enrollment). Create a master annual HR calendar to schedule special projects.

✔ **Companywide:** Seeking change companywide can be a more of an uphill battle. Begin by making sure they understand what your new certification means. Tell the decision-makers what you studied and how you felt it could benefit the company. This conversation isn't one way either. Make sure that you're listening to the executives, managers, and supervisors to avoid being labeled an academic. Some of the concepts you have learned during your studying aren't a one-size-fits-all solution. Common ground is where the meaningful change occurs.

Focusing on staying relevant: Continuing your education

The expectation of the newly certified HR professional is that you continue to engage in professional development activities; therefore, both the PHR and SPHR certificates are valid for three years. That means that you must recertify your credentials in one of two ways: retake the exam or earn credits. Not surprisingly, many choose to earn the 60 recertification credits over the three-year active window rather than sit for the exam again.

Recertification credits aren't difficult to obtain, but you need to be on the lookout for opportunities. Approved activities may fall into any of the following categories:

✔ **Continuing education:** Part of the HRCI code of ethics is that HR professionals commit to professional development. Taking classes, attending seminars, and participating in webinars are all activities that can go toward recertifying your credential.

✔ **Instruction:** Teaching an HR class or a topic of which you're an expert is a great way to reinforce your learning while mentoring others. Perhaps you can guest speak at your local university or present at an HR networking luncheon.

✔ **On-the-job training (OJT):** The classic OJT works for recertification credits. They typically need to be for tasks or responsibilities that are new to your role.

✔ **Research/publications:** With the abundance of online publishing, blogs, and e-newsletters, plenty of opportunities are out there for you to write on an HR topic that may be trendy or of interest to other professionals. Conducting field, boots-on-the-ground research and sharing your findings is another creative and job-related way to get recertified.

✔ **Leadership:** Leading teams or projects are not only bonus worthy, but they also will earn you recertification credits with proper documentation.

✔ **Professional membership:** Log any professional memberships you have such as SHRM or ATD for additional credits.

There is also no need to only look for approved programs. After you're certified, you'll be able to go into your HRCI profile and log work activities or educational activities to submit along with your recertification application.

Demonstrating knowledge: Positively impacting your employer

Business as usual isn't always the best policy, but wanting to change too much too fast can actually damage your credibility. Think carefully about what is book smart compared to changes that your employer or teammates can reasonably be expected to tolerate. There will come a time however when you really must speak up and advocate for a change. How you do so will be the difference between being a hero or viewed as the office pariah. Ways to constructively offer feedback to your team or company include

✔ **Seek to understand.** Asking the right questions about why a process is in place can help you understand the desired outcome.

✔ **Know the facts.** After you understand what the company needs from a person or process, you can data gather. Strive to *be the expert* when it comes to the numbers and statistics to ensure that your idea is the best course of action. You must not only know your job, but also the industry and business functions that you support. Do things such as work the line, answer the phones, ship the widgets, work the night shift; in short, live the impact your suggestions may have on your people or processes.

✔ **Be flexible.** After you comprehend the outcome and have all the facts, you may have to abandon your attempt, because it may not be the right option. You may also work with the management team on a *buffet solution,* where you take a little bit from here and a little bit from there and mash it all together. A commitment to a collaborative, flexible effort will help you gain trust.

✔ **Time it right.** Timing has two issues that you must consider:

 • **How you present your ideas:** Trying to gain permission in the hallway while your boss is walking into a meeting isn't the time to articulate your thoughts. You're bound to shortchange your ideas.

 • **When you present your ideas:** Many business have seasons, so proper planning can help you and your management team work around these peak times of year. For example, the best time to introduce new point-of-service software in retail is not November or December.

✔ **Speak their language.** HR people often have to be chameleons, blending into all organizational environments and departments. Know the priorities of the groups that you serve and speak to those needs before anything else. If the VP of HR needs business metrics, be sure to include a system to deliver in any proposed change.

✔ **Study change management techniques.** *Change management* (the process of systematically coordinating and managing change in the workplace) is a well-researched topic. Become the change management guru at your organization, bringing others along with you. Most people fear change, and fear is a powerful deterrent to any behavior, no matter how well designed. Teaching your company to embrace the new can help them compete — a win for all who work there.

Know that your long-term impact may take time to materialize. It may even take a change of leadership or business strategy to launch your ideas. Having a consistent, flexible approach can help you gain trust and create a successful business partnership.

Constructively criticizing: What to do when you disagree

Constructive conflict is the fuel that drives the corporate engine. If everyone always agrees when a new topic is introduced, you should question whether you have an engaged management team or workforce. The good news is that docile compliance isn't a typical state of work; opportunities abound for lively disagreements about people, products and services, or work procedures. Not only will you need to help facilitate these conversations, but you also will often be the instigator of the conflict. For this reason, in any disagreement, you should first understand your role. Determine if you're there to facilitate the dialogue in a neutral fashion, or if you're there to provide constructive feedback about why you disagree.

Here I discuss a few important topics to guide you through this process of communication, which includes the ability to facilitate dialogue rather than teach a topic and provide constructive feedback and guidance where necessary.

Grasping the role of facilitation

Facilitation is the art of suspending your own opinions and beliefs while delicately extracting tiny little bombs of information from others without detonation. It requires the ability to ask questions, reform comments, and keep participants focused on the business at hand. Start by identifying the common goals and shared rewards, and then work backward to identify what must be done to get there. In facilitation, you aren't the expert.

Providing constructive feedback

Constructive feedback is similar to facilitation, except that you're now a participant in the arena. Although the focus must still be on business needs, you're now actively trying to modify behavior. The foundation of this feedback must be courtesy, dignity, and respect. Most individuals aren't devising diabolical plans of disruption at work in the morning while brushing their teeth. They have a reason for behaving the way they behave, and they deserve the courtesy of understanding their motivation and reasoning before being expected to jump on the bandwagon of change. Consider using humor, asking for their opinions on how to make something better, or trying self-deprecation.

Keep in mind that providing constructive feedback isn't punitive. Find a way to show the individual why his work life will be better if he takes your feedback and applies it to his job. Then be sure to follow up to see how it's working for him. This approach to coaching becomes a flexible win-win for both parties.

Chapter 6

Examining the Core Areas of Knowledge

In This Chapter

▶ Getting familiar with the core knowledge requirements (CKR)

▶ Studying with the CKR

▶ Distinguishing between CKR and the body of knowledge (BOK)

▶ Using the knowledge in your study plan

*T*he core knowledge requirements (CKR) are part of the fundamental HR principles that serve to expand upon the exam objectives. They reflect best practices in human resources and business. Many test takers aren't aware that the connection between the core knowledge requirements and exam objectives exist, which means they aren't using them to guide their preparation efforts. This chapter shares study strategies with you to help you capitalize on that connection, while describing the CKR in detail.

Relating the Core Knowledge to Exam Objectives

As an experienced HR practitioner, you're probably familiar with the process of creating job descriptions. It begins with a thorough analysis of the tasks, duties, and responsibilities of the job, followed by an in-depth compilation of the individual knowledge, skills, and abilities that an individual must have for successful performance.

In designing exam objectives, HRCI uses a *practice analysis study* (PAS), in which a job analysis of sorts is conducted on the work of HR, producing the industry's job description. Two primary elements make up this job description:

✔ **Exam objectives:** They describe the responsibilities of a HR professional and are independently numbered for each functional area.

✔ **Core knowledge requirements:** They describe the knowledge necessary to execute the responsibilities. The CKR are consecutively numbered, representing all exam functional areas.

The PAS is boots-on-the-ground action, which means that HRCI uses a taskforce to review the exam objectives and knowledge statements to remove obsolete items or make the necessary changes to keep the objectives relevant. HRCI also conducts a validation survey, in which HR professionals are asked to rate the percent of time spent on each task in the current BOK and the importance of the knowledge statements. The PAS is conducted approximately every five years, with any changes reflected in the exam updates.

This information is important to you because it underscores the importance of *both* the exam objectives and CKR as you prepare for the PHR and the SPHR. The following sections explain what you need to know about the CKR and how to apply it while you study.

Understanding the differences

Both the PHR and SPHR exams have a shared body of knowledge that measures the ability of the individual to perform the tasks, duties, and responsibilities of an HR professional, as well as to apply sound business and HR principles to their performance. Although the responsibilities and knowledge of components are different, they're still connected. These links include the task that needs to be completed and the knowledge necessary to do so. You'll benefit from using the connections to study.

Table 6-1 gives you a few examples directly from the Human Resource Development (HRD) area of the BOK.

Table 6-1	The Difference between BOK Responsibilities and Knowledge
Responsibility	*Knowledge of*
01. Ensure that HR development activities are compliant with all applicable federal laws and regulations.	27. Applicable federal laws and regulations related to HR development activities; for example, Title VII, ADA, Title VII (Copyright law).
02. Conduct a needs assessment to identify and establish priorities regarding HR development activities.	28. Career development and leadership development theories and applications; for example, succession planning and dual career ladders.

As you the table demonstrates, there are direct links between the tasks and responsibilities, and the knowledge required to perform these tasks.

Take note of their numbering system. In this example, HRD has nine exam objectives described under the responsibilities, yet the *knowledge of* section begins at number 27 (not 10) because the core knowledge responsibilities are written as one master list that runs through all of the functional areas. So you'll see the first *knowledge of* component in the first functional area (Business Management and Strategy), and they follow numerically. I list them later in the "Identifying the CKR" section in one continuous flow. You should study them from the functional area perspective to ensure that you're connecting the right dots.

Relying on experience

Both the PHR and SPHR exams are based on experience performance, not rote memorization. As a result, it's unreasonable to expect that any one exam preparation system will completely prepare you to take these tests. I suggest that you view the CKR areas through the filter based on your experience. If you lack in any area, you should focus on resources to fill the gap.

For example, look at this example

Functional area: Workforce Planning and Employment

Exam Objective: 05. Influence and establish criteria for hiring, retaining, and promoting based on job descriptions and required competencies.

Knowledge of: 13. Recruitment sources — for example, employee referral, social networking/social media — for targeting passive, semi-active, and active candidates.

Work experience application: In this case, the objective is asking you to use job descriptions to find qualified applicants, hire new employees, and establish the performance criteria necessary to promote them. The *knowledge of* component tells you what resources you may tap to complete the tasks described in the objective. For this example, think about how you have used social media in the past to recruit and hire. What websites did you use and what were the results? Were there challenges associated with the recruiting source or risks at hiring that needed to be mitigated? Consider the legal implications such as privacy laws. Screen your experience by the results. Who did you find on websites such as LinkedIn versus a website such as Instagram? Where did you find working baby boomers or the newly educated?

 If a particular concept or relationship is muddy, reach out to a mentor and ask. For this example, every HR professional probably knows someone who is in the staffing industry. If you don't, find your local HR association and reach out to a board member. Ask about how she uses social media and what works versus what doesn't. This commitment to your studying can help you master the experience component of both exams.

Applying the Core Knowledge Requirements to Your Study Plan

The exam content is less murky then you may think. The Human Resource Certification Institute (HRCI) has established the exam components in a very systematic way. Your ability to take what HRCI is telling you and apply it to exam conditions is directly correlated to a pass or fail. For this reason, it behooves you to train yourself to the exam objectives and core knowledge requirements. For that, you need to know what they are.

HRCI has published the BOK along with the CKR on its website (www.hrci.org), and I include it here, along with a short description after each area that gives you a summary of what follows.

Business Management and Strategy

This functional area of Business Management and Strategy (BMS) relates to having working knowledge of general business principles. It includes the development of the mission, vision, and values; the process of strategic planning; the creation of business plans; and the knowledge of the roles of different business units and structures. It also places heavy emphasis on metrics. The HRCI knowledge items for BMS are

- 01 The organization's mission, vision, values, business goals, objectives, plans, and processes.

- 02 Legislative and regulatory processes

✔ 03 Strategic planning process, design, implementation, and evaluation

✔ 04 Management functions, including planning, organizing, directing, and controlling

✔ 05 Corporate governance procedures and compliance; for example, Sarbanes-Oxley Act

✔ 06 Due diligence processes; for example, M & A and divestitures (SPHR only)

✔ 07 Transition techniques for corporate restructuring, M & A, offshoring, and divestitures (SPHR only)

✔ 08 Elements of a cost-benefit analysis during the life cycle of the business (such as scenarios for growth, including expected, economic stressed, and worst-case conditions) and the impact to net worth/earnings for short-, mid-, and long-term horizons

✔ 09 Business concepts; for example, competitive advantage, organizational branding, business case development, corporate responsibility

Workforce Planning and Employment

Approximately 9 of the 16 knowledge objectives in Workforce Planning and Employment (WPE) relate to the recruiting and selection process. WPE makes up 24 percent of the PHR exam, so it's wise to spend a good bit of your study time on recruiting and selection. Other elements include the unwinding of employment, forecasting labor, and assessing talent for business re-organization or growth. The HRCI knowledge items for WPE are

✔ 11 Applicable federal laws and regulations related to workforce planning and employment activities; for example, Title VII, ADA, EEOC Uniform Guidelines on Employee Selection Procedures, Immigration Reform and Control Act

✔ 12 Methods to assess past and future staffing effectiveness; for example, costs per hire, selection ratios, adverse impact

✔ 13 Recruitment sources for targeting passive, semi-active, and active candidates; for example, employee referral and social networking/social media

✔ 14 Recruitment strategies

✔ 15 Staffing alternatives; for example; outsourcing, job sharing, and phased retirement

✔ 16 Planning techniques; for example, succession planning and forecasting

✔ 17 Reliability and validity of selection tests/tools/ methods

✔ 18 Use and interpretation of selection tests; for example, psychological/personality, cognitive, motor/physical assessments, performance, and assessment center

✔ 19 Interviewing techniques; for example, behavioral, situational, and panel

✔ 20 Impact of compensation and benefits on recruitment and retention

✔ 21 International HR and implications of global workforce for workforce planning and employment (SPHR only)

✔ 22 Voluntary and involuntary terminations, downsizing, restructuring, and outplacement strategies and practices

✔ 23 Internal workforce assessment techniques; for example, skills testing, skills inventory, and workforce demographic analysis

✔ 24 Employment policies, practices, and procedures; for example, orientation, on-boarding, and retention

✔ 25 Employer marketing and branding techniques

✔ 26 Negotiation skills and techniques

Human Resource Development

After employment has been launched in the workforce planning stage, it becomes necessary for HR practitioners to develop and retain the employees. Human Resource Development (HRD) communicate the need for career development, management, and executive coaching, and in the case of SPHR candidates, a solid understanding of global issues and training metrics. The HRCI knowledge items for HRD are

- ✔ 27 Applicable federal laws and regulations related to human resources development activities; for example, Title VII, ADA, and Title 17 (Copyright law)

- ✔ 28 Career development and leadership development theories and applications; for example, succession planning and dual career ladders

- ✔ 29 Organizational development (OD) theories and applications

- ✔ 30 Training program development techniques to create general and specialized training programs

- ✔ 31 Facilitation techniques, instructional methods, and program delivery mechanisms

- ✔ 32 Task/process analysis

- ✔ 33 Performance appraisal methods; for example, instruments and ranking and rating scales

- ✔ 34 Performance management methods; for example, goal setting, relationship to compensation, and job placements/promotions

- ✔ 35 Applicable global issues; for example, international law, culture, local management approaches/practices, and societal norms (SPHR only)

- ✔ 36 Techniques to assess training program effectiveness, including use of applicable metrics; for example, participant surveys, and pre- and post-testing)

- ✔ 37 Mentoring and executive coaching

Compensation and Benefits

In Compensation and Benefits (CAB), candidates are asked to understand concepts related to pay practices and structures. It's not just about base pay either. Knowledge of variable pay plans, non-cash compensation, and employee benefits is necessary to successful navigate this area. The HRCI knowledge items for CAB are

- ✔ 38 Applicable federal laws and regulations related to compensation, benefits, and tax; for example, FLSA, ERISA, FMLA, and USERRA

- ✔ 39 Compensation and benefits strategies

- ✔ 40 Budgeting and accounting practices related to compensation and benefits

- ✔ 41 Job evaluation methods

- ✔ 42 Job pricing and pay structures

- ✔ 43 External labor markets and/or economic factors

- ✔ 44 Pay programs; for example, variable and merit

- ✔ 45 Executive compensation methods (SPHR only)

- ✔ 46 Noncash compensation methods; for example, equity programs and noncash rewards

✔ 47 Benefits programs; for example, health and welfare, retirement, and Employee Assistance Programs (EAPs)

✔ 48 International compensation laws and practices; for example, expatriate compensation, entitlements, and choice of law codes (SPHR only)

✔ 49 Fiduciary responsibilities related to compensation and benefits

Employee and Labor Relations

Striving for balance between employees and their employers, and in some cases, the union, is the information you need to understand for the Employee and Labor Relations (ELR) content area. Immerse yourself in relationship management in the form of retention strategies, union practices, and management of the separation process. The HRCI knowledge items for ELR are

✔ 50 Applicable federal laws affecting employment in union and nonunion environments, such as laws regarding antidiscrimination policies, sexual harassment, labor relations, and privacy; for example, WARN Act, Title VII, and NLRA

✔ 51 Techniques and tools for facilitating positive employee relations; for example, employee surveys, dispute/conflict resolution, and labor/management cooperative strategies

✔ 52 Employee involvement strategies; for example, employee management committees, self-directed work teams, and staff meetings

✔ 53 Individual employment rights issues and practices; for example, employment at will, negligent hiring, and defamation

✔ 54 Workplace behavior issues/practices; for example, absenteeism and performance improvement

✔ 55 Unfair labor practices

✔ 56 The collective bargaining process, strategies, and concepts; for example, contract negotiation, costing, and administration

✔ 57 Legal disciplinary procedures

✔ 58 Positive employee relations strategies and nonmonetary rewards

✔ 59 Techniques for conducting unbiased investigations

✔ 60 Legal termination procedures

Risk Management

Spend your study time wisely in the Risk Management (RM) content area, because it's a low percentage of content for both the PHR and SPHR exams. Go deep in the labor laws, such as OSHA, ADA, ADAAA, and HIPAA, because they're cross-functional. Make sure and take an expanded view of these concepts with information on workplace violence, injury and illness prevention programs (IIPP), and substance abuse in the workplace. The HRCI knowledge items for RM are

✔ 61 Applicable federal laws and regulations related to workplace health, safety, security, and privacy; for example, OSHA, Drug-Free Workplace Act, ADA, ADAAA, HIPAA, and the Sarbanes-Oxley Act

✔ 62 Occupational injury and illness prevention (safety) and compensation programs

✔ 63 Investigation procedures of workplace safety, health, and security enforcement agencies

✔ 64 Return-to-work procedures; for example, interactive dialog, job modification, and accommodations

✔ 65 Workplace safety risks; for example, trip hazards, and blood-borne pathogens

✔ 66 Workplace security risks; for example, theft, corporate espionage, and sabotage

✔ 67 Potential violent behavior and workplace violence conditions

✔ 68 General health and safety practices; for example, evacuation, hazard communication, and ergonomic evaluations

✔ 69 Organizational incident and emergency response plans

✔ 70 Internal investigation, monitoring, and surveillance techniques

✔ 71 Employer/employee rights related to substance abuse

✔ 72 Business continuity and disaster recovery plans; for example, data storage and backup, alternative work locations, and procedures

✔ 73 Data integrity techniques and technology; for example, data sharing, password usage, and social engineering

✔ 74 Technology and applications; for example, social media, monitoring software, and biometrics

✔ 75 Financial management practices; for example, procurement policies, credit card policies and guidelines, and expense policies

Other knowledge requirements

The PHR and SPHR exams have 23 other components for two possible reasons:

✔ They may not fall neatly into just one of the previous functions, or

✔ They apply to facets of *all* of the previous categories for studying.

For this reason, you should allocate a good portion of your study time on these knowledge requirements by checking to see where and toward what they apply. From HRCI, these include

✔ 76 Needs assessment and analysis

✔ 77 Third-party or vendor selection, contract negotiation, and management, including development of requests for proposals (RFPs)

✔ 78 Communication skills and strategies; for example, presentation, collaboration, and sensitivity

✔ 79 Organizational documentation requirements to meet federal and state guidelines

✔ 80 Adult learning processes

✔ 81 Motivation concepts and applications

✔ 82 Training technique; for example, virtual, classroom, and on-the-job training

✔ 83 Leadership concepts and applications

✔ 84 Project management concepts and applications

- ✔ 85 Diversity concepts and applications; for example, generational, cultural competency, and learning styles

- ✔ 86 Human relations concepts and applications; for example, emotional intelligence and organizational behavior

- ✔ 87 Ethical and professional standards

- ✔ 88 Technology to support HR activities; for example, HR information systems, employee self-service, e-learning, and applicant tracking systems

- ✔ 89 Qualitative and quantitative methods and tools for analysis, interpretation, and decision-making purposes (for example: metrics and measurements, cost/benefit analysis, financial statement analysis)

- ✔ 90 Change management theory, methods, and application

- ✔ 91 Job analysis and job description methods

- ✔ 92 Employee records management; for example, electronic/paper, retention, and disposal

- ✔ 93 Techniques for forecasting, planning, and predicting the impact of HR activities and programs across functional areas

- ✔ 94 Types of organizational structures; for example, matrix and hierarchy

- ✔ 95 Environmental scanning concepts and applications; for example, Strengths, Weaknesses, Opportunities, and Threats (SWOT) and Political, Economic, Social, and Technological (PEST)

- ✔ 96 Methods for assessing employee attitudes, opinions, and satisfaction; for example, surveys and focus groups/panels

- ✔ 97 Budgeting, accounting, and financial concepts

- ✔ 98 Risk-management techniques

Using the Core Knowledge to Study

After you're on the right path, the clues become obvious. It may take some digging, but you can find so much of what you need to apply these CKR online. These sections mention several examples of what may be on the exam, straight from HRCI's website (www.hrci.org).

No one can tell you exactly what is going to be on the exams, but I can make a pretty educated guess based on the BOK and CKR. Because these authors and resources are recommended to build into your study plan, getting to know them better is well worth your time.

HRCI's suggested authors

In addition to publishing the BOK and CKR, the HRCI gives you hints and tips on what material to study. They include must-reads by authors such as:

- ✔ **Warren Bennis:** Bennis is a management theorist in the areas of leadership and behavior management. In general, he states that the traditional organization structure of top-down authority is less effective than democratic or collaborative leadership. Although he has authored several books, you should take a strong look at his work on Douglas McGregor, one of the fathers of humanistic behavior management in the field of industrial psychology. The principles of both of these authors are very likely to be in one form or another on the exams.

✔ **Charles Handy:** Handy is best known for his work on organizational strategy, so SPHR candidates should accord special study time to studying his theories. In short, he discusses the need for businesses to function as a community, with rights and shared responsibilities.

✔ **Geert Hofstede:** A well-respected social psychologist, Hofstede pioneered work in the field of organizational culture. He developed the idea of dimensions of culture, specifically that individuals are "group animals" responding to a moral code of conduct and values that must exist in an organizational community. Familiarize yourself with the concepts of power distance, individualism versus collectivism, masculinity versus femininity, long- versus short-term orientation, and indulgence versus restraint.

✔ **Henry Mintzberg:** The author of several management books, Mintzberg talks quite a bit about balancing the power of economic structures, in which he includes organizations. For purposes of the exams, take a look at his model of 10 managerial roles.

✔ **Kenichi Ohmae:** Ohmae may be best known for his role in illuminating the lean manufacturing principles in the West. Started by Toyota in Japan, lean is a quality management program with the goal of stripping out waste and engaging in just-in-time production. His work, however, is quite broad and focuses on both operations and strategy, making him a necessary read for both PHR and SPHR exam takers.

✔ **Michael Porter:** If you've taken any management strategy classes, you probably have heard of Porter's five forces. His work proved to be part of the foundation of scanning the environment during the strategic planning process for factors influencing a company's success or failure. They include supplier power, buyer power, competitive rivalry, threat of substitution, and threat of new entry. Also, be familiar with his five generic strategies.

✔ **C.K. Prahalad:** Prahalad makes for good company on this list of pioneers. Much of his work was focused on corporate strategy and the need for business to break through traditional competitive boundaries and invent new markets. A great example of this is his book titled *The Fortune at the Bottom of the Pyramid,* which discusses how organizations can compete and profit while eradicating poverty.

✔ **Edgar Schein:** A prolific author, Schein's work in organizational culture, leadership, and management theory is quite broad. PHR candidates will benefit from his work on modern career pathing and leadership development. SPHR candidates should go deep in his works about organizational culture and its impact on outcomes.

✔ **Peter Senge:** Organizational learning is the focus of Senge's work. He viewed organizations as one whole system with inter-related parts (departments) that are completely dependent upon organizational health. Called *systems thinking,* it's the fifth discipline of how organizations learn, integrating the other four that include personal mastery, mental models, shared vision, and team learning.

✔ **Dave Ulrich's Scorecards:** You must spend time on business and HR scorecards, and Ulrich is the man to help you. As HR practitioners, it's your responsibility to develop measurements that help your company make data-driven decisions. His work talks about what must be measured and the tools you may use to do so.

Online business journals

The exam BOK is updated every five years, and item writers use popular business research sources (along with field studies, peer-reviewed research, and a host of other techniques) to increase the relevance of the exam to the current business climate. Here are three credible sources listed by HRCI that are a must-visit for supplemental exam materials:

- ✔ **McKinsey & Company:** An international management consulting firm, this company doesn't just consult, it researches and shares findings online at www.mckinsey.com. Sign up for its tweets or emails and incorporate its articles in your daily mash of studying. Its topics are quite diverse and relate to broader issues, such as global business to more topical issues like the impact of obesity on the workforce.

- ✔ **The Boston Consulting Group:** The BCG publishes information through its website (www.bcg.com). It includes a host of business-related information, including global perspectives, CEO engagement, technology, and business transformations. You can view the group's information online or sign up for its magazine to strengthen your studying efforts.

- ✔ **Deloitte & Touche:** Another global company, Deloitte is most relevant to the exams based on its surveys and business articles. Some of the topics covered at Deloitte University Press include CFO focus, business analytics, risk management, and performance. Check out www.deloitte.com.

Employing the Principles: Going Deeper

You may be wondering how you're going to find the time to go deep and study all of the material on the PHR and/or SPHR exams. At this stage of your studying, I must emphasize how critical your daily commitment is to success. Reading all of these books and absorbing enough to apply to the exam is ideal, but probably not necessary. Instead, consider implementing the following study goals:

- ✔ Commit to spending 10 or 20 minutes each day outside of your normal study time to research the authors from the previous section "HRCI's suggested authors" and their work.

- ✔ Watch videos online where the authors give lectures, which may be the best way to immerse yourself in what *they* believed was important about their work.

- ✔ Create a master document or flashcards of what you believe is most relevant, focusing on themes of leadership development, company culture, metrics, and strategy.

- ✔ Look for common threads between these authors and articles, and extract what best applies to the exam objectives.

As with so many other facets of these tests, proper planning and development of meaningful study tools can ease your mind and get you ready for exam day.

You're not studying for an MBA, so focus your time on the application of these principles to the exam objectives. Taking a broader view of this material may be interesting, but not purposeful to the one goal that you're focusing on — getting a passing score.

Finally, trust yourself and your talent. What seems overwhelming at first glance will eventually come together in an identifiable shape, and you can see how these pieces fit together in your job as an HR professional. That awareness can help you apply the knowledge to the exam questions, so don't give up if at first it seems fragmented and unconnected. Build the foundation, and the "a-ha" moment will come.

Part III
The Ins and Outs of the PHR/SPHR Exams

Top five fundamentals of the exams

- ✔ Review all of the exam objectives that build exam content so that you know what to study.

- ✔ Focus your preparation efforts on key exam topics to ensure that you're studying the right things.

- ✔ Maximize the Internet to expand your knowledge base and create depth in critical exam concepts.

- ✔ Identify common HR tools and reports that the exam will test you on.

- ✔ Discover government resources for ancillary study material that will help you better understand how labor laws apply to the workplace.

Refer to www.dummies.com/extras/phrsphrexam for more information to help you prepare for the PHR and SPHR exam.

In this part . . .

✔ Review HRCI's exam functional areas and exam knowledge objectives, which are the most credible sources of what may be on your exam.

✔ Discover ways to use the Internet to expand your resources and knowledge so you can go beyond a textbook (and this book) for success.

✔ Become knowledgeable about common HR reports and tools that are used in day-to-day operations. These exams are experienced based, so get ready by learning how to interpret and apply these fundamental reports and formulas.

✔ Focus on exam-specific topics that are likely to show up on your test based on the exam objectives, knowledge components, and reports of other exam takers.

✔ Practice your test-taking skills on a few example questions while studying critical HR topics.

✔ Familiarize yourself with the language and acronyms of both business management and human resources so you can successfully interpret the exam questions.

Chapter 7

The Key to Success: Business Management and Strategy (BMS)

· ·

In This Chapter

▶ Examining five important areas of BMS

▶ Identifying additional resources for help with BMS

· ·

*B*usiness Management and Strategy (BMS) is the functional area of the exam that focuses specifically on the need for human resources to be strategic business partners. It requires a thorough understanding of the relationships between human resources and the stakeholders. These stakeholders may include

- ✔ Executive management
- ✔ Employees and their families
- ✔ Suppliers and vendors
- ✔ Investors
- ✔ Community

For purposes of BMS, the stakeholders are anyone within or outside of the organization that has an interest in the future of the company.

HRCI defines this functional area as follows:

"Developing, contributing to, and supporting the organization's mission, vision, values, strategic goals, and objectives; formulating policies; guiding and leading the change process; and evaluating organizational effectiveness as an organizational leader."

This chapter helps you prepare for BMS questions, so that when you encounter them on the exams, you aren't surprised.

Eyeing the BMS Exam Objectives

The BMS exam objectives can be categorized as related to general business principles and best practices and the process of strategic planning. The objectives also are heavily oriented toward the need to create and utilize various business metrics to assess the effectiveness of organizational efforts. Here are the PHR and SPHR Bodies of Knowledge (BOK) defined by the Human Resource Certification Institute:

- 01 Interpret and apply information related to the organization's operations from internal sources, including finance, accounting, business development, marketing, sales, operations, and information technology, in order to contribute to the development of the organization's strategic plan.

- 02 Interpret information from external sources related to the general business environment, industry practices and developments, technological advances, economic environment, labor force, and the legal and regulatory environment, in order to contribute to the development of the organization's strategic plan.

- 03 Participate as a contributing partner in the organization's strategic planning process; for example, provide and lead workforce planning discussion with management and develop and present long-term forecast of human capital needs at the organizational level (SPHR only).

- 04 Establish strategic relationships with key individuals in the organization to influence organizational decision-making.

- 05 Establish relationships/alliances with key individuals and outside organizations to assist in achieving the organization's strategic goals and objectives; for example, corporate social responsibility and community partnership.

- 06 Develop and utilize business metrics to measure the achievement of the organization's strategic goals and objectives; for example, key performance indicators, balanced scorecard (SPHR only).

- 07 Develop, influence, and execute strategies for managing organizational change that balance the expectations and needs of the organization, its employees, and other stakeholders.

- 08 Develop and align the human resource strategic plan with the organization's strategic plan (SPHR only).

- 09 Facilitate the development and communication of the organization's core values, vision, mission, and ethical behaviors.

- 10 Reinforce the organization's core values and behavioral expectations through modeling, communication, and coaching.

- 11 Provide data such as human capital projections and costs that support the organization's overall budget.

- 12 Develop and execute business plans — for example, annual goals and objectives — that correlate with the organization's strategic plan's performance expectations to include growth targets, new programs/services, and net income expectations (SPHR only).

- 13 Perform cost/benefit analyses on proposed projects (SPHR only).

- 14 Develop and manage an HR budget that supports the organization's strategic goals, objectives, and values (SPHR only).

- 15 Monitor the legislative and regulatory environment for proposed changes and their potential impact to the organization, taking appropriate proactive steps to support, modify, or oppose the proposed changes.

- 16 Develop policies and procedures to support corporate governance initiatives; for example, whistleblower protection and code of ethics.

- 17 Participate in enterprise risk management by ensuring that policies contribute to protecting the organization from potential risks.

- 18 Identify and evaluate alternatives and recommend strategies for vendor selection and/or outsourcing (SPHR only).

- 19 Oversee or lead the transition and/or implementation of new systems, service centers, and outsourcing (SPHR only).

- 20 Participate in strategic decision-making and due diligence activities related to organizational structure and design; for example, corporate restructuring, mergers and acquisitions (M&A), and divestitures (SPHR only).

- 21 Determine strategic application of integrated technical tools and systems; for example, new enterprise software, performance management tools, and self-service technologies (SPHR only).

Both the PHR and the SPHR explore these relationships in depth; however, BMS makes up 30 percent of the SPHR exam and 11 percent of the PHR exam, which means that the SPHR exam has approximately 53 questions related to this exam content, and the PHR exam has approximately 19 questions.

Focusing on What You Need to Know about BMS

BMS, as the title suggests, is broken up into two parts:

- **Business management:** Human resources is not only a function of business, but also a champion of business, which requires professionals have a solid understanding of basic business principles and a working knowledge of other departments within the company. Not only are you tasked with managing your own department, but also you're also responsible for helping other department managers do the same. Think about what you know about finance or ponder the productivity standards of your workforce. As this chapter discusses, you must have enough working knowledge of these other business functions to add value and support your company's outcomes. These outcomes are a major part of the development of a business strategy.

- **Strategy:** *Strategy is* another term for action plan or map. Think of a strategy in terms of military action:

  - The mission is established.

  - The environment is scanned for obstacles or threats.

  - A plan and timeline is developed to achieve the goal and deal with the obstacles.

  - The financial, equipment, and people resources are mustered.

  - Training is completed.

  - The tactical action steps begin.

  - All efforts are measured for success or failure.

A *strategic plan* is a high-level and long-term approach to business that includes the tactical steps necessary to succeed. The following sections break down some of the most important concepts common to both exams. Remember that the SPHR exam has more questions related to BMS than any of the other functional areas.

Exploring the strategic planning process

In no other functional area does the strategic planning process have the most significance than in BMS. However, the outcomes of this process are distributed throughout the HR department and certainly throughout the organization.

The strategic planning process is a series of events that result in a master plan. This plan is designed to achieve the corporate mission. Leaders collect data from multiple resources from inside and outside the organization to help write the plan. From there, tactical goals and actions are created.

During the planning process, threats and obstacles come to light, and it becomes necessary for the planners to create additional strategies, called *interventions*, to address these problems. These interventions address issues is all of the functional areas of HR. Options include re-structuring jobs (Workforce Planning), developing training programs (Human Resource Development), designing effective compensation plans (Compensation and Benefits), and conducting risk assessments (Risk Management). Throughout these interventions, you're responsible for helping corporate leaders, managers, and employees work through the multiple changes that occur as part of these interventions.

These next sections go into a bit more detail of the stages common to most strategic planning processes.

Interpreting strategic planning objectives

Several of the exam objectives address the strategic planning process. For example, BMS exam objective 03 gives clear direction for you when deciding what to study:

> "Participate as a contributing partner in the organization's strategic planning process; for example, provide and lead workforce planning discussion with management, develop, and present long-term forecast of human capital needs at the organizational level."

In this exam objective, you must be familiar with both the strategic planning process and workforce planning efforts. A case in point are the education trends in human resources. Most universities are addressing the market for online and virtual learning centers. From a workforce planning perspective, doing so requires skilled professors who are able to lead classes online or in virtual environments. This strategy will also require the technological capability to deliver the training. In this case, it may be necessary to add staff to an online environment or train the professors in the software necessary to teach and track virtual students.

In another example, 02 directs you to be able to

"Interpret information from external sources related to the general business environment, industry practices and developments, technological advances, economic environment, labor force, and the legal and regulatory environment, in order to contribute to the development of the organization's strategic plan."

Breaking this down, you may be called upon on the exams to deal with this information in three ways:

- ✔ **Collecting the information:** Consider where you would collect information related to industry practices if you are the HR manager for a large dairy farm. You decide to attend classes on food safety delivered by the Innovation Center for US Dairy.

- ✔ **Interpreting the information:** Now that you have plenty of information regarding food safety practices, you educate your management team on the best practices and help them identify any gaps between what is required and current practice.

- ✔ **Applying the information:** After these gaps are identified, you help create an action plan to address the deficiencies. Your team identifies the need for new tools and equipment, employee training, and safety inspections to ensure on-going compliance.

Preparing to plan

The *pre-planning stage* requires decisions be made about the data that will be collected and how it will be collected. It includes factors such as who will participate, how long it should take, and what tools will be used.

As the nearby sidebar shows, the collection of data comes from multiple sources. They include industry trends, technological advances, the economic climate at a local and national level, the skill availability of the labor force, and of course, the effort necessary for compliance with labor law or industry-specific regulations.

The pre-planning stage requires a strong data-mining effort on your part. Although you may not be responsible to collect all of the data, you may be called upon to spearhead the effort, and most certainly be required to help interpret and apply the information that is gathered.

Conducting an environmental scan

An *environmental scan* reviews the internal and external factors that influence an organization's ability to compete in its space. Internal strengths and weaknesses and external threats and opportunities are identified, and plans then are generated to respond to these conditions on a short-term and long-term basis. This process explores the technological, economic, social, and political factors that influence success.

Both exams require an understanding of the different types of environmental scanning formulas, including the following:

- ✔ **PEST:** Political, economics, social, and technological analysis to collect data for the strategic planning process.

- ✔ **PESTLE:** Political, economic, social, technological, legal, and environmental assessment of the business climate.

- ✔ **Porter's five forces:** Michael E. Porter's description of the competitive influences of business success and failure listed as rivalry, supplier power, the threat of substitutes, buyer power, and the threat of new entrants into the market. A good business strategy collects this data and analyzes it for a better understanding of competitive position in their relevant market.

- ✔ **SWOT:** A SWOT audit is a scan of the environment to identify internal strengths and weaknesses and external opportunities and threats. A strong strategic plan maximizes strengths and mitigates weaknesses, while capitalizing on opportunities and taking steps to reduce or eliminate threats.

Formulating the strategy

The mission statement, vision statement, and values statement (MVV) are at the foundation of *strategy formulation.* You probably already know what they mean, but here is what they can tell about an organization:

- ✔ The *mission statement* answers the question: Why do we exist?

- ✔ The *vision statement* answers the question: Where do we want to be?

- ✔ The *values statement* answers the question: What do we believe in?

In addition to the MVV statements, a company's core competencies are often identified at this stage of the strategic planning process. *Core competencies* answer the question "at the end of the day, what do we do?" For example, a car wash company's core competencies statement would be "at the end of the day, we wash cars." Or a construction company's statement would be "at the end of the day, we build things." Although these examples are simplified, they explain that the core competencies set the direction of action for a company in their strategic plan year. By reducing down a company's thinking to the core, an organization can then identify, corral, and focus on the resources necessary to accomplish what, at the end of each day, is at the heart of their business.

Finally, no strategic formulation of a plan is complete without the identification of goals. If the MVV and core competencies are at a 50,000-foot view of the organization as a whole, the goals bring them back to boots-on-the-ground action.

The SMART model is a useful way to remember how to write effective goals. The acronym stands for goals that are specific, measurable, attainable, relevant, and time-based. Clearly articulated goals are more likely to be achieved, and applying the SMART model will guide you through the process. From the perspective of the exams, you must be familiar with setting annual goals and objectives that correlate with the company's strategic direction, including the MVV. Other goals specifically mentioned in the exam objectives are growth targets, new programs and services, and net income expectations. After the goal setting is complete, the implementation of the strategy can begin.

Both the PHR and SPHR exams require that you have a thorough understanding of all stages of strategic planning. But a plan with no action becomes an exercise in futility. A helpful way to remember is to visualize a regular piece of paper folded in half. Above the fold, you have listed all of the steps in this process that occur while sitting in a conference room. Below the fold are the action steps that will require you to be in your office or on the production floor — it's time to get to work.

Implementing the action items

Strategy implementation is the execution of the business plan that is an outcome of the planning process. For human resources, it means taking the relevant portion of the plan and doing the work necessary to achieve the goals. Strategy implementation is a focus on the operational elements necessary to achieve the company goals. The final stage of the strategic planning process is the measurement of outcomes. SPHR candidates must be prepared for questions related to metrics. In fact, BMS exam objective 06 specifies SPHR only in the exam objective to develop and utilize business metrics to measure the success or failure of strategic objectives.

Evaluating the outcomes

Strategy evaluation is the process of measuring how well or how poorly an organization is doing when compared to the strategic plan. The timing of the evaluations are important because they shouldn't be completed only at the end of the plan year. When the proper tools are identified and built, an organization can regularly collect data that will allow it to respond to deficiencies quickly and adjust course as necessary — thus the importance of finding the right tools for measuring success.

You should be familiar with several evaluation tools in preparation for the exam. They include the following:

- ✔ **Financial measures:** In simplest terms, these reports follow the money — how it comes in and where it goes out. An example is the company budget.

- ✔ **Company overview:** A *company overview* is focused on performance and is often broken down by department. Examples include dashboards or a balanced scorecard.

- ✔ **Quality initiatives:** These efforts exist both on a macro and micro level, meaning the focus can be on overall product/service quality or a unit-by-unit quality. Quality is often cited as a company value, launching initiatives such as Total Quality Management (TQM) or the International Organization for Standardization (ISO).

> ✔ **Productivity standards:** These standards measure the outputs of effort and include calls tended or cubes per hour.
>
> ✔ **Sales targets:** These targets are set for several reasons, including identifying the break-even point and providing a plan for business growth. Sample reports include comparing year over year, month over month, and individual product growth or decline.

Working with other business functions

For purposes of the exam, knowing information related to the operational functions of business is important. These functions include a general understanding of finance, accounting, production, sales and marketing, customer service, purchasing, and information technology (IT).

Finance and accounting

Some people commonly misperceive accounting and finance as one and the same. Unfortunate for the amount of studying that you have to do, that's simply not true. The *finance* function of business management deals with elements, such as making data-driven decisions using financial information. It may also include establishing banking relationships to meet both current and future needs. The *accounting* function is more operational in nature, dealing primarily with accounts receivable and accounts payable. HR supports the accounting function through the development of key metrics, including budgets to execute workforce planning or human capital management plans.

Look for keywords and variations to the terms strategic and operational. *Strategy* is a fundamental component to the SPHR core knowledge requirements, whereas the term *operational* often refers to the PHR exam. For example, the finance elements are important to building and evaluating the strategic plan, so you may anticipate questions related to this business function on the SPHR exam. The accounting function, however, is more operational, often describing tasks that are critical to day-to-day operations, an essential concept to the PHR body of knowledge. Although studying all of these concepts is important, identifying these key terms will help direct your attention to foundational material for your particular exam.

Production

Production deals with producing the widgets from which a company generates revenue. It can be either products or services. Production is often considered the most important function of business because it remains firmly rooted at the heart of the company's core competency.

Because production (or services) is often a core competency, both the PHR and SPHR exams require working knowledge of how HR can support productivity and the ancillary needs, such as quality, performance management, employee relations, and risk management.

Sales and marketing

Similar to finance and accounting, sales and marketing are separate yet related business functions. *Marketing* deals with issues, such as determining what products or services to introduce to the market, branding the products and the company, and providing the collateral necessary to get the message into the marketplace. In turn, the *sales* department is responsible to sell the items that production is producing and marketing is offering. Symbiotic, as it were — it's all related.

Sales and marketing are conduits to profit. Therefore, on both exams, expect to see questions related to the recruiting and selection of qualified professionals, commission-based pay structures, plus ongoing performance management of the behavior of these employees to positively impact growth.

Customer service

Customer service serves multiple roles within an organization, but viewing it is easiest from the perspective of pre- and post-sale. Customers may have many questions before making a decision to buy, ranging from product details to purchase policies or warranties. After a sale, a customer may have issue with damaged product or the need to return. For this reason, HR best supports the customer service department through the hiring of talent, training on the skills necessary to problem solve, and being able to answer questions successfully regarding the products and services. The areas of HR support are topics that you can expect to see on both of the exams.

Purchasing

Purchasing is tied closely to the inventory management system that is in place within the organization. It's primarily a support function of production, solving issues related to incoming raw materials and the ancillary components necessary to build a product or operate a business. The PHR exam more than likely asks questions related to operational issues about conducting inventory or hiring purchasing agents. On the SPHR exam, prepare for questions related to higher level strategy of the interrelatedness of purchasing technology and its impact on other corporate systems, and know how to respond to the threat of supplier availability in the marketplace.

Information technology (IT)

The impact of technology in the workplace is far reaching. In human resources, the use of Human Resource Information Systems (HRIS) helps to tie together the various elements present in the life cycle of the employee, as Figure 7-1 shows.

An HRIS system serves as a resume database for recruiting, a compliance repository for training materials, and documentation of compensation and benefits as the employee matures within the company.

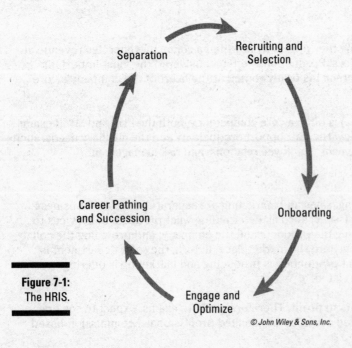

Figure 7-1:
The HRIS.

© John Wiley & Sons, Inc.

IT is also important in that it's the frontline of defense in the protection of customer and employee information.

Finally, IT provides the infrastructure necessary for the execution of most business operations.

On both exams, prepare for content related to confidentiality issues and the electronic storage of records. It's also likely that you will be asked questions related to workforce planning, because technology can replace part of the existing workforce due to streamlined processes, or questions about the need to staff a new department with technical, noncore skillsets of talent.

Establishing internal and external relationships

Relationships are how business gets done, simply because people are at the core of work and how people work together affects outcomes. *Internal relationships* exist between departments and co-workers as well as between supervisors and employees. Several exam components deal with these relationships, including the following:

- **Managing change:** Because change is a natural outcome of strategic planning, the SPHR exam more than likely will have more questions related to this activity. When studying change management, you can easily identify solutions by looking at the functional areas of HR. For example, paying more for higher-level skill sets is a consideration of compensation and benefits. Another example is shoring up your knowledge about union avoidance strategies when introducing change to a skeptical workforce, a function of employee relations.

- **Motivating workers:** Among the core knowledge requirements of both exams is the need to motivate people to do the work that needs to be done. Behavior management has several theories that are grounded in scientific research. B.F. Skinner's *operant conditioning* and Abraham Maslow's *hierarchy of needs* are two examples of such theories that Chapter 6 covers in greater detail.

- **Managing development:** Both exams have the objective of helping supervisors and managers model and communicate expected standards of behavior. Some supervisors will need help, and it's up to HR to identify opportunities for management development in this area.

External relationships reflect other stakeholders, such as customers, investors, and communities. On the exams, you should anticipate questions related to the *employer brand*, which is just a fancy name for the company reputation. There will also be questions related to financial oversight, such as the Sarbanes-Oxley Act and whistleblower protection. Finally, in the area of communities, the exams cover elements of *corporate governance* and *sustainability*, both of which are values-based business practices.

Managing these relationships is often classified as the need to be both the employer and employee advocate. This role serves to remove obstacles, communicate shared responsibilities, and move the proverbial ball of business forward toward goals.

A few notes about the *PHR-only* or *SPHR-only* exam objectives in the BOK:

- If you're taking the PHR exam, note that not all exam objectives in the area of BMS are labeled *SPHR only*, which means that you still need to be able to understand and apply strategic concepts. Start by studying the objectives in this chapter that are universal.

✔ Similarly, if you're taking the SPHR exam, you need to know *all* of the BMS concepts. However, you should plan to invest additional study time to the material labeled SPHR only — especially in the BOK with a total of 11 out of 21, or about half of the exam — labeled as such. This is as close as you can get to having a map to the content of your exam.

✔ The BOK only has two PHR-only areas, and they're found in the functional areas of Compensation and Benefits (refer to Chapter 10) and Risk Management (flip to Chapter 12). If you're an SPHR candidate, you need adequate time to prepare for 99 percent of the exam BOK, regardless of the label.

Managing metrics

The SPHR exam in particular is heavily focused on the use of metrics. *Metrics* are measurements that communicate the cost and impact of HR processes to evaluate the effectiveness of company activities. Established in the strategic planning process, these accountability factors serve to measure progress toward reducing the gap between where the company is and where the company wants to be. Being able to measure action assumes that the strategic planning process has adequately defined the vision, goals, and objectives. If you're sitting for the SPHR exam, you should be extremely familiar with the following industry metrics.

Return on investment (ROI)

The language of business communicates the consumption of resources, written specifically in terms of cash or percentages. A *return on investment (ROI)* calculation identifies the cost of an investment compared to the return. ROI is best calculated as a percentage with the following:

$$\frac{Benefit - Cost \times 100}{Cost}$$

A company had ten employees turnover last year at the cost of $5,000 per employee for a total of $50,000. HR recommends the purchase and implementation of an employee retention program, software, and tracking system for an initial cost of $30,000, and ongoing maintenance over a five-year period of another $30,000 for a total investment of $60,000. HR believes this system will reduce annual turnover by 50 percent. What would be the total savings?

(A) $25,000

(B) $55,000

(C) $65,000

(D) $125,000

The correct answer is (C). The anticipated savings is 50% of $50,000, which is $25,000. Over a five-year period, the total savings would be $125,000. Subtract the cost of the investment (125,000 – 60,000) and you arrive at $65,000. In this scenario, you can translate this savings into an ROI percentage by using the initial investment of $60,000:

$$\frac{125,000 - 60,000 \times 100}{60,000} \qquad \frac{125,000 - 60,000 \times 100}{60,000} \qquad \frac{6,500,000}{60,000}$$

108% ROI over 5 years

Turnover cost

Turnover occurs when an employee separates from the organization. It can be functional or dysfunctional. *Functional turnover* is often described as a relief; the employee needed to leave. *Dysfunctional turnover* occurs when key personnel leave the organization, often to the detriment of people or processes. Although the exact cost of turnover can range from one to three times the exiting employee's annual salary, there is no dispute that there is more value in retaining current workers than trolling for new talent. HR must successfully communicate that fact in order to

✔ Justify retention efforts and expenses

✔ Justify training expenditures (payroll, lost productivity, direct costs)

✔ Highlight departmental issues such as lack of supervision or lack of compliance

A simple turnover analysis can help achieve this. The following formula calculates companywide turnover and turnover by department. The lower the rate, the better:

$$\frac{\text{Number of employees terminated}}{\text{Total number of employees}} \times 100 \ \left(\text{to express as a \%}\right)$$

A company has 300 employees in the production department over a one-year period. Within that same time frame, 50 employees were terminated. What is the turnover rate that year in production?

(A) 16.67%

(B) .167%

(C) 600%

(D) 16.6%

The correct answer is (A). You get it by taking 50 terminated employees by 300 total employees and then multiplying by 100. (B) is incorrect, because it didn't multiply the division solution by 100 to arrive at the correct percentage. (C) is incorrect because it was divided improperly. (D) is an underestimation.

Cost per hire and time to hire

Cost per hire is the amount of direct and indirect costs of hiring new employees. An HR department uses it to capture the costs of filling open positions, which is helpful to determine future recruiting/selection budgets and to compare the value of developing current employees to the cost of hiring externally. In 2012, the Society for Human Resource Management (SHRM) partnered with the American National Standards Institute (ANSI) to develop a standard formula for calculating these costs:

$$\frac{\text{External costs} + \text{Internal costs}}{\text{Total number of hires in that time period}}$$

Cost per hire is often used in conjunction with *time to hire,* which calculates the amount of time it takes from the time the position opens to an employees first day of work. *External costs* include costs associated with outside referral agencies, advertising, and travel. *Internal costs* are associated with salaries consumed through recruiting, interviewing, and other ancillary components such as technology.

Recruiting for engineering positions at Business Technology Solutions, Inc., seems to be a nonstop endeavor. The HR director is preparing the budget for the new year and has decided she needs to ask for an increase in recruiting dollars to continue to support the engineering hiring efforts. Which of the following calculations should she use to estimate future costs?

(A) Time to hire

(B) Return on investment

(C) Cost-benefit analysis

(D) Cost per hire

The correct answer is (D). A *cost-per-hire analysis* will allow the director to demonstrate how much it costs to hire engineers. When combined with cost-per-hire data for other positions, it will lead the discussion on workforce planning efforts and ensure that enough dollars are allocated to support company needs. Although useful, (A) doesn't adequately communicate a budgeting need. (B) and (C) are too broadly focused to estimate a line item category for an annual budget.

Break-even analysis

A *break-even analysis* determines at what point sales of a product or service will begin making a profit. It requires data, such as sales price per unit, the cost per unit to produce, and the amount of fixed costs. The formula for calculating the break even point is

$$\frac{\text{Average price per unit} - \text{Average cost per unit}}{\text{Fixed costs}}$$

Knowing common reports and tools

Other more subjective tools determine the value of business activities. Make sure that you're familiar with these as you prepare to take the PHR and SPHR exams.

Cost-benefit analysis (CBA)

A *cost-benefit analysis* (CBA) measures the effectiveness of a community of intervention activities focused on company operations. Basically, a cost-benefit analysis takes a more global, whole-system view. Although a bottom-line dollar figure is used to communicate the results, a CBA seeks to measure both tangible and intangible outcomes in terms of money. Factors to evaluate include

- **Alignment with company's mission, vision, and values:** Does the suggested intervention strategy serve the MVV?

- **Management engagement in the trenches (operational):** Is there sufficient buy-in of the managers for successful implementation of the activity, and if not, what does HR need to do to develop the management team?

- **The direct costs of the program specifics:** Does the company's cash flow support the outcome, whether negative or positive?

- **The indirect costs of implementation:** Have you considered the indirect costs of implementation, including wages, benefits, and lost productivity of the personnel involved?

- **Risk factors of failing to implement:** What will happen if you don't implement this particular strategy?

- **Revenue and profit:** What revenue will be generated as the result of these efforts, and what will be the profit margin?

CoolerCorks is a large scale American manufacturer of wine storage cooling units. As part of this year's strategic plan, the company decided it would undertake a Lean Manufacturing transformation, where the focus is on streamlined operations and elimination of waste. Michaela, the quality manager, has questioned whether or not the inconvenience and cost of this transformation is really necessary. Which of the following statements is TRUE?

(A) Michaela should be given the option to step down, and a more committed replacement found.

(B) Michaela should be allowed to continue on as a manager; she'll come around eventually.

(C) Michaela should be coached through the process, seeking buy-in and commitment.

(D) Michaela should be fired.

The correct answer is (C). HR provides support to the management team during the change that often is the result of the strategic planning process. (B) isn't a viable solution, because it doesn't clearly communicate the performance expectations and solutions. (A) and (D) may become necessary, but not until she has been given adequate time and support to perform successfully.

Forecasting

A crystal ball in human resources would come in handy at times, but the information may be less magic and more available than you may think. As I discuss earlier in the chapter in the "Conducting an environmental scan" section, data is collected both internally and externally for use in planning. If done properly, you now have at your disposal much of the information you need to properly forecast human resource needs at your place of employment. Consider the following examples:

- ✔ **Political:** Who holds office at a national and local level can strongly influence organizational objectives. For example, in 2000 then President Bill Clinton passed a national ergonomics safety standard. In 2001, when George W. Bush took office, he signed an order from Congress to repeal. Based on the current political climate, immigration reform will continue to be an emerging compliance issue for employers.

- ✔ **Economic:** Swinging gas prices affect commerce on multiple levels, not the least of which is the cost of getting product from A to B. The economy is further deteriorated when companies must pass this cost along to consumers, increasing the cost of living. If wages don't keep up, American workers can't afford to buy. If workers can't afford to buy, company profits suffer, leading to negative outcomes such as furloughs or layoffs. Based on the current economic climate, employers should seek out tax and training credits for workforce expansion and other government efforts to get individuals back to work.

- ✔ **Social:** Cultural trends and patterns are often useful gauges toward the practice of human resources. One of the best examples is the 1960s civil rights era. The mood of the country was that of diversity, and Congress responded by passing the Civil Rights Act of 1964, which led to changes in workplace hiring practices and legal compliance, just to name a few. Based on the current social climate, anti-discrimination regulations will continue to emerge for groups not currently protected and depth in coverage for others.

- ✔ **Technological:** Employers can count on technological advances to emerge at a fairly fast pace. From enterprise resource planning (ERP) systems to radio frequency (RF) inventory scanners, multiple tools are available to increase quality and productivity. Based on the current technology climate, anticipate the need for virtual work space and clearer telecommuting policies and procedures.

Which of the following statements is TRUE?

(A) Strategic planning is an executive level activity.

(B) Analyzing the political climate is part of an environmental scan.

(C) Calls per hour is a type of quality measurement.

(D) The mission statement identifies where a company wants to be.

The correct answer is (B). PEST and PESTLE audits scan the environment for the political, economic, social, technological, legal, and environmental factors that must be addressed as part of an organization's strategic plan. (A) isn't the best answer, because midlevel managers are often part of the planning process and certainly become involved at the implementation stage. (C) is incorrect, because calls per hour are a measure of productivity. Mission statements (D) identify why a company exists.

Scorecards

The use of scorecards in one form or another is a useful way to see a snapshot of how the company is doing as a whole when compared to the desired outcomes identified during the strategic planning process. One widely accepted approach is the use of a balanced scorecard.

A *balanced scorecard* defines the accountability factors for each of these areas and collects data to measure how well or how poorly an organization is doing in addressing the deficiencies defined during the strategic planning process. The results allow for on-the-spot decision making and adaptability, rather than waiting to see if the intervention measures worked at the end of some arbitrary period of time.

Which of the following measurement tools would best capture an overview of how well a company is doing when measured against the strategic plan?

(A) An ROI calculation

(B) A break-even analysis

(C) A balanced scorecard

(D) A financial dashboard

The correct answer is (C), a balanced scorecard, which pulls together data regarding the organization as a whole and compares it to the goals identified as part of the strategic planning process. (A) and (B) are incorrect because these types of calculations are best used on a micro level for smaller interventions. (D) is incorrect because it's specific to a function, not a company overview.

Using the Internet for Additional Resources

Finding resources that address both knowledge and practical application has never been easier than it is today with the availability of information online. This section identifies credible Internet resources that you can use to go deeper in your studying efforts.

One or two exam preparation resources isn't enough for you to ensure a passing score. Many of the exam objectives simply scratch the surface of business application. Reach out for more information on unfamiliar topics or on topics that represent the largest percentage of the exam. In the case of BMS, SPHR candidates need to create depth to these strategic concepts.

The Balanced Scorecard Institute

This website (www.balancedscorecard.org) is an excellent place to seek out additional information regarding strategic planning, intervention strategies, and most important for the SPHR candidate, tools of metrics. It includes videos, white papers, Q&As, and more to help you understand both the process and the tool. Click on the Resources tab to read articles, success stories, and frequently asked questions.

Society for Human Resource Management

The Society for Human Resource Management (SHRM) is a distinguished and highly credible resource for HR professionals. Go to www.shrm.org. Although membership is required for full access to the information relevant to today's practitioner, you can access some free resources.

Part of SHRM's academic initiatives is to further the education of the emerging HR worker. As such, the website offers free educational resources, which include case studies and learning modules available for download, written by subject matter experts throughout the United States.

SHRM also partners with other reliable agencies such as ANSI to define industry standards. These publications are also available on SHRM's website.

The Free Management Library

The Free Management Library is an robust resource for all things business. As the title indicates, it's a library of information related to approximately 650 topics and more than 10,000 links to additional information and resources. For purposes of BMS, you can access the library at http://managementhelp.org and search for the term "all about strategic planning."

Chapter 8

Perfecting Process: Workforce Planning and Employment

● ●

In This Chapter

▶ Eyeing what's essential about Workforce Planning and Employment (WPE)

▶ Tackling labor law and standards

▶ Tapping into an employee's lifecycle

▶ Getting a firm grasp of the selection process

▶ Using the Internet to study WPE

● ●

*I*n analyzing the exam function of Workforce Planning and Employment (WPE), understanding the term *human resources* is important. Similar to the heavy use of acronyms in the industry, this term and its uses can be an obstacle to learning.

Human resources in the first context refers to the people of the organization. Also referred to as the *human talent* and the *human capital,* these terms refer to the people who do the work of the company. From brawn to brains, individual contributors to executives, these people are the resources toward which workforce planning efforts are applied.

The second phrasing of the term applies to three areas:

✔ **Profession:** The *profession* is that of a human resources professional — those individuals who are educated, certified, and professionally positioned to execute the best practices of the field.

✔ **Field:** The *field* refers to the industry of human resources where vendors, suppliers, networks, associations, and experts exist to evolve the profession through research, education, and publication.

✔ **Department:** The *department* is the functional area of an organization that takes the knowledge skills and abilities of the professional and applies the best practices of the industry toward the work of business.

Noting What's Important about WPE

As with the other exam functional area, HRCI publishes the exam objectives, which are in addition to the core knowledge requirements that I discuss in Chapter 6, and should be used together as you study this section. The priorities of WPE, according to HRCI are as follows:

"Developing, implementing, and evaluating sourcing, recruitment, hiring, orientation, succession planning, retention, and organizational exit programs necessary to ensure the workforce's ability to achieve the organization's goals and objectives."

Here are the PHR and SPHR Bodies of Knowledge (BOK) defined by the Human Resource Certification Institute:

- 01 Ensure that workforce planning and employment activities are compliant with applicable federal laws and regulations.

- 02 Identify workforce requirements to achieve the organization's short- and long-term goals and objectives; for example, corporate restructuring, workforce expansion, or reduction.

- 03 Conduct job analyses to create and/or update job descriptions and identify job competencies.

- 04 Identify, review, document, and update essential job functions for positions.

- 05 Influence and establish criteria for hiring, retaining, and promoting based on job descriptions and required competencies.

- 06 Analyze labor market for trends that impact the ability to meet workforce requirements; for example, federal/state data reports.

- 07 Assess skill sets of internal workforce and external labor market to determine the availability of qualified candidates, utilizing third-party vendors or agencies as appropriate.

- 08 Identify internal and external recruitment sources — for example, employee referrals, diversity groups, social media — and implement selected recruitment methods.

- 09 Establish metrics for workforce planning; for example, recruitment and turnover statistics and costs.

- 10 Brand and market the organization to potential qualified applicants.

- 11 Develop and implement selection procedures; for example, applicant tracking, interviewing, reference and background checking.

- 12 Develop and extend employment offers and conduct negotiations as necessary.

- 13 Administer post-offer employment activities; for example, execute employment agreements, complete I-9/e-Verify process, coordinate relocations, and immigration.

- 14 Develop, implement, and evaluate orientation and on-boarding processes for new hires, rehires and transfers.

- 15 Develop, implement, and evaluate employee retention strategies and practices.

- 16 Develop, implement, and evaluate the succession planning process. (SPHR only)

- 17 Develop and implement the organization exit/off-boarding process for both voluntary and involuntary terminations, including planning for reductions in force (RIF).

- 18 Develop, implement, and evaluate an affirmative action plan (AAP) as required.

- 19 Develop and implement a record retention process for handling documents and employee files; for example, pre-employment files, medical files, and benefits files.

Keep these exam objectives by your side every time you crack open a textbook to study. Use them to compare what you are reading with what the exam objective is asking for.

WPE makes up the *most* content for the PHR exam, coming in at 24 percent, or approximately 42 out of 175 exam questions. Not to be outdone, the SPHR counts WPE as third in line for content, making up 17 percent of the exam, or 30 or so questions. Because this functional area of HR (the industry) weighs so heavily on the exam, it's a critical study area for all exam takers.

Recognizing What Subjects to Study for WPE

The workforce planning subject on the exam places heavy emphasis on the legal issues governing the work of business, so these sections share with you some of the broader strokes of fundamental labor law. Refer to the appendix for a more complete list.

In addition to labor law, workforce planning efforts play an important role in the execution of business strategy, so these sections discuss some of the more salient points of this effort, along with some of the more common types of business metrics used to evaluate success.

Applying US labor law

The purpose of labor law is to govern the relationship between the employer and the employee by protecting the employee from harmful or unfair employer actions. Labor laws exist in all of the functional areas of HR, but create significant job responsibilities for Human Resources in the area. WPE because employer workforce planning efforts address the employment relationship from the time a person applies with a company to the time the employee separates, and everything in between.

Pause for a moment and revisit the WPE exam objectives, and see if you can name the labor law that affects the exam objective. Test your knowledge using Table 8-1 for a few examples of the laws you must be familiar with by test day.

Both the PHR and SPHR exams are unique in their question writing. Hoping for questions with answers that require simple regurgitation of facts isn't a good strategy. Your ability to *apply* the relevant labor laws to exam questions should be the focus of your exam preparation in WPE, not rote memorization of dates and numbers. Here is an example using the Americans with Disabilities Act (ADA).

The Americans with Disabilities Act applies to employers with 15 or more employees, prohibiting unlawful discrimination against qualified individuals with a disability. An individual with a disability is someone who has a physical or mental impairment that substantially limits a major life activity (such as walking, breathing, hearing, and seeing), who has a record of such impairment (such as successful treatment), or who is perceived to have such impairment (such as a facial disfigurement).

Table 8-1	Considering Some WPE Exam Objectives
WPE Exam Objective	**Applicable Labor Law**
04 Identify, review, document, and update essential job functions for positions.	Americans with Disabilities Act
05 Influence and establish criteria for hiring, retaining, and promoting based on job descriptions and required competencies.	Uniform Guidelines on Employee Selection Procedures; Title VII of the Civil Rights Act of 1964
11 Develop and implement selection procedures; for example, applicant tracking, interviewing, and reference and background checking.	Uniform Guidelines on Employee Selection Procedures; Employee Polygraph Protection Act, Fair Credit Reporting Act
13 Administer post-offer employment activities; for example, execute employment agreements, complete I-9/e-Verify process, coordinate relocations, and immigration.	Immigration Reform and Control Act

A qualified individual is one who has the knowledge, skills, and ability to perform the tasks, duties, and responsibilities of the job with or without reasonable accommodation.

Employers may claim undue hardship for failing to accommodate an otherwise qualified individual, but only on a case-by-case basis when considering the employer's size, financial resource availability, and the business structure in general.

CPR Real Estate Investments has more than 300 independent real estate agents across the entire state of California that work on a commission basis only. Administrative and management support is housed out of the corporate offices in the Central Valley with three brand managers, three regional exempt–level managers, and five administrative support workers. One of the administrative support workers was recently diagnosed with fibromyalgia and needs every Friday and Monday off to seek treatment and recuperate until her follow-up appointment in four months. CPR refused to accommodate, because it is too small to absorb the new schedule. The worker quit and then filed a claim of unlawful discrimination under the ADA. Which of the following statements regarding this situation is true?

(A) CPR violated the employee's rights under the ADA.

(B) CPR did not violate her rights under the ADA.

(C) CPR violated her rights under the Family Medical Leave Act.

(D) CPR was correct in claiming undue hardship because nobody else could cover the responsibility.

The correct answer is (B). CPR didn't violate the employee's rights under the ADA for several reasons, making (A) incorrect. The Family Medical Leave Act doesn't apply here because the employer doesn't have more than 50 full-time equivalent employees, making (C) incorrect. (D) is more difficult, because it's possible it's correct, but you don't have enough information to know if it's correct.

Arriving at this answer requires knowledge of the ADA on several levels, including

- ✔ **The number of employees:** CPR employs 300+ independent agents, meaning they're not employees. The ADA's threshold of 15 employees wasn't met by the 11 corporate workers.

- ✔ **The definition of a qualified individual:** The employee was a qualified individual with an actual disability. _Qualified_ means the individual can, with or without reasonable accommodation, perform the essential duties of the job. Depending on the severity and individual symptoms (such as the degree of limitations), this employee may be considered a qualified individual with a disability.

- ✔ **The concept of undue hardship:** _Undue hardship_ doesn't apply because she wasn't covered by the ADA. If she had been, the argument could be made that the employer didn't engage in an interactive process to find alternatives.

- ✔ **Awareness of other labor laws:** Answer (C) was meant to distract you from the ADA issue. If you have knowledge of the FMLA, you would know that job protection is granted for up to 12 weeks for a serious health condition. However, the FMLA applies to employers with more than 50 full-time employees, so answer (C) is incorrect. Refer to the book's appendix for a more comprehensive list of the labor laws to study in preparation for these exams.

As you can see in the example, your study activities for the multitude of labor laws may begin with the detailed facts, but they must end with application, application, application.

Tackling executive orders

The President of the United States (POTUS) signs an *executive order (EO)*, and it carries the full weight of law. An executive order isn't passed by an act of Congress; POTUS bypasses Congress. These executive orders only apply to federal employees and federal contractors. You should know eight or so EOs, and they include

- ✔ **11246:** Passed in 1965, it prohibits unlawful discrimination based on race, creed, color, or national origin, requiring affirmative steps be taken in employment activities by federal contractors.

- ✔ **11375:** It bans discrimination on the basis of sex for federal workers and for federal contractors in 1967.

- ✔ **11478:** It prohibits discrimination in employment on the basis of race, color, religion, sex, national origin, handicap, and age for federal employees. Also mandated affirmative action to reach EEO goals.

- ✔ **12138:** It created the National Women's Business Enterprise policy in 1979.

- ✔ **13087:** It expands protected class status to sexual orientation in 1998.

- ✔ **13152:** It includes status as a parent to the list of protected characteristics in 2000, referencing the care of dependents who can't care for themselves.

- ✔ **13279:** Offers some relief of 11,246 to faith-based organizations in 2002.

- ✔ **13672:** It amends prior executive orders, preventing discrimination on gender identity (federal employees) and both gender identity and sexual orientation (for hiring by federal contractors).

Familiarizing yourself with the EOs is an act of context, not memorization, based on the fact that you can infer the answer by the leading numbers. They're numbered chronologically, so the orders that begin with the number 11 were passed prior to those that begin with 12 or 13. If you know then that the first relevant EO was passed in the 1960s, you can infer that it had something to do with civil rights. Align your studying methods of the EOs with these numbers, and your recall will be more meaningful than it would be through rote memorization.

If the President of the United States wants to create a law without Congress's approval, which of the following tools would he use?

(A) A bill

(B) An executive order

(C) An amendment

(D) A joint resolution

The correct answer is (B). An executive order is a rule signed by the President of the United States that carriers the weight of law. It differs from bill (A) or a joint resolution (D) in that a bill and joint resolution must proceed through Congress in order to become a law. An amendment (C) is a Congressional change to existing law.

Looking at the life cycle of the employee

The function description published by HRCI in the BOK focuses on the life cycle of the employee, beginning with recruitment and ending with organizational exits. Chapter 7 explains the stages that individuals go through in their tenure.

A lot of workforce planning efforts exist within each cycle, so understanding the activities from this perspective is important. Workforce planning efforts begin with the strategic plan, where decisions about hiring needs are often made based on new business growth, including mergers and acquisitions or new product offerings. Decisions regarding layoffs or divestitures may also be identified during the planning process. Consider it as two sides of the mirror: what is created at the beginning of the life cycle must be unwound at the end or the opposite of expansion is reduction. At minimum, a strong strategic plan will have benchmarks that determine whether hiring or firing is financially the right decision and what data should be collected and measured that will trigger those WPE decisions.

In addition, the common thread that links each of the functional areas together is that of *legal compliance,* which is the effort by employers to abide by the law. WPE is the section of the BOK that addresses compliance. Table 8-2 gives you examples of each of the exam functional areas as they relate to the employee lifecycle.

Table 8-2	The Life Cycle Represented throughout the Exams
Stage in the Life Cycle	*Related Functional Exam Area*
Recruiting and Selection	Business Management and Strategy, Workforce Planning and Employment, Compensation and Benefits
Employee Onboarding	Workforce Planning and Employment, Human Resource Development
Engage and Optimize	Human Resource Development, Compensation and Benefits
Career Pathing and Succession	Business Management and Strategy, Human Resource Development, Compensation and Benefits
Separation	Business Management and Strategy, Employee Relations

Which tool is primarily focused on gathering data about the internal talents of the employees?

(A) Labor market data

(B) Skills inventory

(C) Job analysis

(D) Performance appraisals

The correct answer is (B). A *skills inventory* is a tool used to gather data about the existing skill sets of current workers. It's an excellent resource to use during the workforce planning process, because it highlights the individual and collective strengths of the existing workforce, which can then be used to fill gaps during hiring or to eliminate redundancies if the company needs to lay off employees. (A) is incorrect because it applies to the external labor market. (C) refers to the tasks, duties, and responsibilities of the jobs, not the knowledge, skills, and abilities of the worker. (D) is a tool used to provide feedback to employees, not to gather data about their skills.

Testing your WPE Knowledge

The SPHR exam weighs heavily on BMS, and the PHR is weighted heavily in WPE. Review Table 8-1 and test yourself on your ability to articulate how the *life cycle* is impacted by the *function*. Do this by thinking about how the exam objectives apply to each stage in the cycle. For example, can you answer the following question?

✔ Q. What strategic processes are supported by the *recruiting and selection* stage of the employee life cycle?

✔ A. Mergers and acquisitions, global expansion, national expansion, changes to products or services requiring different employee skill sets

With the exception of natural attrition, recruiting and selection are about growth. Exam content in this area likely will deal with the skills sets of the existing workforce when compared to strategic growth initiatives.

Initiatives that prompt a spotlight on recruiting and selection activities are those mentioned in the answer. If you require further convincing, look no further than exam objective number 02 from the exam BOK for both the PHR and SPHR exams:

✔ 02 Identify workforce requirements to achieve the organization's short- and long-term goals and objectives; for example, corporate restructuring, workforce expansion, or reduction.

Now try another:

✔ Q. What strategic processes are supported by the *separation* stage of the employee life cycle?

✔ A. The opposite of the answer in the first question, separation activities of the Workforce Planning and Employment function of HR.

Comparing orientation versus onboarding

Orientation and *onboarding* are terms that are often used interchangeably because some employers practice both as though they're one activity. However, they really are separate employee experiences. The simplest way to distinguish between the two is to note that orientation is an *event,* whereas onboarding is a *process.* For example, filling out post-hire paperwork is often done at orientation and only needs to be completed once. Mastering the tasks, duties, and responsibilities of the job occurs over time, as is often part of the onboarding process. Table 8-3 describes more of the differences.

Orientation is reflected on the exams through the administration of post-hire activities such as completing Form I-9, which verifies a new employee's identity and eligibility to work in the United States. Both exams ask questions about the onboarding process, including how to develop the processes, implement the systems, and evaluate their effectiveness. Keep in mind that the affected employees include new hires, rehires, transfers, and potentially, the newly promoted.

Table 8-3	The Difference between Orientation and Onboarding
Orientation	**Onboarding**
Is one to three days	Is 30 to 90 days or longer depending on the position (consider expatriation activities for example)
Doesn't provide a fluid mechanism for employee feedback	Ends with a 30-, 60-, or 90-day, two-way review
Focuses on compliance training	Focuses on skills identification and development needs
Proper hiring forms are filled out, such as Form I-9 and W-4	Embeds employee in company culture through development plans and objectives

Creating a recruiting process

The process of recruiting launches an employee's life cycle. It's often the first exposure an individual has to the *employer brand*. Figure 8-1 shows the steps in the recruiting process from the perspective of the exam objectives. Note that the recruiting process is separate from the selection process. Recruiting focuses on identifying workforce needs and marketing open positions and is reflected in exam objectives 02 through 10. The selection process begins with WPE exam responsibility 11 — "develop and implement selection procedures," beginning a new HR process.

One important step in the recruitment process is the development of the employer brand. The *employer brand* is the company's reputation as an employer that the candidate experiences, which may include several facets related to effective communication such as:

- ✔ **Application process:** So much of the recruiting process is now done online. Sources include social media, job boards, and the company's website, giving the applicants a glimpse into how the employer does business.

- ✔ **Responsiveness:** After an application has been submitted, an individual will expect to hear back. Do applicants receive an automated email thanking them for their application? Is a nonselection letter sent if they aren't qualified? Too often, applicants submit their résumé into what feels like an inky void, never to be heard from again, which affects the employer's reputation.

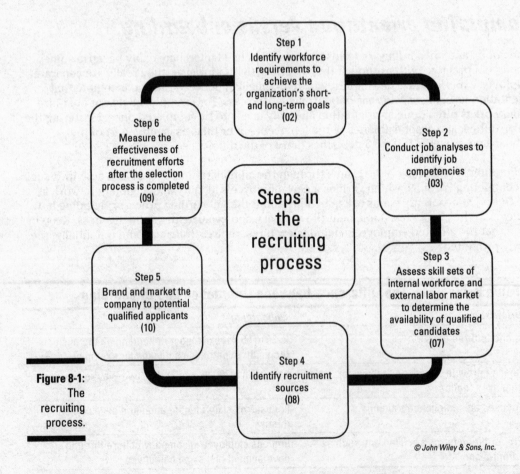

Figure 8-1:
The recruiting process.

© John Wiley & Sons, Inc.

✔ **Availability of information:** Communicating the employer brand requires access to information about the company. Many employers have their own social media pages and utilize videos for maximum effect on why a candidate should come and work there. Applicants can read about the employer's mission, vision, and values, or find out about the benefits the company offers. They can see how many positions are open and view the locations and requirements of the jobs.

✔ **Employee referrals:** A large percentage of consumers shop online. Next to price, product reviews rank high in searches. This concept applies to employers as well. People want to work for companies that they can trust or that they know something about. Employee testimonials are quite effective at communicating the employer brand. Employee referrals can be done in person at job fairs, via a company résumé, or by online videos.

These communication factors are dependent upon a well organized HR department, and the exams vary with what they will ask about communicating hiring data, depending upon the test. I use a *human resource information system* (HRIS) as an example. If you're taking the SPHR, an HRIS can be used to run reports and track metrics, such as time to hire, cost per hire, and applicants by recruitment source. If you're taking the PHR, understand that most systems are a one-stop shop for recruiters, allowing the recruiter to update job descriptions and job postings, run searches in the résumé database, and track applicants through the hiring process.

Building Blocks is a technology start-up that has to continuously recruit for specialist roles in the highly competitive Silicon Valley of California. The company's major challenge was lack of name recognition, making it highly dependent on third-party vendors for placement solutions. As the new HR director, which of the following strategies should you recommend first?

(A) Contact the staffing agencies and negotiate better pricing on their fees.

(B) Start a company social media page and pay for exposure.

(C) Research HRIS solutions to better organize applicants.

(D) Develop an employer-brand campaign starting with videos of current employee testimonials.

The correct answer is (D). The lack of name recognition is this company's biggest challenge, and an employer-brand campaign utilizing videos and employee reviews is the best place to start. Neither (A) nor (D) address the employer brand, and (B) should be part of the larger brand campaign.

Operationally, this activity matches candidate knowledge, skills, and abilities with job tasks, duties, and responsibilities. Strategically, this process communicates company culture and accurately predicts future success on the job.

Selecting the right employees

Imagine a world where you have hundreds of résumés to review and they all have the skills for which you're seeking. The applicants are properly educated, have a strong work history, volunteer in their communities, and are reasonable about the starting salary. And then you wake up. The simple fact is that many employers are competing in two markets: the unemployed and the currently employed. Without the proper filters, recruiters will be forced into a review of hundreds of résumés of individuals who may or may not be qualified to do the job. After the résumés are filtered for deal breakers such as salary and skills (preferably through the recruiting process), the imagined scenario in the previous section is made more possible, albeit on a much smaller scale.

Using pre-employment tests

The Uniform Guidelines on Employee Selection Procedures (UGESP) state that *any* employment requirement is a test, and therefore, subject to two factors:

- **Reliability:** *Reliability* is that the test consistently delivers similar results of a candidate when measured over a period of time.

- **Validity:** *Validity* is a process of ensuring that the test measures what you say it measures.

For example, an applicant takes a personality assessment as part of the selection process and scores very high in teamwork. This would be a reliable measure if at a future date, the employee retakes the test and scored very similarly to round one. This test would be valid if the individual is hired and found to be a collaborative worker. If the test results are inconsistent or don't accurately measure the behavior of the person on the job, the results and the test itself would be found to be unreliable and invalid.

Distinguishing between the different types of validity

The Uniform Guidelines specifically address the different types of validities. Here is a list of the types of validity studies you should be familiar with for the exams:

- **Face validity:** *Face validity* simply addresses whether the test appears to be measuring what it's supposed to be measuring. Thus, a driving test for the position of bus driver would be high on face validity. A math test for bus driver would be low.

- **Criterion validity (concurrent versus predictive):** *Criterion validity* refers to whether the employment test predicts job performance either now (*concurrent validity*) or in the future (*predictive validity*). In general, the *pure ability* of a test to predict performance now and in the future is criterion validity.

- **Content validity:** *Content validity* is often the most important for defending a lawsuit. If an employment test measures the same content as on the job, then it's high on content validity. For example, if you create an employment test using the job description for the content of the questions, you're likely to result in a test that is high on content validity.

In addition to being reliable and valid, employment tests must be job related (as demonstrated by content validity) and avoid unlawful discrimination based on protected class status. (Refer to the nearby sidebar for a court case that relates to pre-employment tests.)

Recognizing common reports and tools

WPE is an area with a lot of documentation requirements. From reporting new hires to analyzing the effectiveness of hiring sources, the need for formal documents and processes is evident all throughout this functional area. Some of the most common reports and tools that are likely to be examined on the tests are explained in these sections.

EEO-1 reporting

The EEO-1 report is a mandatory compliance survey for employers who meet the threshold requirements. It's a collection of employment statistics categorized on the Standard Form 100 by race/ethnicity, gender, and job category. The Equal Employment Opportunity Commission (EEOC) and the Office of Federal Contract Compliance use these findings for support enforcement and civil rights activities and to analyze employment trends across industries.

Examining Griggs vs. Duke Power

Griggs vs. Duke Power is a landmark Supreme Court decision made in 1971 that shaped the use of pre-employment tests. Its outcome: Even seemingly neutral employment requirements must be job related and not result in adverse impact against a protected class group. *Adverse impact* occurs when there is a significantly different rate of selection of protected class groups. Selection is not just about who is hired; it's selection for promotion or participation in training programs as well.

Note that Duke Power had a history of discriminatory practices prior to the passage of the Civil Rights Act of 1964 by segregating black workers in one of its many departments, the labor department, and hiring only white people for the better jobs in other departments at significantly higher pay rates. Post 1964, Duke Power implemented a high school diploma requirement for all positions available in the labor department. The high school diploma became a condition of employment or to be eligible for transfer to other positions claiming that it would enhance the overall quality of the company employees.

Furthermore, understand that the diploma and baseline skills testing became a requirement after Title VII was passed, effectively precluding African American workers to transfer to better jobs. Thirteen employees filed suit under Title VII of the Civil Rights Act of 1964, stating that this requirement resulted in discriminatory practices against African Americans, because they have a substantially lower rate of graduation from high school than whites.

These charges were upheld, with final commentary focused not on the requirement itself, but the impact. The diploma requirement in and of itself was a neutral hiring tool, however; the impact of this tool resulted in disparate impact or substantial underrepresentation of a protected class group, rendering the outcome discriminatory.

You should understand five important principles for the exams that are the result to this landmark case:

✔ A test or other selection practice must be job related, and the burden of proof is on the employer to demonstrate that they didn't discriminate against an individual.

✔ An employer's intent not to discriminate is irrelevant. Having an otherwise neutral employment requirement that results in discrimination — regardless of intent — is unlawful.

✔ If a practice is "fair in form but discriminatory in operation," the court won't uphold it.

✔ Business necessity is the defense for any existing program that has adverse impact. Business necessity typically can be shown for safety sensitive positions or for religious positions that require a certain faith of their employees.

✔ Title VII doesn't forbid testing. However, the test must be job related or valid, in that performance on the test must be related to performance on the job. Refer to the earlier section, "Distinguishing between the different types of validity" regarding the different types of validity for more information.

You can find an audio version of the oral arguments in this case online at the NAACP's Legal Defense and Educational Fund (www.naacpldf.org/case/griggs-v-duke-power-co).

Make sure that you're familiar with completing this form in preparation for the exam, even if you aren't currently required to use it on the job.

Form I-9

Form I-9 is a post-hire document that verifies two things:

✔ An employee's identity

✔ An employee's eligibility to work in the United States

Required as part of the Immigration Reform and Control Act of 1996, this document must be completed within 72 hours of the new employee's first day of work for wages.

For guidance on how to complete this one-page form, you can refer to the 66-page Handbook for Employers (M-274), published by the United States Citizen and Immigration Services. It's a great addition to your study materials. Download a copy now at www.uscis.gov and see if you can find the answers to the following questions in Part 7, FAQ section of the M-274.

✔ How should you correct a mistake on Form I-9?

✔ Do you need to fill out this form for independent contractors?

✔ In general, photocopies of documents aren't acceptable. What is the exception?

Fines for failing to complete this form properly range from $100 to $1,100 per error. Your bigger concern now however is to ensure you are prepared to answer questions about this process — including e-verify — for the exams.

Recruiting analysis

A *recruiting analysis* is a very simple document that you can create to track the effectiveness of various recruiting resources. This data is tracked by job and is helpful for future openings to know where qualified candidates are sourced from, the amount of time it takes to make the hire, and the overall cost to recruit. This information can then be translated into department budgets for anticipated openings, shrinking the amount of money and time spent on nonproductive recruiting sources in the future. Understanding a recruiting analysis is an example of a WPE measurement in accordance with exam responsibility 09, establishing metrics.

You can measure the effectiveness of your recruiting efforts in these ways:

✔ **Metrics:** *Metrics* refers to the number of candidates per source, number of hires per source, and ratio of resumes to interview. Define for your organization what is useful to measure and apply a formula for data collection, review, and application.

✔ **Feedback:** Interviewing new hires to get their opinions and feedback on the recruiting process is helpful to ensure the desired message is being sent during the process.

✔ **Quality of hire:** Turnover ratios and performance measures are just two of the many ways that you can measure to ensure that the hires you're making are a good fit for the organization. Consider that you may hire ten employees from one source, but if they all turn over in the first six months, the recruiting source isn't effective.

✔ **Validation of measures:** Looking for patterns of effective hires and determining which recruitment methods are more able to differentiate better from worse candidates is a worthy effort. Doing so helps narrow your focus and find qualified candidates for your employer the first time around in future hiring efforts.

Going Online for Additional Resources

The Internet is a significant advantage, regardless of exam selection. From the perspective of exam preparation, you can pop online anytime, anywhere. Perhaps you're waiting in line at the grocery store or for the rice to cook. Or you have a few minutes on the subway or while on the treadmill. Multitasking has the benefit of increasing your retention, because you'll recall where you were when you were studying that particular piece of information. Here are my favorite websites that can help you quite a bit when studying WPE concepts.

The United States Department of Labor

The Department of Labor (DOL) (www.dol.org) is the stronghold of all things labor law, administering and enforcing more than 150 employment standards. Visiting this website gives you access to information related to the major labor laws that you need to understand for these tests, including the Fair Labor Standards Act (FLSA), Occupational Safety and Health Act (OSHA), Employee Retirement Income Security Act (ERISA), and the Consolidated Omnibus Budget Reconciliation Act (COBRA).

The DOL is sorted by sections, such as wage and hour laws and safety, along with unions and military protections. My recommendation is that you access this website *daily* and immerse yourself in the fact sheets. If you're less motivated by going online, print out the fact sheets all at once and review them in chunks or transfer the information to index cards for portable use.

The Equal Employment Opportunity Commission

The Equal Employment Opportunity Commission (EEOC) (www.eeoc.org) exists to enforce Title VII of the Civil Rights Act of 1964, prohibiting discrimination in the workplace. It's been around for about 50 years and has the authority to sue companies for illegal discrimination on behalf of workers. In its original form, the law prohibited employment discrimination on the basis of race, ethnicity, national origin, and gender.

The website is a goldmine of information, ranging from videos sharing the history of the agency and antidiscrimination laws to statistics and trends that justify the need for enforcement. I have used it for classroom research on real-world case studies into what is and isn't unlawful discrimination. Go to the publications page for fact sheets on discrimination related to religion, age, disability, and more. Cross-reference these fact sheets with how these protected classes were added to law. It may have been as amendments to Title VII or by executive order. This site creates depth in your knowledge and provides insight into the process that will serve you on the exams.

The Uniform Guidelines on Employee Selection Procedures

The Uniform Guidelines on Employee Selection Procedures (UGESP) is yet another acronym related to WPE. It is the result of a need to have uniform guidelines recognized by agencies such as the DOL and the EEOC when considering the proper (translation, nondiscriminatory) use of tests and other hiring criteria during the selection process. At this site (www.uniformguidelines.com), you can find information related to the different types of validity, the concept of reliability, to what employment actions the criteria apply, and more.

O*Net

O*Net (www.onetonline.org) is possibly the best kept secret of a free HR resource on the web. O*Net is short for Occupational Information Network and is a database sponsored in part by the DOL. This database houses hundreds of occupations and their job-related content from tasks, duties, and responsibilities to both the cognitive and physical skills and abilities that are necessary for successful completion of each job.

HR professionals use this site to build job descriptions, link to local salary survey information, and identify employment trends in specific job classifications. For exam preparation, focus on the content model, which describes the anatomy of an occupation. It's also helpful to jump into the numbers provided by the Bureau of Labor Statistics (BLS) to get a sense of the job climate by the numbers. Study this information with an eye toward exam objectives 03 and 06, analyzing trends and jobs, and 05, establishing hiring criteria. All of this preparation should round out your reasoning and application of this information to a day in the life of an HR professional.

Chapter 9

Sharpening Your Tools: Human Resource Development

In This Chapter

▶ Recognizing the exam objectives

▶ Training and developing employees

▶ Managing employee performance and providing feedback

▶ Utilizing Web resources to study

*J*ust as the domain of Business Management and Strategy focuses on the function of the business units and processes, Human Resource Development (HRD) is all about the people. Using this analogy can help you see the parallels between managing the business and managing the talent. For example, an organization needs a strategic plan to guide it over a period of one to five years, just as an employee needs a career path that points her in the direction that you need them to go. A *gap analysis* may be used to identify the differences between where a company is and where it wants to be, a tool that may also be used for disparity in employee performance. Keep this analogy in mind as you read through the exam objectives that describe both the responsibilities of HR and the knowledge required to perform.

No matter whether you're taking the PHR or SPHR, this chapter examines the HRD content area and helps you recognize what subject areas you need to study and how you can handle these types of questions.

Identifying What's Essential About HRD

In HRD, the term, *human resources,* applies in two ways: the responsibilities of the human resources department and the people of the company. The HR Certification Institute (HRCI) describes this function as

> "Developing, implementing, and evaluating activities and programs that address employee training and development, performance appraisal, and talent and performance management to ensure that the knowledge, skills, abilities, and performance of the workforce meet current and future organizational and individual needs."

Here are the PHR and SPHR bodies of knowledge (BOK) defined by the HRCI:

✔ 01 Ensure that human resources development activities are compliant with all applicable federal laws and regulations.

✔ 02 Conduct a needs assessment to identify and establish priorities regarding human resource development activities.

✔ 03 Develop/select and implement employee training programs — for example, leadership skills, harassment prevention, and computer skills — to increase individual and organizational effectiveness.

✔ 04 Evaluate effectiveness of employee training programs through the use of metrics; for example, participant surveys and pre- and post-testing (SPHR only).

✔ 05 Develop, implement, and evaluate talent management programs that include assessing talent, developing career paths, and managing the placement of high-potential employees.

✔ 06 Develop, select, and evaluate performance appraisal processes — for example, instruments, and ranking and rating scales — to increase individual and organizational effectiveness.

✔ 07 Develop, implement, and evaluate performance management programs and procedures (includes training for evaluators).

✔ 08 Develop/select, implement, and evaluate programs — for example, telecommuting, diversity initiatives, and repatriation — to meet the changing needs of employees and the organization (SPHR only).

✔ 09 Provide coaching to managers and executives regarding effectively managing organizational talent.

The HRD shares an almost equal weight in terms of content: 18 percent for the PHR and 19 percent for the SPHR. If you're taking the SPHR, take note because the HRD makes up one of the top three functions for content, second only to Business Management and Strategy. You should allocate a minimum of two weeks to review this related content.

Examining What You Need to Know for the Exam Related to HRD

The exam objectives explore HRD as an evolution of the people of the organization for maximum *effectiveness* (able to do the work well). Although the objectives address training specifically, the content also demands that you understand employee development beyond simple training, such as through development activities and providing performance feedback. The following sections describe this process in more detail.

The PHR/SPHR materials have changed the term definitions of *training* and *development* over time, and there are many different definitions in existence. Basically, *training* is teaching workers skills that they need now for the job, and *development* includes required competencies that will be needed in the future.

Training as an intervention

"He needs training" is a common refrain of frustrated supervisors everywhere, and yet, training as a solution isn't always the right answer. The exam objectives tell you that a needs assessment is the first thing that you need to do to determine if training is the appropriate intervention. A *training needs assessment (TNA)* is a tool used to identify the goals of training. A TNA can be used on a macro level to view the company from 50,000 feet during the strategic planning process. For example, if the company is introducing a new product or installing new software, the training need is fairly obvious. On a smaller scale, the training needs are generally viewed from three perspectives:

✔ **Compliance:** So many labor laws, so little time. Training is often the second step to demonstrating compliance with various labor laws, bowing only to establishing a policy. Areas where training is required by law include harassment prevention and safety.

✔ **Technical:** How to perform the work is another reason for training. Although most companies seek to hire individuals with at least some level of skill or experience, all jobs usually require a learning curve that must be nurtured through training efforts.

✔ **Retention:** Many employers simply attempt to hire employees with the necessary skills required for the job. When this is impossible (or impractical), they may find that training current workers with the specific skills needed for new jobs is more effective. Training costs may prove to be much lower than recruitment costs. Also, employees may be less likely to leave an organization that is willing to offer more job security through training.

True organizational development activities take into account the third prong of training, the humble soft skill, helping employees develop in areas of communication, leadership, change management, and more. So many companies unfortunately are forced to allocate their training dollars and time to compliance and technical training, leaving this third option woefully unexplored.

Regardless of the type of training, the exams ask you to apply your knowledge to a broad range of training applications, which include

✔ **Instructional design:** Defining the objectives of the training must be the focus of any solid *instructional design* (a process to identify the systems, methods, and strategies of training). Exam prep materials often use a helpful acronym called ADDIE:

- **A**nalyze the need.

- **D**esign the training objectives.

- **D**evelop the training material.

- **I**mplement the training by teaching.

- **E**valuate the outcomes.

  Find a more detailed description of these steps in the later section, "Making the most of common reports and tools."

✔ **Training delivery:** How the training is delivered is actually an important consideration. When training is selected as an intervention, a company must make many decisions. One decision is to identify if the training should be formal, such as conducted by an outside expert, or informal, such as self-paced. You need to be familiar with training terms, such as *vestibule* (near the job training), *computer-based* training (online, CDs, software), and *contract learning* (self-identified competency learning at one's own pace).

✔ **eLearning:** *eLearning* is the formal name for any training that students attend online or at a computer. Terms you should know for the exam include asynchronous and synchronous. *Asynchronous* training occurs when student and teachers are online at different times, whereas *synchronous* training is when participants are required to be online at the same time.

✔ **mLearning:** A relatively new term, *mLearning* refers to mobile learning, or the ability of elearners to access training material on mobile devices. For training developers, mLearning requires decisions to be made about how the information will be delivered and upon what devices in order to modify content as necessary. For example, web-based learning that relies on mouse click selections won't work on tablets that are touch screen. HR professionals need to become familiar with authoring tools that support this mode of training delivery.

✓ **Measurement of training effectiveness:** The goal of most training activities is to transfer learning to the job, which requires that you're able to measure the effectiveness of a training program through the use of established metrics. If you're an SPHR candidate, take heed. Your exam requires that you're able to demonstrate knowledge in the evaluation of the success or failure of a training program in terms of knowledge or skill transfer.

Nancy Jones created a measure of satisfaction with the training program using a 1 to 5 scale, with 1 being not at all satisfied to 5 being completely satisfied. This would be an example of what type of scaling:

(A) Nominal

(B) Ordinal

(C) Interval

(D) Ratio

The correct answer is (C). (D) is incorrect because a 4 isn't twice as good as a 2. It isn't (A) because the measures aren't categories. The answer isn't ordinal (B) because this measure doesn't order the responses from higher to lower.

Developing employees

The content for the PHR and SPHR exams is updated every five years. The last update made a significant change to functional area 05: "Develop, implement, and evaluate talent management programs that include assessing talent, developing career paths, and managing the placement of high-potential employees." What used to be SPHR only was changed, meaning that PHR (as well as SPHR, you're not off the hook) candidates should strongly expect to see content related to the following:

Examining adult learning styles

All trainers should take into account the learning styles of their employees. Many of them haven't been in a formal classroom in years, and yet HR professionals often hustle them into a conference room for the latest PowerPoint presentation without regard to how well they will absorb the material. Effective trainers know that people learn with their senses, and some senses are more dominant than others. Imagine for example, that a child enters a playground with his mother. A *visual learner* will watch how the other kids are playing and then mirror their behavior. An *auditory learner* may ask his mother what he should do, seeking verbal direction. A *tactile* or *kinesthetic learner* is likely to jump right in, grabbing a ball or digging his hands in the sand.

Now, imagine that this same child is all grown up and is required to learn a new software program. The visual learner will be most comfortable using a reference chart or reading the training manual. The auditory learner would benefit from watching a video on the key program features, listening to the trainer's voice. And the tactile learner just wants to get started, tap, tap, tapping away on the keyboard or clicking his way through the demo.

According to the adult learning theory, adults are different than children in their process and approach to learning in the following ways:

✓ Adults have the need to know why they're learning something.

✓ Adults have a need to be self-directed.

✓ Adults bring more work-related experience into the learning situation.

✓ Adults enter into a learning experience with a problem-centered approach to learning.

✓ Adults are motivated to learn by both extrinsic and intrinsic motivators.

✔ **Assessing employee performance:** A good employee or bad employee classification isn't sufficient for an organization to successfully compete. HR professionals must be able to help their organizations drill down into the core of what knowledge, skills, or abilities are necessary for benchmarked performance. The gap between the core and the talent may then be addressed, focusing resources on the root causes rather than the symptoms of employee performance.

✔ **Creating career paths:** The term *career paths* was actually added to this objective. The field research or other studies used to update the exam content indicated that this aspect was important to the daily life of an HR professional. *Career path* is simply a plan of development for employees that address both strengths and weaknesses. Figure 9-1 illustrates the concept of *forced distribution*, where supervisors are asked to *distribute* their employees on a curve based on current status. This practice *forces* them to think through who their top performers are that should be developed for promotion, those that are to remain at status quo, and those that are underperforming. Note that the stars represent individual employees and that they can be at varying degrees of your career-pathing efforts. You should also know for the exams the different types of career paths. Employees may choose

- **Traditional:** Promoting up the ladder within chosen field

- **Expert:** Focusing on being the best in their industry

- **Spiral:** Developing new skills over time, or combining new skills with old skills to create a new career

- **Transitory:** Developing skills by constantly moving into new positions or companies

✔ **Managing high potential employees:** *High potential employees (hi-po)* are those employees that, if not properly managed, will take their talent and go. These individuals tend to not only have the skills and abilities to do the work that they're assigned, but they have a high degree of internal motivation and drive. Often they have a career plan in mind and will exert the necessary effort and time commitment to learn new things or take advantage of opportunities. Allowing these employees to wilt on the vine is something that HR professionals must help their employers avoid through development plans, mentoring, and new skill development.

A supervisor has grouped her employees into three performance categories: develop for promotion, stay in current position, and needs improvement. Which strategy should she apply to the group of workers classified as needs improvement?

(A) Direct and assess

(B) Sustain and support

(C) Discipline and exit

(D) Retain and transfer

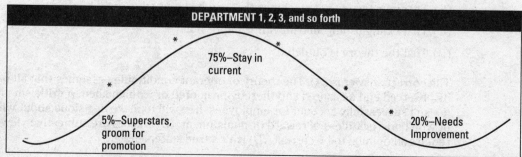

Figure 9-1: Forced distribution.

© John Wiley & Sons, Inc.

The correct answer is (A). In this strategy the supervisor would provide clear direction to the employees needing improvement while assessing them for retention. (B) isn't correct because sustaining poor performing workers doesn't solve the issues. (C) may not be the best strategy for all of the employees, especially for employees that need improvement who just need a bit of coaching to perform better. (D) isn't a good strategy, because transferring poor performers into another department doesn't address the performance deficiencies.

Picture in your mind a slot machine player in Vegas. She inserts a few quarters, pushes a button or pulls a lever, and suddenly music is playing and lights are flashing. Every once in a while, she receives a payout — a reward for continued play. The lights, sounds, and reward all encourage her to continue putting money in the machine. B.F. Skinner used gambling as an example to describe his theory of *operant conditioning*, in which a specific action has a reward, conditioning people to expect certain outcomes.

Apply behavior management to your employees. They have — through individual and organizational behavior — been conditioned to act a certain way based on the rewards. The rewards may be *tangible,* such as pay or benefits, or *intangible,* such as supervisor praise or co-worker esteem. Harnessing these rewards and using them to encourage productivity is at the core of the successful management of employee behavior. You need to understand this theory and other theories of motivation in order to execute the responsibilities of this domain, a line item in the core knowledge. You can find more information about the use of rewards and discipline, along with the influence of company behavior on employee performance in Chapter 11.

With regard to HRD specifics, training and employee motivation programs aren't just about training and managing behavior. It's the management of a larger network of programs and procedures that must be identified, developed, implemented, and evaluated. It includes the need for train-the-trainer programs to ensure proper facilitation or teaching of the class. For SPHR candidates, this exam objective includes the need to measure whether or not these programs are effective through the use of surveys and tests.

Don't forget about the vast amounts of videos online. A favorite of mine is one of Skinner that describes how he taught pigeons to read. It's well worth a few minutes of your time. Pick up on keywords such as *conditioning,* schedules of *reinforcement,* and *reward,* and think about how this theory ties into employee behavior management. Other important concepts to Skinner's theory are

- ✔ **Positive reinforcement:** Behaviors that are followed by a reward tend to be repeated

- ✔ **Negative reinforcement:** Behaviors that are followed by undesirable consequences tend to disappear

- ✔ **Extinction:** The elimination of behaviors through failure to reward

What is a frequent criticism of the theory of operant conditioning?

(A) That it does not take into account free will

(B) That humans are not machines that can be counted

(C) That extinguishing all behavior is impossible

(D) That the theory is outdated

The correct answer is (A). The theory of operant conditioning assumes that all behavior can be observed and measured and thereby promoted or extinguished. A criticism is that it doesn't successfully account for employees' free will to make decisions about what they will or won't do, regardless of reward or punishment. (B) and (C) are subjective views that require an opinion to be correct. (D) isn't a true statement.

Providing performance feedback

The dreaded performance appraisal. Supervisors don't want to write them, and employees look forward to them only if they think that they're getting a raise. Supervisor and employee reports of dissatisfaction with the performance appraisal process continue to abound, and the dissatisfaction often is related to many things such as the following. You can also read more about performance appraisals in the later section "Performance appraisals" where I discuss the actual form.

- **Lack of clearly defined measurables:** Chapter 8 mentions that the effort that must go toward defining the tasks, duties, and responsibilities of the job must be matched with the knowledge, skills, and abilities necessary to perform. If this activity hasn't been successfully completed, having meaningful feedback system in place for employees is nearly impossible.

- **Rater errors:** Similar to the bias interviewers must avoid, performance rater errors dilute the effectiveness of the review process.

  - The *recency effect* — where raters allow recent events to drive the feedback without looking at performance for the whole rating period — is especially prevalent, generally because most supervisors are crunched for time and often haven't properly documented employee performance for the entire year or quarter, thus being held hostage by their own memory.

  - Another problem can be the *error of central tendency*, in which all employees are rated as average — no highs, no lows. Central tendency is the middle child of "all my employees are amazing" and "everybody needs to improve" — two other rater issues that HR must be on the lookout for when managing the process.

  - Another error is the *primacy effect*, when raters allow first events to drive ratings. For example, when interviewing ten people in a row there is often the tendency for raters to remember the first person that they interviewed more clearly than others.

  - The *halo effect* refers to assuming that there are many positive things about a person based on one positive thing, such as a person with excellent attendance must also be productive.

  - Similarly, the *horn effect* refers to assuming many negative things about a person because there is an area in need of improvement.

  The rater errors apply not only to the rating of employee performance, but also to interview bias that occurs during the hiring process. Study these errors from both perspectives for the exams.

- **Perceptions of fairness:** Equity is a shared issue through all of the functional areas of HR. From discriminatory hiring practices to disparity in compensation decisions, *fairness* is a concept in which you must become well-versed. Performance appraisals — especially when tied to pay increases — are quite the large target for claims of supervisor favoritism. HR can combat claims of favoritism by helping the raters understand the job criteria, by creating objective measurement criteria, and by training management on the expectations and purpose of the review process.

  Employees may experience two types of inequities. They are important to mention for the exams because they apply in two of the functional areas — HRD and C&B. They are as follows:

  - **Procedural justice:** Employees consider an outcome acceptable if they believe the procedure used to make the decision is fair. For example, differences in pay are acceptable if the employees perceive the process to arrive at the disparity is both clear and reasonable or a performance rating is fair if the right criteria was used to arrive at the final rating.

- **Distributive justice:** *Distributive justice* refers to the perception of fairness in the distribution of outcomes. If employees feel like their performance review was fair in comparison with how their peers did, their satisfaction with the outcome is likely to be perceived as acceptable. In compensation, distributive justice refers to the perception that the employees got the proper reward when compared to their effort.

Although the performance appraisal is probably the most recognized way of providing employee feedback, the exam doesn't stop there. Studiers should be prepared to review informal feedback as well, which includes daily, on-the-job comments, gaining feedback from employees through 360-degree reviews and employee suggestion systems. You also should study giving and receiving constructive criticism and handling difficult conversation.

Which of the following sources would be consulted in a 360-degree review of a accounting clerk?

(A) The production manager

(B) The accounting manager

(C) A vendor

(D) All of the above

The correct answer is (D). In a 360-degree review, performance ratings are gathered from many different sources to evaluate the performance of an employee. The goal of this type of review is to measure how well a support function relates to all of the individuals affected by her performance.

Making the most of common reports and tools

Several useful reports, tools, and processes support the function of HRD. They range from specific documents such as the performance appraisal to the more detailed process of applying the ADDIE model to the process of training. Keep reading for more detail on how these tools apply to your exam.

Performance appraisals

If ever there was a need to break the mold and start over, the performance appraisal form is the place to start. Kick up the dust at your company by starting the dialogue about what makes its performance appraisal forms irrelevant or meaningless. Be open to rewriting the document, but only do so after you have received feedback from your supervisors and employees about what they really want to know about how well or how poorly they're doing.

The actual performance appraisal tool should reflect what the company deems the most important of employee behavior, which may include quantifiable information, such as attendance and productivity and the more subjective elements such as teamwork and attitude. The performance appraisal document should be both simple for the supervisor to complete and thorough enough to provide meaningful feedback to the employee.

The information gathered as part of the performance appraisal process can be used as a resource to identify training needs.

Training needs assessment (TNA)

A *training needs assessment* is an analysis tool used prior to the design or delivery of training. It answers questions about whether there is a need for training. Strategic training needs assessment focuses on whether the employee knowledge, skills, and abilities (KSA) and performance support desired business outcomes. These objectives must be very clearly defined. Table 9-1 shows you an example using a problem-solving technique of the whys.

In this example, a company needs to improve customer satisfaction ratings for consumers who call in with a problem with a product.

Table 9-1	Remembering Why When Determining Training Needs	
Why Question	*Answer*	*Note*
Why does the company need to improve these ratings?	The company received poor reviews online about its customer service.	If you stop asking why here, the training may be designed around communication or problem-solving, and you still don't have enough information to make a diagnosis.
Why did the company receive poor reviews?	The customer service representatives didn't have enough technical knowledge about the products to answer the consumer questions.	If you stop asking why here, you may only address part of the problem.
Why were there issues related to certain products?	The issues were with new products that went to market before everyone was trained, and the product went out with faulty wiring.	So then, who needs to be trained? The correct answer is both the customer service reps in technical knowledge and the production workers in quality.

Training design

After the training participants and the business outcomes have been identified, training design can begin, including what core competencies need to be improved and who should facilitate the training. In the example from Table 9-1, you can continue asking why until you drill down to the root, in which training may not be the only identifiable solution. When designing training, consider three primary considerations:

- **Determining learner readiness:** Knowing the levels of readiness of learning participants is an important consideration when designing training. *Learner readiness* helps to design training that meets the specific needs of the workgroup being trained. For example, if you have an entry-level workforce, the training may need to be designed to teach baseline knowledge that then sets the employee up to learn more detailed principles. Another factor may be language barriers in the workplace. Employees whose first language isn't English may struggle to keep up, so you may need to conduct the training in another language or work with the employees to teach them basic English terms that will be used in the training.

- **Understanding different learning styles:** All adults have different learning styles, and the basics are auditory, visual, and tactile. Quality training is designed to incorporate strategies for all learning styles, such as the use of charts and graphs for visual learners, lecture and discussion for auditory learners, and hands-on exercise for the tactile learners in the training group. Refer to the earlier sidebar that discusses adult learning styles for more information on this important exam consideration.

- **Designing training for transfer:** The third consideration is to prepare the content for transfer onto the job. The goals of training are to modify behavior and outcomes, so establishing learning objectives and supplying tools for transfer should be of utmost priority. Cross-reference the upcoming section on Kirkpatrick's four levels of training evaluation to discover more about the modification of behavior and results as a goal of training.

Training development

After the training needs have been identified and the design of training addressed, choose and create (or purchase) the appropriate training tools. For purposes of the exam, copyright issues may come up, so it's important for trainers to use tools only for the purpose intended. It may be a violation of copyright laws if you don't.

Training implementation

The implementation of training is all about the action — how it will be delivered, when it will be scheduled, and who to invite as the participants. Method matters at this stage, and a few training delivery options you should be aware of for the exams include

- **On-the-job training:** This training occurs when the employee is working. It may be through *job shadowing* (when an employee observes another employee doing the work) or doing the work while a trainer watches him, correcting the trainee as mistakes occur.

- **Role-playing:** *Role-playing* is useful when there are relational duties as part of a job. Role-playing asks participants to act out a scenario, with the facilitator and other participants evaluating and discussing their responses. It can be uncomfortable for some to work in front of a group or be critiqued by others, so the use of role-playing should be limited to employees that will gain maximum benefit such as sales reps or customer service agents.

- **Computer-based training (CBT):** CBT has continued to grow in popularity. CBT occurs online or is delivered via software. It's most beneficial for training that can be quantifiably measured through the use of review questions or scores. An extension of CBT is online training that may occur at the same time as the instructor is online (*synchronous*) or when the instructor and student are online at different times (*asynchronous*).

Training evaluation

Training isn't successful simply because you held the event, regardless of how fun or relevant the content was. Successful training occurs when participants are able to apply the knowledge or skill gained to their work environment, thus achieving the desired state. Thus the *E* in Addie standing for *evaluation*.

Donald Kirkpatrick in the 1950s developed a method of evaluating training that includes four levels: reaction, learning, behavior, and results. Figure 9-2 shows these levels along with common tools used to successful evaluate the training. Measuring training is highly dependent upon the identification of training objectives prior to design or delivery. Without these objectives, evaluating whether or not the training hit the targets is difficult.

Several books and papers support the Kirkpatrick model at www.kirkpatrickpartners.com. These resources can help you go deeper into the concepts of training evaluation for the exam. At minimum, go online and review the site's thoughts on how this model has evolved and remains relevant in today's workplace.

Mary Jones managed Acme's Customer Service training program in which Mary reviewed the proper way to greet customers. After all the employees went through the program, she asked the trainees' managers to measure how many times the employee greeted a new customer with a smile and welcome as they walked into the door. This form of measurement is at what level of Kirkpatrick's levels of training evaluation?

(A) Reaction

(B) Learning

(C) Behavior

(D) Results

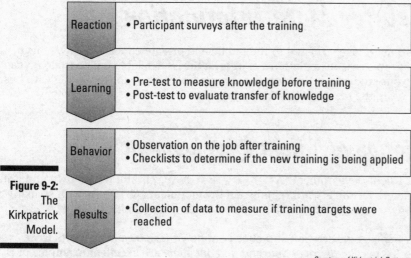

Courtesy of Kirkpatrick Partners

Figure 9-2:
The
Kirkpatrick
Model.

The correct answer is (C). Kirkpatrick's evaluation of training level of behavior measure the impact of training on the employees' work actions. In this case, the manager was measuring how the employees' conduct changed in direct relationship to what the employees had learned in class. An employee's reaction to training is measured by what he thought of the class, so answer (A) is incorrect. Learning is measured by evaluating what knowledge was transferred, not behavior, so (B) is incorrect. Results in this example would be evaluated by determining whether the training efforts made a difference to customers or how many of the employees was able to successfully apply the new behaviors, so (D) isn't the best choice.

Studying for comprehension in six hours

Print out the nine exam objectives and the additional core knowledge requirements for the HRD function (numbers 27–37). Look at your study schedule and allocate at least six hours as such:

✔ **Hours 1 and 2:** Search the Internet for documents related to *each* exam objective and save or print the information. Sort this stuff by the exam objective, not their headings or titles. You must decide how the information applies to the test. This is transferring *knowledge*.

✔ **Hours 3 and 4:** Read through your saved documents from the first two hours, looking for common threads, themes, trends, or patterns in this field. Use highlighters or sticky notes to relate concepts and draw conclusions on where the functional area is heading. Draw conclusions about what information makes each exam objective related to the other, creating a web of connectivity. This activity teaches you *critical thinking*.

✔ **Hours 5 and 6:** Try and put each exam objective into a work context. Ask yourself questions about how the exam objective and related content would translate into your workplace. What are the obstacles? If already in place, how is it working? What measurements could you design to communicate effectiveness? This process supports your efforts toward applying *experience* to this domain.

You now literally have much of the information required to tackle this exam subject. Spread this exercise over a period of a week, and the knowledge, critical thinking, and experience perspectives will create depth to your learning. See if you can apply Kirkpatrick's four levels of training evaluation to this effort. What was your *reaction* to the exercise? Did it result in *learning*? How did it change your studying *behavior*? Were your *results* better on the assessment in HRD post training?

Surfing the Web for More Information

HRD in an organization is closely related to the public and private educational systems of the United States. For this reason, a plethora of information is available online that you can utilize to shore up your studying in this area. Here are a few of my favorites, along with best practices to incorporate the research into your studying.

The Association of Talent Development

The Association of Talent Development (ATD) (www.astd.org) is still well known under its former name, the American Society of Training and Development (ASTD). As with so many HR organizations, there was a need for a more global focus, prompting a rename.

Click on any ATD's webcast description and check out how these training experts write learning objectives. Terms like *discover how* and *find out about* are excellent examples of how to accomplish the HRD task of writing training outcomes.

One of the great things about HR is that if you don't enjoy all aspects of the job, you can choose to specialize. Many HR professionals decide that training and development is their cup of tea. ATD offers several *communities of practice* for support. These communities consist of subject matter experts in multiple areas of relevance for these exams. For PHR candidates, I recommend that you visit the communities of

- **Learning and Development:** Although this section has a lot of great information regarding training interventions for performance management, one of my favorite aspects is the learning blog. Written by multiple experts, it allows for a rich experience-based perspective of training and the real-world challenges faced in the design and delivery of effective programs.

- **Career Development:** Exam objective 05 refers to career pathing. This community focuses the spotlight on taking control of careers and using coaching to underscore training. Free webcasts and descriptions of a trainer competency model illustrate the need for a broad skill set. Skills for trainers include change management, coaching, and the ability to manage learning programs. If you're a member, you can also explore the career navigator tool, which assesses your current self-described skill set and compares it to your dream job requirements and competencies.

- **Learning Technology:** Training programs must be agile, and old-school methods of teaching in a brick-and-mortar classroom are no longer the obvious nor best solution. This community engages visitors with elearning, innovation, mlearning, and social learning concepts just to name a few.

In addition, SPHR candidates should go even deeper into communities made up of

- **Management:** This area is devoted to helping managers respond to the moving targets that make up most of their days. Topics include tackling succession planning, implementing change , dealing with productivity issues conflict management, and managing a multigenerational workforce.

- **Human Capital:** The description of this community is that of helping employers manage the employment life cycle. Although fairly broad in application, it makes sense in that the human capital — also called people, talent, and resources — must be effectively managed at all stages from recruiting to separation. Strolling through this digital community takes you to topics such as coaching, diversity, and executive coaching (another SPHR favorite).

- ✔ **Senior Leaders and Executives:** This section has some great blogs dedicated to developing both future leaders and current CEOs. Other attention-getting headlines in this community include selecting the right team members for projects and examining the different leadership styles of executives such as transactional, transformational, and laissez faire.

- ✔ **Global HRD:** One core knowledge requirement in this area suggests that SPHR candidates be able to apply information relating to international law and societal norms, so be sure and search for related data in this community. Other issues examined are how to communicate with global teams and the how to handle unique management differences cross countries.

Even though much of the content is available only to members, you can still access plenty of it for free, which makes this site a worthwhile stop on the prep journey. Options include scrolling through its blogs or signing up for its newsletters to stay connected to emerging content in this very important exam domain for both the PHR and SPHR.

Chief Learning Officer Magazine

I prefer to get this magazine mailed to me, because I already have a crowded email inbox that has me approaching information overload. Having a hard copy magazine delivered to the office or home sets the content apart from email, providing a psychological nudge that it's important that I pick it up and look at it, rather than simply hit delete.

You may instead however prefer to visit www.clomedia.com. On this site, spend the bulk of your time on the research and results pages. You can download many of the documents for review. If you're taking the SPHR, search for work related to learning metrics, the learning organization, and organizational development. If you're taking the PHR, seek out information relating to training development and design and performance appraisals.

Talent Management

Similar to the Chief Learning Officer Magazine, Talent Management, a subscription service, offers a plethora of HRD information that goes both deep and wide. At www.talentmgmt.com, you can find research and reports about how to manage high-potential employees, develop succession plans, and identify the emerging trends of the field. This site is your full-service resource for all things HRD. Use it to gain clarity on unfamiliar exam objectives or simply to freshen up your resources when you're feeling burnt out on others.

The International Society for Performance Improvement

At www.performancexpress.org, you can find several great articles under "Performance Express." This site also has the option for a paid membership, but the newsletter is free and contains all sorts of relevant and timely information related to this exam function. Recent examples include holding managers accountable for results and how to test what you teach.

American Evaluation Association

At this site (www.eval.org) you can find a free elibrary that you can access to download academic and peer-reviewed research related the HRD function of these exams. The elibrary features scientific research that both directs and supports the efforts of professional trainers and evaluators; it's well worth a regular visit as you study this section of the exam.

Chapter 10

Paying Your Dues: Compensation and Benefits

•••

In This Chapter

▶ Identifying the exam objectives

▶ Knowing what the exam will test

▶ Utilizing common reports and tools

▶ Maximizing Internet time while studying

•••

The impact of compensation and benefits (C&B) in the workforce is intense. Compensation is one of the primary reasons employees get up and come to work each day (some may say the only reason). Employee benefits can add a burden of 30 percent or more to the cost of having workers. The regulatory environment spends a lot of time in these areas, with many of the top reasons employers get sued related to wage and hour violations. And payroll remains one of the top outsourced functions of HR. This chapter gives you an overview of the C&B category and provides some example questions to help you be ready when you encounter them on the PHR or SPHR exam.

Identifying the Exam Objectives for C&B

Compensation and benefits is known by another term — *total rewards*. In fact, this functional area has changed names within the last 15 years — from *Compensation and Benefits* to *Total Rewards* and back to *Compensation and Benefits* for the last exam updates in 2012. One possible reason for the change back to a split title is that the organizational component of the activities continue to grow in distinction rather than merge into a blended activity.

Another example is in exam objective 05, in which the term *compensation* was added to the original phrasing "benefits programs needs assessment." This clue increases the likelihood that the exams have questions about compensation and benefits needs assessments. The area description reads as follows:

> "Developing/selecting, implementing/administering, and evaluating compensation and benefits programs for all employee groups in order to support the organization's goals, objectives, and values."

Here are the PHR and SPHR Bodies of Knowledge (BOK) defined by the Human Resource Certification Institute:

✔ 01 Ensure that compensation and benefits programs are compliant with applicable federal laws and regulations.

✔ 02 Develop, implement, and evaluate compensation policies/programs; for example, pay structures, performance-based pay, and internal and external equity.

✔ 03 Manage payroll-related information; for example, new hires, adjustments, and terminations.

✔ 04 Manage outsourced compensation and benefits components; for example, payroll vendors, COBRA administration, and employee recognition vendors (PHR only).

✔ 05 Conduct compensation and benefits programs needs assessments; for example, benchmarking, employee surveys, and trend analysis.

✔ 06 Develop/select, implement/administer, update, and evaluate benefit programs; for example, health and welfare, wellness, retirement, and stock purchase.

✔ 07 Communicate and train the workforce in the compensation and benefits programs, policies, and processes; for example, self-service technologies.

✔ 08 Develop/select, implement/administer, update, and evaluate an ethically sound executive compensation program; for example, stock options, bonuses, and supplemental retirement plans (SPHR only).

✔ 09 Develop, implement/administer, and evaluate expatriate and foreign national compensation and benefits programs (SPHR only).

For these operational reasons, C&B makes up 19 percent of the content of the PHR exam and 13 percent of the content for the SPHR. Note that C&B is in the top three weighted functional categories for PHR. Conversely, it's second to last in terms of content for SPHR candidates. Regardless, you still need to prepare for this key functional area of HR.

One of the two PHR-only exam objectives lives in this functional area. If you're a PHR candidate, be sure and work into your study plan extra activities related to managing compensation and benefits vendors such as payroll, COBRA administration, and leaves of absences. If you're an SPHR candidate, spend a portion of your allocated time researching executive compensation, expatriate, and foreign national compensation packages.

Another clue to exam content is in the description. Note the / sign between develop/select and implement/administer. That symbol is a nod to exam objective 04, managing outsourced compensation and benefits.

If you're a PHR candidate, expect some exams to have questions related to

✔ **Vendor selection criteria and the implementation/administration of outsourced programs and functions:** Think about how to write requests for proposals (RFP) and reading through service agreements.

✔ **Liability:** Consider adding extra research on liability and who is ultimately responsible for compliance with laws governing tax deductions and FMLA or COBRA notification compliance.

✔ **The protection of confidential information:** Payroll and medical files both have a high level of confidentiality associated with the administration, so take steps to discover how to protect this delicate information.

If you're an SPHR candidate, consider the phrasing "support the organization's goals, objectives, and values" in the description. Based on this you may anticipate questions related to

✔ **A company's compensation philosophy:** The decision to lead, lag, or match the market with regard to compensation is directly related to supply and demand. You may have to recommend higher pay strategies for positions requiring in-demand or difficult to find skills. Other issues that arise from a company's compensation strategy include pay compression, red/green-circled employees, and the system for offering pay increases.

Around the world: Benefits practices in other countries

The United States isn't the leader in offering social or other welfare benefits to its workers. Examples of excellent benefits practices in other countries include

✔ **Netherlands:** All employees are entitled to four weeks of paid holidays.

✔ **Argentina:** Employees receive ten continuous days of leave for the qualifying event of marriage, and overtime may not exceed more than 30 hours a month or 200 hours per year.

✔ **Slovakia:** New mothers are entitled to 34 weeks of maternity leave to care for a newborn, and they can request up to three years of time off to care for a new child.

Although the exams aren't likely to quiz you on these kinds of specifics, you should have a general understanding that compensation and benefits packages in other countries must take into account differences in minimum wages, holiday pay, social welfare benefits, and extended leave rights.

✔ **Value-added benefits:** With the rising cost of benefits and the uncertainty of how the Patient Protection and Affordable Care Act (PPACA) will operationally play out, the exam spends a lot of attention on employee benefits packages. Being a resourceful business partner requires that you have knowledge of alternatives to traditional benefits and that you can recommend strategies to, at minimum, help employers keep their annual benefits offerings budget-neutral. That may include recommending financial options, such as increasing the employee shares of the burden or switching providers. Behavioral health options are also possible strategies, such as health and wellness programs for smokers or programs for employees who desire to lose weight.

✔ **Market rates, including global C&B practices:** As companies operate on a more global scale, you must have working knowledge of expatriate compensation and international compensation laws. Look for study material related to applying the Equal Pay Act outside the United States. Note the special issue in global compensation of compensation discrimination, which is prohibited under Title VII and will apply under certain circumstances. Find resources to help you understand the differences between American benefits and other countries (refer to the nearby sidebar for more information). Other issues to research include the cost of living; expatriate compensation should take into account the cost of living in another country to ensure equity.

Tackling the Key Points about C&B

C&B is about much more than processing payroll. Programs that are tied to the organization's strategic plan will have influence in all of the functional areas of the exams. Consider Workforce Planning and Employment. Chapter 8 discusses the objectives from the perspective of the employee life cycle that begins with recruiting and selection. Compensation influences a company's ability to compete for talent. The following section discusses some of the other main things you should know about the C&B function of the exams.

Packaging strategic compensation

The purpose of strategic compensation and benefits packages is to support organizational outcomes, so paying attention to the company's strategic plan is important.

For example, a company will be expanding into California from the Midwest. The company's current minimum wage is out of compliance with California's minimum wage laws, and its sick time policies will need to be updated to comply with the state's sick leave law that requires all employees to accrue one hour of paid sick time for every 30 hours worked. CalCobra is a bit different, and overtime is accrued on an 8 and 40 basis, not just a straight 40 per week. This HR department has a lot of work to do to support its company's strategic objective.

After a company's strategy is set, departmental goals in C&B can be designed, implemented, and measured. One example is the use of *variable pay plans*, in which cash and noncash options are considered. For instance, customer service has been tasked with increasing its revenue generated from selling warranty services by 25 percent in the coming fiscal year. To do so, the company is offering a $100 swag per month to the top-selling customer service representative.

These exams have a lot of information to digest regarding variable pay plans. A few items to understand are as follows:

- **Bonuses:** Bonuses can be a win-win for all involved. Because *bonuses* are above and beyond the base pay rate, employers can offer these pay incentives without a long-term increase of payroll or overtime. When timed properly, employers can leverage the dollars for maximum effect, such as tying it to end-of-calendar year performance paid to employees during the holidays.

- **Team incentives:** *Team incentives* can be an effective way to motivate a group of workers that is required to achieve shared objectives. Examples include assembly stations in manufacturing or marketing groups working together on a project. They can be offered to nurture teamwork or increase productivity.

- **Stock options:** The opportunity to own shares of a company is an equity compensation strategy. They can be effective for start-up company that can't afford to pay market rates to attract (or keep) talent. They're also useful in fostering an *ownership culture* (where employees behave as though they own the company) and sharing the profitability where possible.

Regardless of the type of variable pay plans, the priority should be for the plans to be *self-funded,* which means that the benefit realized through the incentive is greater than or at minimum is equal to the cost of the payout.

Which of the following compensation strategies would you recommend a technology start-up in need of finding affordable yet highly qualified talent?

(A) Pay the average going rate within its industry to ensure pay fairness.

(B) Create a pay for performance system built to the average industry rates.

(C) Offer a C&B package that is above average to entice applicants to leave their existing employer.

(D) Use a combination of strategies including cash and noncash options, such as lower base pay with ownership equity options.

The correct answer is (D). The availability of cash is often a challenge for new start-ups, which means their compensation strategies often must be a blend of cash and noncash options. It's not unusual for technology companies to offer ownership equity options to find the talent they need to aggressively compete. Answers (A) and (B) are incorrect, because matching the industry pay practices isn't sufficient enough to motivate the highly qualified to leave their existing employers. (C) is incorrect because most start-ups don't have the ability to pay above average.

Making pay decisions

After the compensation strategy has been established, decisions need to be made on how to execute the plans. I discuss the main features related to making pay decisions here.

Job evaluation

A *job evaluation* seeks to value the findings of *job analysis* (the process of identifying the tasks, duties, and responsibilities of each job within the company) in an effort to make decisions about pay. The job evaluation process looks at the common factors between all jobs within the company and the market values for the positions. This data is then used to set pay rates. Common methods for evaluating jobs are

- **Point:** The *point* method of job evaluation assigns a value to the *compensable factors* of a group of jobs (job element that is common among a group of similar work).

- **Classification:** The *classification* method uses the job descriptions (written document from the job analysis process that identify the tasks, duties, and responsibilities of the job) to group similar jobs into grades of pay. From this, a minimum and maximum pay level is set.

- **Factor comparison:** More difficult than the other methods for job evaluation, the factor-comparison method assigns points to the job tasks, duties, and responsibilities as well as ranks jobs from highest to lowest according to their worth.

- **Ranking:** The easiest of all evaluation methods, jobs are placed in order of importance.

What is one of the major disadvantages of using the ranking method to conduct a job evaluation?

(A) The data collected cannot be legally validated.

(B) The information collected is highly subjective.

(C) The entire job is considered, rather than the individual elements.

(D) Employees with similar jobs may perform them in different ways.

The correct answer is (C). The ranking method of job evaluation uses the whole job rather than the individual tasks, duties, and responsibilities. Validation studies refer to pre-employment tests, so (A) is incorrect. The job data used for the job evaluation method isn't subjective, because it refers to the output from a job analysis or job description, so (B) is incorrect. In (D), understanding how the work gets done so that it can be properly designed and compensated is important, so this answer isn't a disadvantage.

Pay structures

After the job analysis and market wage surveys (see the later section "Conducting wage surveys" for more about wage surveys) are complete, a company can begin to design *pay structures* (the framework that organizes how employees' pay is calculated). Considerations for the exam include understanding concepts related to exempt versus nonexempt workers (the employers' obligation to overtime and rest breaks), creating pay *grades* or *bands* (grouping similar jobs together and setting minimum and maximum pay levels), and evaluating exiting pay rates to ensure equity. The result of these efforts may identify employees who are out of range for their positions. These employees are known as

- **Green-circled employees:** Green is the color of money, and in the case of green-circled employees, their pay falls short of the established range. Exam candidates should understand strategies to address this deficiency, including a one-time increase or gradual increase until the employees' pay rate matches the pay grade.

✔ **Red-circled employees:** Red means stop, as in, stop paying these employees above the range set for their position. HR can address employee pay rates that are above the grade by freezing wage increases or looking for opportunities to increase employee job responsibilities to account for the increased pay.

Pay compression

Pay compression occurs when the gap between *incumbents* (those currently doing the job) and new hires becomes small. This can happen for a variety of reasons, all generally related to the employer's lack of systems-based decision-making when it comes to company pay practices.

Pay adjustments

After a pay structure is in place, a system to account for pay adjustments must be established. Common pay adjustments include legal processing of *wage garnishments* (court ordered withholdings from employee pay to settle a financial obligation) and pay *increases* (giving an employee a raise or compensating for new job tasks through pay bumps).

According to the Department of Labor, more than 25,000 workers contact the DOL in a typical year with questions about employer pay practices (www.dol.gov/whd/resources/ABAReferralPolicy.htm). This statistic doesn't account for the number of private litigation that employees pursue as the result of employer wage and hour violations. With new healthcare laws, expansion of leave rights, and gender pay equity hitting the headlines, this continues to be a hot issue for which HR practitioners to stay up-to-date.

Conducting wage surveys

Wage surveys, a tool used to collect data about average pay practices of the relevant market, are an important consideration when designing compensation plans for the following two main reasons:

✔ **Labor as a percentage of overhead:** Paying too much for talent impacts the ability of a company to compete in the market. Increased overhead drives the cost of building the widgets or offering services. With inflated overhead, companies are forced to pass bloat to the consumer or compromise other important business outcomes such as quality. A subset to this concept is the decision to *lead* the market in pay rates, which ties directly into organizational strategy. A company that chooses a *differentiation strategy* (designing new or substantially different products from the competition) for its products or services may need to pay more for talent, but the expectation is that its products will be of superior quality, allowing the company to charge more to the consumer.

A strategy of *cost leadership* (in which being the lowest price in the market is the goal) is going to require compensation rates that lag or only matches market pay in order to keep consumer prices down. Leading the market in pay rates increases overhead and therefore increases the cost of goods sold. Nevertheless, a company must conduct external wage surveys to align its pay practices with strategy.

✔ **The ability to compete for talent:** Regardless of organizational strategy, companies need to be able to compete for and retain talent in order to stay in business. Similar to executive compensation, supply and demand drives these decisions. Conducting regular wage surveys allows for greater agility in pay practices, giving businesses the opportunity to get ahead of issues before they become challenges that must be dealt with. In short, it's the difference between *managing* a pay practice and *handling* a pay issue.

Market surveys come with special issues of their own. *Benchmarking* (the practice of comparing jobs to similar work in the industry) jobs is the focus of conducting a pay survey, which can lead to charges of *collusion* (discussing pay practices with competitors) or *wage fixing* (artificially holding down wages or benefits). Any time competitors get together to exchange information, they must be careful not to artificially hold down wages for a group of workers. For that reason, many industries participates in wage surveys conducted by third parties with privacy firewalls.

If you're a PHR candidate, you need to be skilled at managing outsourced vendors, so utilizing and managing a third-party vendor to conduct wage surveys may be an area for increased review.

Several large technology companies agreed to not poach talent from a select group of competitors in order to avoid wage inflation in their industry. Affected employees sued and won based on a violation of which act?

(A) Sherman Antitrust Act

(B) Fair Labor Standards Act

(C) Employee Retirement Income Security Act

(D) The Portal-to-Portal Act

The correct answer is (A). Several major technology companies were accused of agreeing to not poach employees from each other in order to avoid paying higher wages. Affected employees sued, accusing these companies of colluding to fix wages, a practice prohibited under the Sherman Antitrust Act. (B), the Fair Labor Standards Act, established rules for minimum wages, overtime, and child labor. (C), the Employee Retirement Income Security Act, regulates retirement plans, and (D), the Portal-to-Portal Act amended the Fair Labor Standards Act to define compensable time under the act.

Shaping executive compensation

Executive compensation has a bad reputation, part of which has been earned. However, executives do have unique needs that must be addressed when creating a total rewards package. Looking at this from the perspective of risk management may be a helpful way to understand the various components an executive package must consider. The risks include

- ✔ **Turnover:** *Turnover* (occurs when employees leave a company) packs a costly punch and is generally calculated as a percentage of salary. Take one to two times the executive base pay (an accepted number to calculate the cost of turnover), and a company is looking at a large expense. More though is the law of supply and demand, in which wages are affected by the availability of qualified talent. Qualified talent shrinks at the top of the talent pyramid, so keeping qualified executives happy is a core function of compensation packages. In reverse, not many executive level positions are available when compared to other levels of management, so executives that leave one company for another are taking a risk.

- ✔ **Retention:** The opposite of turnover, *retention* (keeping key employees) efforts are built into executive employment contracts usually in the form of golden handshakes or golden handcuffs. A *golden handshake* (also referred to as a *parachute*) means that a *C-suite* (chief officers, such as chief executive officer or chief financial officer) executive is contractually guaranteed a severance package should the company be acquired or she is fired or asked to retire early. A *golden handcuff* is also part of an executive contract, in which the individual is incentivized to stay in an executive position for a specified period of time in exchange for some financial reward.

✔ **Taxes:** With high levels of compensation comes higher tax obligations, costing executives a pretty penny when accepting a lucrative contract. This financial risk can be mitigated through *deferred compensation* in which an employee is paid a portion of their earnings at a later date. Deferred compensation is often built into an employee pension.

As with any other human resource activity, organizations should seek options in which the reward outweighs the risk, which translates into executive compensation that is tied to organizational and individual performance indicators. Both exams cover performance based pay and noncash compensation methods, whereas the SPHR exam goes in greater depth on concepts related to executive compensation.

Selecting and communicating employee benefits

Employee benefits include a long list, including health and wellness, retirement, employee assistance programs (EAP), workers' compensation, Medicare, protected leave, Social Security. Some benefits such as retirement are voluntary but are still regulated after an employer selects them as part of its benefits packages. The laws for which you should have working knowledge for the exams include

✔ **Employee Retirement Income Security Act (ERISA):** ERISA in the context of employment law governs retirement contributions. ERISA requires that plan administrators provide participants with retirement plan details, including a written summary plan description. It also sets standards for plan decision-makers, charging them to act in the best interest of the beneficiary (in this case, the employee enrolled in the plan). A worthy amendment to ERISA that you should be aware of is the Consolidated Omnibus Budget Reconciliation Act (COBRA), which requires employers to offer continued health insurance coverage to employees that experience a qualifying event, such as termination of employment or loss of insurance due to divorce. The employer isn't obligated to pay for the continued insurance.

✔ **Social Security & Medicare (SSI):** Passed in 1935 during the Great Depression, SSI is a form of social insurance in which the government supplies financial assistance to eligible people. Medicare amended the Social Security Act in the 1960s, providing medical insurance for those who qualified. Both SSI and Medicare are taxes paid by both the employer and employee, calculated on a percentage of wages and deducted from each paycheck until the maximum amount is met.

✔ **Workers' compensation:** Workers' compensation is required by federal law; however, individual states administer it. It offers medical care, wage replacement, and rehabilitation and survivor payments to employees injured on the job. Workers' compensation is a form of mandatory insurance that is entirely employer funded.

✔ **Family Medical Leave Act (FMLA):** The FMLA provides job-protected leave to employees with a serious health condition. It applies to employers with 50 or more employees. Eligible employees are entitled to 12 weeks of unpaid leave for the birth of a child, for their own serious health condition, or for the serious health condition of a spouse, child, or parent. If an employee is the caregiver of an injured member of the military, the employee is entitled to 26 weeks of unpaid leave within a 12-month period to provide care. Eligible employees are those who have worked for a covered employer for more than 12 months and at least 1,250 hours.

✔ **Patient Protection & Affordable Care Act (PPACA):** The PPACA (also known as the Affordable Care Act or Obamacare) is the outcome of the government's attempt at healthcare reform. It requires that employers with 50 or more employees provide affordable health insurance options to their full-time equivalent (FTE) workforce or be subject to a penalty.

With the exception of ERISA, the rest of these benefits are mandatory. After they have been implemented, your employer has the option to offer several different types of voluntary benefits such as sick time, vacation leave, tuition reimbursement, or flexible scheduling. After your employer has decided which benefits to offer, HR must communicate to employees why they should take advantage of these benefits. With a diverse workgroup, these conversations can feel discombobulated. For example, baby boomers may be highly interested in the retirement match, but Millennials not yet so concerned. Employees with young families and part-time college students may appreciate flexible scheduling. Ultimately, conducting employee surveys to identify which benefits they prefer is a helpful way to offer and potentially pay for benefits that will increase employee satisfaction.

Taking advantage of common reports and tools

Streamlined reporting supports an employer's efforts toward compensation and benefits communication. Often, the practice of collecting the data can be quite revealing, and it can help employers make decisions about what benefits to offer in the future. The following sections are a few of the more common data collection and communication tools used in administering C & B efforts.

Hidden paychecks

Also called *total rewards statements, hidden paychecks* allow employers to communicate the true value of an employee's pay. It summarizes individual employee base pay, incentives, and benefits. For example, an employee's base pay is $50,000 per year; however, the employer contributions to health insurance and retirement plans adds an additional $16,000, making the total value of their employment $66,000. This information is important for the employee to have, especially if she is considering leaving for what appears to be a better paying job. Total rewards statements are often given at the end of the calendar year.

Benefits surveys

With increasing benefits costs outpacing inflation, the decision to offer benefits has a direct link to the profit and loss statement. Conducting an employee-needs survey to ask employees which benefits they would prefer helps employers offer options that are fully utilized. Surveys can be used to identify both the financial and nonfinancial desires of the workforce. Popular survey questions relate to additional health insurance, coverage for same-sex partners, family-friendly benefits like flexible schedules, the need for tuition reimbursement, and employee wellness incentives for weight loss or smoking cessation.

Exempt checklists

The FLSA allows employers to exempt certain workers from the payment of overtime wages if certain criteria are met. In some cases, a whole class of workers are exempt, such as outside salespersons. Other positions may require a more in-depth look at whether they're truly qualified for this exemption. Factors to consider include

- ✔ **Salary level:** The FLSA mandates that all employees paid less that $23,600 per year be non-exempt and eligible for overtime.

- ✔ **Salary basis:** Salaried employees are those who are paid a guaranteed minimum amount of pay on a weekly basis for performing any work. Employers may still apply a leave policy without violating this requirement. For example, an employee is paid a weekly amount of $880. She takes a vacation day, and the employer deducts eight hours from her accrued time. As long as her paycheck is still $880, the employer is in compliance with the FLSA. Use the FLSA fact sheets to help you study the conditions under which a salaried employees wages may be reduced. You can find them at the Department of Labor's website by searching the term "FLSA." Refer to the later section, "Department of Labor" for the URL and more helpful information.

✔ **Job duties:** Meeting the salaried basis test isn't enough. To be correctly classified as exempt from overtime law, the employee must also meet the job duties requirement. Described by the FLSA as "high-level," the law further breaks down the exemption categories into the following:

- **Executive:** Defined by who is in charge. Even if a supervisor is a working supervisor, if she is the one who is in charge and truly has influence over personnel matters, she may qualify for exemption.

- **Professional:** Creative professionals and those jobs that are highly intellectual requiring an advanced degree such as lawyers or architects aren't entitled to overtime pay.

- **Administrative:** Administrative professionals support the work of business and are considered staff workers (as opposed to line workers who produce the goods or services). HR and finance are two examples of qualified administrative professionals. General clerical workers aren't.

FLSA standards specify that a job is exempt from overtime payments when:

(A) The employees are paid on a commission basis.

(B) The work is done by a tipped employee.

(C) The work is conducted by an independent contractor.

(D) The minimum pay rate equals at least $455 per week.

The correct answer is (D). In order for any position to be classified as exempt under the Fair Labor Standards Act (FLSA), the pay rate must equal at least $455 per week. (A) is incorrect because commissioned employees must be paid a minimum of one and one half times the minimum wage for each hour worked. (B) isn't a factor if exempt or non-exempt, so it's incorrect. An independent contractor isn't an employee, and therefore, not subject to labor laws, so (D) isn't true.

To meet the job duties requirement for exempt workers, you can't rely on job titles. The employee's tasks, duties, and responsibilities (TDR) and knowledge, skill, and abilities (KSA) required to perform the work determine whether the employee is exempt (or not).

Using the Internet for Additional Help

C&B is a complex area of study. Unless you're an expert in the field, more than likely you'll need to work additional resources into your study plan so that you can dive deeper into the concepts. In other words, just reading one section of a textbook isn't enough. Leverage the Internet to develop study material that relates to the exam objectives. Here are some sites that I suggest as you begin your search.

Department of Labor

The United States Department of Labor (DOL) (www.dol.gov) is the government agency charged with oversight of the pertinent information related to C&B including

✔ **Wage and hour laws:** Minimum wage, child labor, and overtime are the big three in terms of wage and hour compliance. As with many other labor laws, the FLSA was passed in 1938 in response to the social climate of the time when employers were taking advantage of individuals desperate for work during the Depression. Similarly, Social Security and Medicare were also passed within this decade. The DOL is the place to find fact sheets and enforcement guidelines to supplement your preparation efforts.

✔ **Health and benefits:** Although employer mandates continue to be defined, the days of voluntary health benefits for employees has been severely diluted in recent years by the passage of the Patient Protection and Affordable Care Act (PPACA), commonly known as Obamacare. The DOL website offers consumers information on what they need to know about ACA health benefits and compliance assistance for employers. The website also includes compliance information for COBRA, the Health Insurance Portability and Accountability Act (HIPAA), and the Genetic Information Nondiscrimination Act (GINA).

✔ **Retirement:** Supplementary retirement continues to be a voluntary benefit offered by employers. However, it becomes heavily regulated after plans are in place. The DOL can offer employer information on how to comply with the ERISA and fact sheets about cash balance plans and traditional pension plans.

As you get more comfortable with the DOL's website, I suspect that you'll agree that a *daily* visit is well worth the time investment. The magnitude of information can be overwhelming, so chunking it into daily bits makes it more easily digestible while serving your long-term retention needs.

World at Work

Formerly known as the American Compensation Association, World at Work (www.worldat work.org) is an excellence resource for all things in the world of compensation and benefits. You can find free information related to compensation strategies and how total reward practices impacts an organization's competitiveness. Use this site as a resource to research pay concepts such as pay equity, distributive justice, and practices for variable pay plans.

World at Work also has membership opportunities. There are many options to specialize in the various practices of human resources. Both functions of C&B have specialist certifications that are excellent options for the developing HR professional.

Internal Revenue Service

The IRS (www.irs.gov) is surprisingly an excellent resource for us when making decisions about compensation. In addition to existing laws, IRS opinion letters are worth a review as you study the area of C&B. Use the site to find information about the following:

✔ **Independent contractors (IC) versus employees:** An *independent contractor* is an individual doing work for your company that isn't an employee. Meanwhile, an *employee* is one for which the employer of record is responsible for taxes and benefits and is granted the protection of general labor law. Properly classifying individuals who do work for your organization has an tax impact, so getting it right is important to the IRS. Improper classification can cost companies a lot of money in penalties and interest. The fundamental factor that distinguishes between an IC and an employee is *degree of control*. The greater the control over the work, the more likely the person is an employee. Factors include behavioral, financial, and type of relationship.

Use the plumber's test to help determine whether an individual is an employee or IC. If you're the manager of a retail store who has a plumbing problem, you probably jump online and search for plumbers in the area; ICs advertise and are licensed. You make the call and the plumber tells you that he can be there between noon and 5:00 the next day — ICs set their own hours and schedule. When the plumber arrives, he brings with him his wrenches and hoses; ICs have their own tools and equipment. After he completes the repairs, he submits a bill. ICs keep their own finances and pay their own taxes. Finally, your core competency is retail sales, not plumbing, meaning that you couldn't have provided the same service that the plumber provided; ICs don't have skills that mirror the key aspects of the business.

✔ **Updated forms:** The IRS publishes new W-4 forms for each calendar year. These forms must be completed upon hire so that proper payroll deductions can be made.

✔ **Employee business expenses:** The IRS website has loads of information pertaining to actual business expenses and employee business expenses. Categories include business travel, mileage reimbursement rates, entertainment expenses, and corporate gifts.

Chapter 11

Connecting the Dots: Employee and Labor Relations

In This Chapter

▶ Recognizing the exam objectives

▶ Living a company culture

▶ Making sense of union organizing

▶ Taking advantage of the Internet

The title of this HR function is telling. Employee and Labor Relations (ELR) is all about relationships. The first relationship is between the employer and the employee. The next relationship is between the employer and a union. The third relationship is between the union and its members. The application of ELR principles will always be toward one of these relationships that exist in the workplace. This chapter examines some of the exam specifics in more detail.

Navigating ELR

One of the fundamental HR directives from the Employee and Labor Relations exam objectives is illustrated by the term *balance*. HR professionals must manage the balance between

✔ **People:** If a work relationship exists, this function addresses it. The exam deals with issues between the company and its employees, managers and their employees, and peer-to-peer relationships. HR will also participate in relationship management if the company is unionized.

✔ **Compliance:** Balancing rights with responsibilities is a critical element of ELR. Employees are granted rights by law (called *statutory rights*) and rights by employment agreements (referred to as *contractual laws*).

Consider these balance factors as you read through the function description defined by HRCI and exam objectives.

"Developing, implementing/administering, and evaluating the workplace in order to maintain relationships and working conditions that balance employer/employee needs and rights in support of the organization's goals and objectives."

Here are the PHR and SPHR bodies of knowledge (BOK) defined by the Human Resource Certification Institute:

- ✔ 01 Ensure that employee and labor relations activities are compliant with applicable federal laws and regulations.

- ✔ 02 Assess organizational climate by obtaining employee input; for example, focus groups, employee surveys, and staff meetings.

- ✔ 03 Develop and implement employee relations programs — for example, recognition, special events, and diversity programs — that promote a positive organizational culture.

- ✔ 04 Evaluate effectiveness of employee relations programs through the use of metrics; for example, exit interviews, employee surveys, and turnover rates.

- ✔ 05 Establish, update, and communicate workplace policies and procedures — for example, employee handbook, reference guides, or standard operating procedures — and monitor their application and enforcement to ensure consistency.

- ✔ 06 Develop and implement a discipline policy based on organizational code of conduct/ethics, ensuring that no disparate impact or other legal issues arise.

- ✔ 07 Create and administer a termination process — for example, reductions in force (RIF), policy violations, poor performance — ensuring that no disparate impact or other legal issues arise.

- ✔ 08 Develop, administer, and evaluate grievance/ dispute resolution and performance improvement policies and procedures.

- ✔ 09 Investigate and resolve employee complaints filed with federal agencies involving employment practices or working conditions, utilizing professional resources as necessary; for example, legal counsel, mediation/arbitration specialists, and investigators.

- ✔ 10 Develop and direct proactive employee relations strategies for remaining union-free in non-organized locations (SPHR only).

- ✔ 11 Direct and/or participate in collective bargaining activities, including contract negotiation, costing, and administration.

ELR makes up 20 percent of the PHR exam, second only to Workforce Planning and Employment, so ELR is an especially critical study area for PHR test takers. If you're an SPHR candidate, you're looking at 14 percent of your exam being made up of ELR content, with an SPHR-only label on exam objective 10.

Focusing on What the Exam Covers in ELR

ELR is about relationship management. These sections explain information about the more salient points of relationships in the workplace, including a discussion about the importance of company culture, the process of gathering feedback, the comprehensive labor laws governing ELR, and a bit about the union-organizing process.

Defining company culture and climate

The term *culture* is used in a few different ways throughout the exam objectives. It includes the diversity perspective of a group of people with a shared national origin that has a collective belief system, customs, and sometimes language that distinct from each other. It also includes the need for HR professionals to manage company culture because negative stereotypes can exist that lead to a lack of team cohesiveness, or worse, unlawful discrimination.

Many conditions define organizational culture. These conditions include beliefs, customs, language, values, artifacts, and both employer and employee behaviors. All of these conditions can be useful in understanding the ELR components in these ways:

- **Beliefs:** In organizational development, the company and employees should share a belief system. These core values are fairly static and serve as the foundation for many corporate decisions and expectations of behaviors. Examples include sustainability, ethical leadership, employee development, and innovation.

- **Customs:** A *custom* is a traditional way of doing things, usually based on a family, religious, or collective belief.

- **Language:** *Language* refers to the systems of communication in place at work. Tone, attitudes, body language, and even the unspoken behaviors communicated by executive decisions set the standard for company culture. Language doesn't refer to the native tongue of the employees.

- **Values:** A company that lives its values is setting a powerful standard for the day-to-day operations and behaviors of employees. Core *values* are guidelines for how a company will behave toward its employees, customers, and other stakeholders. Values serve organizational culture by creating a shared commitment to a set of beliefs.

- **Employer and employee behaviors:** How people act toward each other is an important indicator of the level of trust that exists within the walls of a business. Employers that do what they say they're going to do goes a long way toward establishing a culture of goodwill. In addition, how employees behave toward each other sets the tone for a team environment working toward a common goal.

An added dimension to organizational culture is the intellectual achievements of a company. Everyone wants to be on a winning team — there is just something important about shared wins. Note that every company has a culture (whether it knows it or not). HR's job is to help the company define and reinforce the factors that build a positive organizational culture.

The exam asks you to be proficient in developing employee relations programs that develop the desired culture. The HR activities you should be familiar with from ELR exam objective 03 include

- **Recognition programs:** Too often, ELR programs focus on what employees are doing wrong. *Recognition programs* seek balance by acknowledging the efforts and successes on the individual, team, and organizational level. The exam objectives direct you to be familiar with employee recognition programs that "promote a positive organizational culture." This is tied to another ELR exam objective that directs you to seek out feedback from employees through the use of focus groups, staff meetings, and surveys. The outcome from this employee feedback can help you create effective recognition programs.

- **Special events:** Similar to recognition programs, *special events* create a positive employment culture by bringing employees (and sometimes their families) together. Events to be familiar with for the exams include annual events such as picnics or holiday parties, company retreats used to communicate or develop business relationships and strategies, as well as regular employee meetings for everyone to keep workers up-to-date on the state of the business.

- **Diversity programs:** *Diversity* is a term that describes the differences among employees. It may be based on personal characteristics, such as age or gender or on employee differences in educational or experience levels. Diversity programs seek to train employees on how to work well with others, both from a *tolerance* perspective (accepting others who aren't like themselves) and from the perspective that seeking out different ideas enhances organizational effectiveness.

A positive organizational culture may be influenced by which employee relations program?

(A) Health and wellness

(B) Diversity

(C) Union avoidance

(D) All of the above

The correct answer is (B). Diversity programs positively impact organizational culture by creating a more inclusive environment. Health and wellness programs are focused on the health, safety, and security of the workforce, so (A) is incorrect. Companies create union-avoidance strategies primarily to avoid the unionization of the workforce, (although a positive organizational culture may be part of those strategies), so (C) is incorrect.

After the culture is established, you need to take steps to monitor the climate and assess the effectiveness of ELR programs. These temperature checks appear in the exam objectives 02 and 04. Based on these objectives you should understand the use of the following:

- **Focus groups:** Employee *focus groups* are a form of research used to gather feedback from workers on different employment issues. They send the message to employees that their feedback is valued and serves the organizational culture by improving employee *engagement* (the degree to which employees feel linked to company success). You should be aware that a focus group is considered a softer, more human way to gather information about employee needs because the results are communicated in words rather than numbers.

- **Employee surveys:** Companies use *employee surveys* to both ask the employees what they need and measure the effectiveness of ELR programs, so devote some of your attention to the fundamentals of employee surveys. These fundamentals include the need to clearly identify the objective of the survey and communicate that objective when asking employees for their input. Management commitment to the findings should also be evaluated, because it's demotivating to ask employees for their feedback and then failing to act.

- **Staff meetings:** ELR exam objective 02 references staff meetings as an assessment tool for reading organizational climate. Staff meetings are cross referenced in the knowledge of component 52 from the perspective of employee involvement strategies. From this, you can deduce that a staff meeting is a tool used to both gather employee feedback on important issues and help employees feel involved. Staff meetings are broader than focus groups in that these meetings are regularly scheduled and serve to communicate information rather than specifically to ask for feedback.

- **Exit interviews:** Exit interviews are another fairly specific form of gathering employee feedback. An *exit interview* is narrowly focused on asking separating workers why they're leaving the company. This data is then used to improve retention rates of the remaining employees.

- **Turnover rates:** When employees leave an organization (voluntarily or involuntarily), it's called *turnover*. For the exams, it's a measure of employee engagement, simply based on the premise that happy workers don't leave. This of course isn't necessarily true, because employees leave for many reasons unrelated to the job or company, such as to relocate or to take care of children at home. This seeming contradiction means that you should understand the concepts of the following:

  - **Voluntary turnover:** When an employee chooses to resign his position

  - **Involuntary turnover:** When the employer terminates an employee

  - **Functional turnover:** When difficult employees or poor performers leave

- **Dysfunctional turnover:** When talented workers or high potential employees exit

- **Controllable turnover:** Turnover that could have been avoided through employee retention and engagement efforts

- **Uncontrollable turnover:** Turnover that could not be avoided, such as employee relocation

For this ELR exam objective 04, which asks you to evaluate the effectiveness of ELR programs, you would be measuring the rates of voluntary, dysfunctional, and controllable turnover.

The benefit of evaluating turnover rates within the first year of employment is that:

(A) HR may evaluate the effectiveness of their recruitment efforts.

(B) HR is able to measure the primary reasons that employees leave.

(C) HR may spot trends in first-year employment, such as attendance issues.

(D) HR may use the information gathered to address management deficiencies

The correct answer is (B). Turnover rates can be measured in multiple ways, and *first-year turnover* (the rate of turnover within an employee's first year of work) is useful to identify the primary reasons why employees leave an organization early in their tenure. (B) encompasses the other answers, including how effective the company's recruiting efforts are at determining fit (A), whether or not attendance is a regular problem (C), and whether or not a specific manager or department needs improvement (D).

Understanding compliance

Some days, it feels like all you do in your job is try to figure out how to comply with labor law. On those days when I feel this way, I remind myself that it's job security! ELR is an especially complex web of regulations, particularly because it applies to the right of employees to form unions. The exams include information related to the labor code made up of three fundamental laws:

- ✔ **The National Labor Relations Act (NLRA):** Passed in 1935, the NLRA gave workers the right to organize, including striking against employers who were treating them unfairly. This act sets restrictions on employers during the union-organizing process, attempting to ensure that workers may collect together unfettered to make a decision about whether to unionize or not. For purposes of this exam, you should understand the two types of lawful strikes protected by the NLRA:

  - **Economic strike:** An *economic strike* is when employees refuse to work because they want higher wages, shorter working hours, or better working conditions. Economic strikers can't be discharged, but the employer may replace them.

  - **Unfair labor practice (ULP) strike:** An unfair labor practice strike occurs when workers are protesting a prohibited employer behavior. Prohibited behavior includes the employer threatening or interfering with a worker's right to organize, or refusing to bargain in good faith. The employer may not discharge or permanently replace ULP strikers.

Visit the National Labor Relations Board's website to find out more about lawful and unlawful strikes at www.nlrb.gov/strikes.

- ✔ **The Labor-Management Relations Act (LMRA):** In 1947, Congress felt compelled to respond to the growing imbalance of power that the unions had gained, so it passed the LMRA. This act focused on defining union unfair labor practices and gave examples of prohibited policies and strikes. These prohibited practices include

- **Wildcat strikes:** When workers walk off the job without union authorization to strike, they're considered to have *gone wild,* hence the name *wildcat strike.* The LMRA prohibits them.

- **Secondary boycotts:** A *secondary boycott* occurs when employees refuse to work at their company because their company buys from another site that is on strike.

- **Jurisdictional strikes:** Think of a *jurisdictional strike* as a territory dispute. They occur when unions are engaged in a turf war over who should be able to represent a group of workers.

✔ **The Labor-Management Reporting and Disclosure Act (LMRDA):** The LMRDA was passed in 1959, and it created a bill of rights for union members. This bill of rights gave equal status to union members in terms of voicing opinions, and the bill restricted the dues increases to those that were passed by a majority vote of members. The LMRDA was necessary because there was evidence of corrupt union practices that didn't serve the interests of the union members.

Context matters on these exams. Think about what was going on in 1935 when the NLRA was passed. The effects of the Great Depression were severe, and worker exploitation was the norm. Employees were looking for security and fair treatment. By the time the LMRA was passed in 1947, the unions had used strikes as threats to shut down businesses and were impacting commerce, so Congress responded with a bill to balance the equation. More than 20 years after unions had been officially recognized, the LMRDA was passed in response to reports of union leadership and corruption. Understanding this context should help you relate exam questions that are tied to reasoning.

In addition to the labor code, ELR deals with employees' rights granted by law, called statutory rights. Examples include the right to be free from harassment in the workplace and the right to privacy. Added to these laws must be a conversation about common law doctrines. A common law doctrine doesn't require an act of Congress to have the force of law; it's based on consistent court interpretations. Because of these court interpretations, HR professionals have to stay up-to-date on new lawsuits and court rulings every year, because the status of HR law changes with each ruling.

More than likely, the PHR and SPHR exams will ask you questions about the common law doctrine of employment at-will (EAW). *EAW* is the right for either party in employment to terminate the relationship at any time. Employers don't have to give a reason, and employees don't have to give notice. The challenge with true EAW are the three exceptions:

✔ **Public policy exception:** Employees may not be terminated for engaging in a protected activity. Examples include filing a workers' compensation claim or refusing to alter employee timecards to avoid overtime payments.

✔ **Good faith and fair dealing:** The duty of *good faith and fair dealing* is simply the expectation that employers should act in a fair manner when making employment decisions. An employer can't fire an employee under the at-will doctrine to avoid paying a large sales commission or fire an older worker to avoid retirement obligations.

✔ **Implied contract:** If an employee has longevity and good performance reviews, an *implied contract* may exist, which means that the at-will doctrine is no longer in effect, and the employee may only be terminated for cause. Implied contracts have been created by statements from supervisors to the effect of "as long as you do good work, you'll have a job here for life."

The exam may give you a scenario-based question that looks for the best answer. Consider the question wording carefully before going for the absolutes. For example, just because you can terminate someone under the at-will doctrine doesn't mean you should. HR is often required to communicate the risk of taking a specific action.

The common law doctrine of at-will employment can be defined as

(A) refusing to hire an individual based on a protected class characteristic

(B) holding the employer liable for the actions of its supervisors

(C) providing an untrue employment reference

(D) being able to terminate an employee at any time, for any reason, unless unlawful

The correct answer is (D). The common law doctrine of employment at-will states that the employer or employee may terminate the relationship at any time, for any reason, unless prohibited by law. (A) refers to unlawful discrimination. (B) is the common law doctrine known as *respondeat superior,* and (C) is defamation of character or slander.

In addition to common law doctrines, there is another set of laws *not* passed by Congress that require employer compliance. They're called *executive orders,* signed off by the President of the United States. The exam-related executive orders mainly identify classes of protected groups. Refer to Chapter 8 for more information about executive orders.

Applying discipline and conducting separations

When Human Resource Development (HRD) efforts such as coaching and employing motivation techniques fail, many employers turn to discipline, up to and leading to termination. The ELR exam content refers to these concepts in three objectives:

- ✔ "Develop and implement a discipline policy based on organizational code of conduct/ethics, ensuring that no disparate impact or other legal issues arise." Part of the employee handbook, a *code of conduct* serves to communicate the expected standards of behavior to employees. Many codes include examples of prohibited behavior such as theft, horseplay, and violent behavior.

- ✔ "Create and administer a termination process — for example, reductions in force (RIF), policy violations, and poor performance — ensuring that no disparate impact or other legal issues arise." This exam objective speaks specifically to protecting employers from the risk of *disparate impact* (unintentional discrimination because of a seemingly neutral employment action) and other legal issues such as unlawful discrimination based on race, age, gender, or disability. You should be familiar with how legal issues can come up in the termination process and best practices to avoid these issues when terminating workers.

- ✔ "Develop, administer, and evaluate grievance/dispute resolution and performance improvement policies and procedures." By providing a grievance or dispute procedure, HR ensures that employees have a fair and neutral way to communicate their needs to the employer. This exam objective *combined* grievance/dispute procedure with performance-improvement polices and procedures. It implies that both activities aren't necessarily related, but most certainly systems driven.

Note the common phrase "ensuring that no disparate impact or other legal issues arise" in the first two objectives. It's a clue to exam content. *Disparate impact* occurs when a seemingly neutral employment policy or practice results in unintentional discrimination against a protected class group. For example, requiring applicants to apply on a Sunday morning for a job may disparately impact those who go to church. So the objectives are telling you that the code of conduct and termination process must be legally defensible and consistently applied to avoid discriminatory practices, intentional or otherwise.

In a termination meeting, managers should be counseled to

(A) Be honest and direct.

(B) Keep the meeting as short as possible.

(C) Avoid conflict.

(D) Have another employee present.

The correct answer is (A). *Termination meetings* can be uncomfortable for both parties involved. It's best for a manager to be as honest and direct as possible without being condescending or combative. Keeping the meeting as brief as possible isn't a priority, so (B) is incorrect. Avoiding conflict (C) may not be possible because employees aren't generally happy to be terminated, so a better choice would be for the supervisor to understand how to handle the conflict rather than avoid it. (D) is a bit trickier because it's a good idea to have another person present; however, the witness should be a member of management, not an employee.

Seeing the connection with other functional areas and ELR

In addition to ELR, the other functional areas of the exam have influence upon the process of employee discipline and terminations. See Table 11-1 for examples of discipline and termination efforts in the exam objectives.

Table 11-1	The Relationship of Discipline to Other Exam Content	
Functional Area	*Exam Objective*	*The Relationship*
Core Knowledge	57 Legal disciplinary procedures 60 Legal termination procedures	Discipline and terminations must be balanced with rights of employees. Brush up on the exceptions to employment at-will and Title VII prohibition against retaliation.
Business Management and Strategy	07 Develop, influence, and execute strategies for managing organizational change that balance the expectations and needs of the organization, its employees, and other stakeholders.	All employees don't react to change in a positive manner, and it may take some longer than others to properly adapt. Review concepts related to gathering employee feedback, the popular theories of motivation, change management, and also techniques for positive employee relations activities such as conflict resolution and co-op programs.
Workforce Planning and Employment	17 Develop and implement the organization exit/offboarding process for both voluntary and involuntary terminations, including planning for reductions in force (RIF).	The truth is that an employer faced with a layoff isn't going to downsize its best workers; the low performers will be cut. The exception would be if there is a union contract that dictate layoffs based on length of service with no regard for quality.

Functional Area	Exam Objective	The Relationship
		For this reason, HR must manage the process of job elimination or re-structure to help avoid dysfunctional turnover. Related to this exam content is the avoidance of calling an employee separation a layoff when it actually is a termination. This may occur when an employer wants to get rid of a low performer, but it desires to avoid a confrontation or wrongful discipline/ discharge claim.
Human Resource Development	06 Develop, select, and evaluate performance appraisal processes — for example, instruments, and ranking and rating scales — to increase individual and organizational effectiveness.	Don't confuse the performance review session with a discipline session. You must hold them separately. Effective performance management programs have systems in place for regular employee feedback, including discipline, outside of the appraisal process. Be familiar with these techniques.
Compensation and Benefits	03 Manage payroll-related information; for example, new hires, adjustments, and terminations).	An employee termination has an operational impact in several pay-related ways. It includes giving the employee his final pay, responding to claims for unemployment benefit eligibility, issuing benefits continuation notices in compliance with laws such as the Consolidated Omnibus Budget Reconciliation Act (COBRA), and issuing Health Insurance Portability and Accountability Act (HIPAA) certificates as applicable, all relevant to both exams.
Risk Management	09 Develop policies and procedures to direct the appropriate use of electronic media and hardware; for example, email, social media, and appropriate website access.	Email, social media, and Internet policies all carry some measure of HR management. Having a clear understanding of employee rights in the areas of privacy and confidentiality is important before disciplining or terminating an employee for his e-behavior.

Calculating disparate impact

Metrics continue to be a valuable tool in the day-to-day operations of HR. To measure disparate impact, you must call upon the definitions from Uniform Guidelines on Employee Selection Procedures:

> "Disparate treatment occurs where members of a race, sex, or ethnic group have been denied the same employment, promotion, membership, or other employment opportunities as have been available to other employees or applicants."

The UGESP provides the formula for calculating when disparate, or an adverse impact has occurred:

> "A selection rate for any race, sex, or ethnic group which is less than four-fifths (⅘) (or eighty percent) of the rate for the group with the highest rate..."

This means that you can calculate the rate of terminations of protected class groups when compared to non-protected class groups by using the four-fifths rule. Here is an example:

Christmas Trees Inc.'s busy season has ended, and as has been past practices, it must lay off workers. Of its 500 employees, 100 employees older than 40 and 75 employees younger than 40 were selected for termination. Of the 500 total employees, 200 were older than 40, with the remaining 300 younger than 40. To calculate if disparate impact occurred against older workers:

1. **Identify the total number of workers older than 40 that were selected for layoff and divide that by the total number of employees in the workforce.**

   $100 \div 200 = 50\%$

2. **Identify the total number of employees selected for layoff who are younger than 40 and divide that by their total number in the workforce.**

   $75 \div 300 = 25\%$

3. **Divide the selection rate to identify the impact ratio.**

   $25 \div 50 = 5\%$

The impact ratio of .5 percent is less than .8 percent, so there is evidence that disparate impact occurred. Find more information on disparate impact (also referred to as *adverse impact*), check out www.uniformguidelines.com.

Making sense of the union organizing process

Unions tend to target the baseline needs of employees — job security, better pay and benefits, and safer working conditions. In their early years, these elements were subject to employer discretion, which led to all sorts of horror stories for employees. Now that these bits are actually addressed via labor law (such as the FLSA, PPACA, OSHA), unions have been in a continually decline. However, the essence of union organizing has remained fairly constant. The process, along with the various types of unfair labor practices (ULP) that can occur at each stage, looks like this:

✔ **The campaign:** A *union campaign* is similar to a political campaign in that the union and the employer are opponents with the winner decided by a majority vote. The union may contact employees at home or hold offsite meetings to woo employees over to its side, which is accomplished when at least 30 percent of the targeted workers sign authorization cards, authorizing a vote. Campaign strategies include signage, mailers, phone calls, town hall meetings, and propaganda — it's an intense time for all involved.

For the exams, note the various unfair labor practices that may occur. An employer may not interfere with, restrain, or coerce employees during a union campaign. Examples of prohibited behavior include promising employees benefits if they remain union free, polling employees to determine their support of the union, and photographing or videotaping employees engaged in protected activities.

✔ **Representation election:** After 30 percent of the targeted workers have signed authorization cards, a representation election is scheduled. A *union ballot* (voting card for employees to cast their vote) is created showing the candidates (the union and the employer) petitioning to be the employee representative. The option that receives the most votes of the majority that voted (not number of employees) wins. For this reason, many employers subject to a representation election encourages *all* affected employees in the bargaining unit to vote.

ULPs that may occur during the representation election include an employer spying on voting activity, threatening employees who vote one way, or trying to bribe workers to vote in the employer's favor.

✔ **Union certification:** The NLRB issues official certification after a successful election. The union is now authorized by the employees to make decisions on their behalf through the collective bargaining process.

✔ **Collective bargaining:** Union employees are no longer at-will; an employment contract governs them. The union and the employer negotiate the contract, which addresses typical issues such as wages, hours, pensions, seniority, working conditions, and cause for discipline or termination. The contract will also stipulate the length of the contract, grievance procedures, and any security provisions desired by the union. A union may file a ULP against the employer during the collective bargaining process if the employer fails to send someone in with the authority to bargain in good faith.

✔ **Ratification:** After an agreement has been reached through collective bargaining, the union representatives take it back to the workers who vote whether to accept the terms. A union may be charged with a ULP if it lacks transparency in presenting the final contract to the union members or changes parts of the agreement after the membership has voted to ratify.

A bargaining unit consists of only the employees eligible to be represented by a union. These employees must have shared interests, such as supervision, wages, benefits, physical location, and industry description

The *community of interest* doctrine established the criteria that must be met in order to be considered a bargaining unit. It states that the proposed members of a bargaining unit have enough shared employment interests that an agent can effectively represent the group without conflict. Supervisors can't be part of a bargaining unit because they're considered part of the management team rather than part of the labor. For follow-up, study the NLRB's definition of a supervisor, which is especially important because there have been several attempts by employers to categorize groups of employees as supervisors (such as nurses) in order to impede their ability to organize.

After the agreement in in place, a union steward who is both an employee of the company and a union official is put into place to handle employee grievances. For larger issues, union members may strike against their employer by refusing to come to work.

Seeing the relevance of common reports and tools

In the area of ELR, the best advice is to remember that "if it isn't documented, it never happened." Most human resource forms and documents are used to establish a paper trail of activity, ensuring that procedures are followed and both parties' interests are protected. These documents and forms are essential in ELR.

Employee handbooks and policy reviews

The words *policy* and *police* share origins, in that they refer to governing a population. In the workplace, policies are designed to communicate employer expectations and to comply with the various laws requiring that employees be notified of certain rights and responsibilities. An *employee handbook* (written employment guide that documents employee rights and responsibilities) is the tool used by employers to document and communicate employment policies.

A special issue for the SPHR: Union avoidance

The ELR has only one exam objective unique to the SPHR, which is No. 10:

"Develop and direct proactive employee relations strategies for remaining union-free in non-organized locations."

Breaking this exam objective down requires that you look at just one facet: engaging in proactive employee relations strategies. You can do so by

✔ **Aligning ELR activities with the company mission, vision, and values.** Writing polices and activating procedures in alignment with the corporate MVV will help to ensure that employees are on the same page with management. Doing so communicates to an employee that she is part of a bigger picture and encourages a direct line of communication between management and employees. Supporting this link reduces the need for a third-party facilitator.

✔ **Training the supervisors to be fair and accurate reflection of the MVV.** An old saying goes "employees don't leave companies, they leave bosses." Twisted up a bit, one could argue that employees don't invite a union in, but rather bad managers open the door. As a result, training supervisors, coaching leaders, and teaching management to model desired behavior is a frontline defense against union organizing.

✔ **Evaluating management and program effectiveness.** Soliciting employee feedback isn't enough. HR must take action. And taking action doesn't mean giving employees everything they ask for, but rather communicating to employees the information used to arrive at a decision.

✔ **Putting policies to good use.** No-solicitation and open-door policies are preventive in nature, but they must be applied judiciously to avoid charges of interference. If you're taking the SPHR, familiarize yourself with how and why policies can help avoid a positive outcome to a union election.

Remember that ELR is all about the relationships, and any efforts made toward fostering a positive culture will help improve employee job satisfaction. This supports union avoidance efforts in that happy employees generally do not seek out union representation.

Be sure to seek out additional information about utilizing third-party union busters as part of the resistance efforts should a campaign get going at your facility.

One example is in the area of sexual harassment prevention. In order for a company to be able to provide an affirmative defense against a charge of sexual harassment, the company first must have a policy in place that prohibits unlawful harassment. The harassment prevention policy would be used to train workers on appropriate conduct in the workplace, and the policy would reside in the handbook for future reference.

From the exam perspective, HRCI's ELR exam objective 05 states that you must understand how to:

"Establish, update, and communicate workplace policies and procedures — for example, employee handbook, reference guides, or standard operating procedures — and monitor their application and enforcement to ensure consistency."

This means that you should be prepared to answer questions about how to create and monitor both policies and *procedures* (standard methods for performing a job task) for all of the jobs within the company.

Because the handbook is a tool for compliance, I recommend that an attorney write or at least review the company handbook on an annual basis because you want the person who will have to *defend* a policy to be the one who *wrote* or signed off on the policy.

Another advantage of having an employee handbook is that is becomes a reference guide for supervisors. Common policies include attendance, benefits, and the company code of conduct. Supervisors are then able to apply consistent practices to the workforce because the handbook has spelled out the specifics. They may also be able to very clearly show employees what is expected with regard to behavior and follow disciplinary guidelines if they're part of company policy.

Another area in the scope of ELR is that of *arbitration agreements* (agreements in which both parties in a dispute attempt to have an independent ruling outside of court). Having an arbitration agreement buried at the back of a policy manual isn't enough. Employers who want to have a legally compliant arbitration system in place should take steps to demonstrate that the employee knew and understood what she was agreeing to.

HRCI's ELR exam objective that tells you what you need to know about arbitration agreements reads as follows:

> "09 Investigate and resolve employee complaints filed with federal agencies involving employment practices or working conditions, utilizing professional resources as necessary; for example, legal counsel, mediation/arbitration specialists, and investigators."

Keeping this in mind, an example question may look like this:

In dispute resolution, what do conciliation, mediation, and arbitration all have in common?

(A) They are all binding legal decisions.

(B) They are all required by the UGESP.

(C) All three are conducted by third-party individuals.

(D) All three are required to be included in employment contracts.

The correct answer is (C). Conciliation, mediation, and arbitration are alternative dispute methods that use neutral third parties to attempt to resolve employee complaints. Conciliation and mediation decisions aren't legally binding, whereas arbitration decisions are, so (A) is incorrect. None of the three options are mandated by the Uniform Guidelines on Employee Selection procedures, nor must they be included as part of employment contracts, making (B) and (D) false.

Standard forms

The list is really quite long of the various types of forms that make up the administrative debris that is part of HR. Some of the more common include

- ✔ **Incident reports:** Employee incidents can be of any kind, running the spectrum from an injury or accident to a near miss to an instance of a quality defect. Being able to track accurately this data allows for a focus on prevention. You can then use it to communicate expected standards of behavior to employees using real-time information.

- ✔ **Disciplinary action:** If compensation and incentives are the carrot in employee motivation, then discipline is the stick in the realm of employee relations. Supervisors that notice negative behavior talk to the employee about what she needs to do to correct it and then document the conversation, which makes them much better positioned to make a longer-term decision about separation. It's fairer to the employees as well. Underperforming workers should be given the opportunity to correct their behavior before being placed on the path of discipline. When necessary, these initial conversations are used to justify more formal disciplinary action, up to and including termination.

- ✔ **Request for time off:** Employees are generally granted time off through policies, and a way to track usage is necessary. The employee can give the request form to the supervisor in advance to approve and adjust scheduling as necessary, and HR can use the form to enter the time used in the recordkeeping system, along with adjusting the pay as necessary.

✔ **Grievance or complaint:** Good employee relations management is paved as a two-way street. Supervisors should have a way to document performance, and employees should have a way to log complaints. From a claim of harassment to dissatisfaction with an employment decision, these objections are documented on a grievance form, which officially begins the grievance procedure.

Good forms aren't multipage documents. They're a quick checklist that reflects the core need of business to document occurrences and track efforts.

Employee suggestion systems

A form of *upward communication* (the direction of information moving up from the employees to management), employee suggestion systems are useful ways for employees to share their thoughts on specific issues with the management team.

One example of the use of suggestion systems is in quality management programs. Employee opinions on the elimination of waste or improved efficiencies is solicited, and a committee meets to evaluate the merit. This information can then be tied to incentives, which pay employees for implemented ideas, or gift cards to recognize employees who gave their opinion.

Encouraging employee suggestions is a worthwhile employee relations effort, because employees are the experts in their jobs and best positioned to provide impactful feedback. Asking for employees' opinions is an indication that the company and management desires to hear what employees have to say.

Agendas

An *agenda* isn't just a good business practice for meeting efficiency. They're also necessary for corporations to communicate and record board of directors activity. Corporations are required to have a board of directors, and boards must have meetings. An agenda announces to the stakeholders what will be covered, and the agenda becomes a part of the meeting record. The meeting frequency varies state by state, but standard protocol for meetings usually holds.

For example, a quorum must exist for the meeting to be held, and certain bylaws require the publishing of the meeting agenda in advance. Most meetings must have a record of the activity, so minutes are kept to accurately reflect the meeting outcomes and general follow up.

Beyond the corporate governance efforts, the ELR exam objectives describe a need for employee involvement strategies through employee management committees, self-directed work teams, focus groups, and staff meetings. You should be familiar with how agendas can keep a meeting flowing smoothly and on topic, but also how an agenda serves as a record of what was discussed should a dispute arise in the future. For example, the National Labor Relations Act (NLRA) doesn't allow employers to dominate a labor organization. A labor organization may be said to exist if an employee committee is used to address policies or practices and the committee represents the opinions of other employees. If the employer directs the efforts or bargains with this group, an unlawful practice likely has occurred. In this example, an agenda can help defend or support this claim.

Going Virtual for Additional Help

Focus your online efforts to study this important exam area on the more objective components of the bodies of knowledge. Use it also to understand labor law and the the process of union organizing and grievance procedures. Plenty of information is available for you to review. The best sources are government resources and those that make a living by educating the workforce on key ELR issues. Check out these sections for good places to start.

The National Labor Relations Board

The NLRB (www.nlrb.gov) is the governing body of the union-organizing process. This site has excellent information and pertinent details of the three major acts (NLRA, LMRA, and LMRDA) affecting unions in the United States. (Refer to the earlier section "Understanding compliance" for more details.) You can also find fact sheets on key amendments and interpretations related to HR issues such as social media. However, you may find most valuable the graphs illustrating the election process as well as the process to filing an unfair labor practice charge.

American Arbitration Association

Found at www.adr.org, the American Arbitration Association is a nonprofit organization tasked with governing the entire arbitration process, from filing to closure. The organization's website offers resources that educate individuals and companies on key concepts related to arbitration and mediation.

You can search for court rulings and common forms used throughout the process to help you visualize and relate the process to your own workplace. This information can add an experience dimension that's vital to both the PHR and SPHR exams.

AFL-CIO

One of the best repositories of information on both the history and relevant current issues affecting unions and workers is the AFL-CIO. The self-described "umbrella federation for America's unions," its website (www.aflcio.org) has videos and blogs full of information.

Although definitely a *biased* viewpoint, the website still can be helpful when viewing the unionizing issues from the other's perspective. Use this checklist to take your studying online to discover

✔ What industries are covered by unions in the United States?

✔ What are worker center partnerships?

✔ When and how did unions rise in the United States?

✔ How has globalization impacted union organizing and coverage of workers?

Chapter 12

Shrinking the Target: Risk Management

• •

In This Chapter

▶ Identifying the exam objectives

▶ Understanding the concepts of enterprise risk management

▶ Preparing plans for safety and emergencies

▶ Taking advantage of the Internet

• •

Several important relationships exist within the framework of employment. With these relationships come several types of risks that pose a threat to the health and safety of the workers and the viability and sustainability of employment processes.

The PHR and SPHR exams deal with the need for HR professionals to anticipate and execute plans that minimize or eliminate business risks such as worker injuries and customer privacy. The exam objectives also describe a need to understand how to return injured employees back to work and stay compliant with specific safety laws at a federal level. This chapter describes these risks and the exam objectives in more detail so that you're ready to answer questions related to this important HR function.

Noting What's Important about Risk Management

Risk Management (RM) is the smallest chunk of content for both exams, coming it at just 8 percent for the PHR exam and 7 percent of content for the SPHR. What used to be all about safety and health has evolved into the concept of *enterprise risk*, a holistic view of all the different ways a company and its employees can be harmed. (*Enterprise* is a fancy word for a business or an undertaking.) This concept is communicated fairly clearly in the functional area description:

> "Developing, implementing/administering, and evaluating programs, procedures, and policies in order to provide a safe, secure working environment and to protect the organization from potential liability."

Here are the PHR and SPHR Bodies of Knowledge (BOK) defined by the Human Resource Certification Institute:

- ✔ 01 Ensure that workplace health, safety, security, and privacy activities are compliant with applicable federal laws and regulations.

- ✔ 02 Conduct a needs analysis to identify the organization's safety requirements.

- ✔ 03 Develop/select and implement/administer occupational injury and illness prevention programs; for example, Occupational Safety and Health Act (OSHA) and workers' compensation (PHR only).

Exam objective 03 is one of the two exam objectives only for the PHR. Although IIPPs and worker's compensation are fairly specific, the third element, OSHA, is very broad. Because 03 will have approximately only 14 questions (8 percent of 175), dedicate a large chunk of your RM study time to the OSH Act, OSH administration, and compliance efforts.

✔ 04 Establish and administer a return-to-work process after illness or injury to ensure a safe workplace; for example, modified duty assignment, reasonable accommodations, and independent medical exam.

✔ 05 Develop/select, implement, and evaluate plans and policies to protect employees and other individuals, and to minimize the organization's loss and liability; for example, emergency response, workplace violence, and substance abuse.

✔ 06 Communicate and train the workforce on security plans and policies.

✔ 07 Develop, monitor, and test business continuity and disaster recovery plans.

✔ 08 Communicate and train the workforce on the business continuity and disaster recovery plans.

✔ 09 Develop policies and procedures to direct the appropriate use of electronic media and hardware; for example, email, social media, and appropriate website access.

✔ 10 Develop and administer internal and external privacy policies; for example, identity theft, data protection, and workplace monitoring.

An interesting note about these exam objectives is the *addition* of objective 09 when the exams were last updated in 2012. Peer-reviewed or field research showed that HR is regularly being asked to address employee behavior in the use of electronic media. Spend some extra study time researching issues related to this exam objective.

Recognizing What the Exams Cover for This Objective

Compliance with federal labor law occurs at three levels: have a plan, train employees, and investigate incidents. This three-step process is an excellent way to approach not only safety laws, but the RM exam objectives as well.

These sections cover the basics of what you need to know to prepare for RM questions on the PHR and the SPHR, including plan development, safety hazards training, and the need for incident investigations.

Managing enterprise risk

You can understand the risks to the business or project through the following filters. With such a small representation on both exams, organize your RM study topics by these big three areas of knowledge:

✔ **Financial risks:** The knowledge requirements are helpful in identifying some of the types of financial security risks you may help your company prevent. Financial risks include corporate espionage, sabotage, and theft. Minimizing these risks may be best accomplished through the use of technology to limit access to sensitive information. The knowledge requirements also ask you to be familiar with procurement policies, credit card and expense policies, and the limit loss from these work efforts.

✔ **Physical risks:** The employees' physical well-being used to be the largest focus of workplace safety efforts, so a lot of information is related to this HR activity. Target your studying on prevention efforts such as compliance with safety standards and commonsense work rules. Areas include hazard communication, workplace safety, emergency response, and violence prevention.

✔ **Information risks:** The loss of critical information can be devastating to both the employer and employee. The exam objectives and knowledge components address information risks through the use of data security techniques, such as passwords and monitoring software.

Although some exam objectives are pretty straightforward, others take a bit of dissection to fully understand what you must study. Look at Table 12-1 for a detailed look at how to expand objectives for maximum study effect. This table involves selecting an exam objective and related knowledge component, then drawing a table to visually break down the information. With Table 12-1, use the following exam objective and the related knowledge component:

✔ 10 Develop and administer internal and external privacy policies; for example, *identity theft*, *data protection*, and *workplace monitoring*.

✔ 73 Data integrity techniques and technology; for example, data sharing, password usage, and social engineering.

As you can see from this table, this exercise is not designed in a right-or-wrong mode. It's a data-dump technique that forces you to think critically about the objective. It helps you pair the objective with the knowledge requirements, identify what you already know, and recognize what information is missing for future research.

Table 12-1	Expanding the Exam Objectives		
	Identity Theft	*Data Protection*	*Workplace Monitoring*
Internal	Protecting employees' information such as Social Security numbers and driver's licenses	Protecting an employer from competitive data loss such as trade secrets or customer lists by limiting access to sensitive information through passwords	Limiting an employee's reasonable expectation of privacy by writing privacy and electronic use policies
External	Protecting customer credit card information by investing in technology	Limiting the success of scammers to trick employees into revealing sensitive information by training employees on social engineering scamming techniques such as phishing and baiting	Protecting customers on company premises by installing video cameras and security lights in company parking lots

The BEST way to protect confidential employee information is to

(A) Not collect it in the first place.

(B) Store it digitally, with no paper trail.

(C) Limit access to only those who need to refer to the data for business purposes.

(D) Create a buddy system in which information is accessed only with witnesses present.

The correct answer is (C). Whether confidential information is stored as paper files or digitally, HR must control access through passwords and keys. (A) is unrealistic, because labor laws require that employers collect and store information. (B) doesn't address protecting the information, just the storage, so it's an incomplete answer. (D) is unrealistic and unnecessary for the types of information collected and stored by HR.

Complying with safety standards in the workplace

The OSH Act and administration are your go-to resources for workplace safety compliance. As with all of the functional areas, they each begin with the need for HR professionals to ensure that activities are compliant with the law. The exam objectives take you on a nice little journey to tell you how to do so, as Figure 12-1 illustrates.

All you have to do is fill in the blanks on the requirements of how to do so. Look at some examples of OSHA standards on how you can accomplish these tasks:

- **Hazard assessment:** Although the exam objective calls them a *needs assessment,* OSHA gets a bit more specific. OSHA requires that you to conduct a hazard assessment to determine, for example, what personal protective equipment is required for each job, and OSHA asks you to conduct a job hazard analysis to identify hazards before they cause injury. OSHA publishes the top ten most cited standards on its website, and it's a good idea to be familiar with these hazards and relevant compliance requirements for the exams. They include fall protection, hazard communication, scaffolding, respiratory protection, powered industrial trucks, lockout/tagout, ladders, electrical, wiring methods, machine guarding, and general requirements for electrical. Find OSHA descriptions of each of these standards on their website at www.osha.gov/Top_Ten_Standards.html.

- **Injury and Illness Prevention Programs (IIPP):** OSHA identifies the common elements that should be present in all company IIPP. Although some states may have differing standards, they all must meet or exceed federal requirements. Therefore, you can confidently assume the baselines will include management leadership, worker participation, hazard identification, hazard prevention and control, education and training, and program evaluation and improvement.

   Obtain a copy of your employers IIPP and compare it to the common elements defined by OSHA. Doing so can give you an experience layer to apply to the exam requirement.

- **Disaster preparedness and emergency response:** Called emergency preparedness by OSHA, compliance efforts focus on both disaster response and recovery. In some standards, OSHA requires companies with more than ten employees to have these plans in writing. I provide a more detailed look at this HR activity in the next section.

- **Training of the workforce:** Most OSHA compliance efforts require some measure of communicating hazards to employees. Communicating hazards is most often accomplished through employee training. Keeping accurate documentation of training efforts include a description of the training content, the date(s) of training, who conducted the training, and signatures of the training participants.

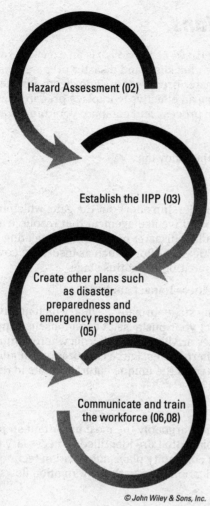

Figure 12-1:
The journey
from hazard
assessment
to training
the work-
force.

Hazard Assessment (02)

Establish the IIPP (03)

Create other plans such
as disaster
preparedness and
emergency response
(05)

Communicate and train
the workforce (06,08)

© John Wiley & Sons, Inc.

✔ **General duty clause:** OSHA states that employers are required to provide their employees with a place of employment that "is free from recognizable hazards that are causing or likely to cause death or serious harm to employees." This is more commonly referred to as the *general duty clause*. The courts have interpreted OSHA's general duty clause to mean that an employer has a legal obligation to provide a workplace free of conditions or activities that either the employer or industry recognizes as hazardous and that cause, or are likely to cause, death or serious physical harm to employees when there is a feasible method to abate the hazard.

How should an employer communicate the contents of an IIPP?

(A) Give it to employees at the time of hire.

(B) Make it available on a company intranet.

(C) Conduct annual training on the various hazards addressed in the IIPP.

(D) All of the above

The correct answer is (D). There are several acceptable methods for communicating the contents of the employer's injury and illness prevention program (IIPP), and they include a need to present it at the time of hire (A), giving employees access if they have questions such as in (B), and conducting compliance training for known hazards that are identified in the document (C).

Creating preparedness plans

The Federal Emergency Management Agency (www.fema.gov/) is an excellent resource for businesses. The agency's website has free checklists and disaster preparedness materials that you can use to brush up on your disaster preparedness knowledge for the exams. FEMA also has a five-step process to designing an effective workplace preparedness plan. This plan is an excellent way to approach the process and compare your organization's current plan.

According to the FEMA, these steps include the following:

1. **Manage the program.**

   The first step establishes a committed leadership effort out the gate, which means that HR may need to make the case to executive management that resource allocation will provide a return on investment should a disaster occur. Communicating customer and financial impacts and identifying mitigation efforts such as insurance coverage are both elements to gaining upper management buy-in at this stage.

2. **Conduct the needs assessment and business impact analysis.**

   Upon getting the green light, the planning stage formally begins, which involves identifying potential hazards that could affect your business. A commonsense approach may be helpful. For example, earthquakes are likely in California whereas hurricane preparedness in more likely in the Southern states. Large corporations in multiple locations must create custom programs suited to the unique natural threats in the communities of business.

3. **Implement the plan.**

   As with all great plans, proper execution is arguably the most important step. It actually begins by writing the multitude of plans that are identified as necessary in the assessment process. Consider business continuity plans, information technology plans to recover data, and the crisis communication plan so that information flows as freely as possible in the middle of a crisis.

   An *ad hoc committee* is one that meets to address a specific need. Identifying participants for an ad hoc crisis management meeting may be a helpful prevention effort. Use job titles rather than employee names for a practical approach to maintenance, but be sure the participants are properly trained on their roles.

4. **Test and conduct simulations and drills.**

   Employee training is a significant element to program effectiveness. Rather than holding classroom-based training, hands-on simulations and exercises are more likely to condition employees on how to respond in an emergency. Where possible, bring in outside experts to validate the company's point of view. These experts are also helpful in spotting program deficiencies before a crisis, enhancing the overall effect of a good response plan.

5. **Update, maintain, and improve the program.**

   As an R & D technician once put it to me, his goal was to "break it, then build it better." This philosophy serves the program improvement step of disaster preparedness well. Running the tests and simulations on a regular basis should identify where the program is deficient. Calendaring this activity on an annual basis allows HR to update the plan based on business changes such as expansions, turnover of key personnel, and training of new hires.

Apply the ADDIE model that I discuss in Chapter 9 to the five-step process recommended by FEMA. Using the ADDIE model gives you practice applying the individual steps when approaching an HR activity such as getting prepared for a disaster. The ADDIE approach includes:

1. **A**nalyze the needs.
2. **D**esign the program to address those needs.
3. **D**evelop the resources necessary.
4. **I**mplement the plans.
5. **E**valuate the program effectiveness.

Reducing the risk of workplace violence

Although the exam content appears to focus on having a plan to respond to workplace violence, OSHA also addresses the issue in the OSHA standards. Refer to www.osha.gov/SLTC/workplaceviolence for OSHA's specific definition of workplace violence. In addition, OSHA has conducted research to identify who most is at risk for workplace violence and concluded that positions that involve an exchange of money, working in isolated locations, and working with unstable individuals all have an increased risk for violence on the job.

As with most safety standards, the employer's response should be aimed at reducing the risk of harm to its employees. This effort begins by having a zero-tolerance policy for any intimidating or violent behavior in the workplace. OSHA also offers support in the development of a workplace violence prevention program, which aligns your work efforts with the exam objective. These programs include policy development, employee training, and administrative controls.

Another area of concern for employers includes the threat of terrorism. FEMA describes several different types of potential terrorism threats including biological, cyber, chemical and nuclear. www.ready.gov/business is an excellent resource for you to visit to find out more about employer responsibilities. This website is a public service campaign affiliated with FEMA. Ready.gov states that more than 40 percent of businesses affected by a natural or man-made disaster never reopen. From an HR perspective, you should anticipate questions on the exam that relate to preparing your company to respond as quickly and effectively as possible to avoid short-term or long-term business impact.

Disaster preparedness is most effective when built on a foundation of what?

(A) Leadership

(B) Regulatory compliance

(C) Business needs

(D) Understanding hazards

The correct answer is (A). A foundation of leadership commitment involves providing the resources necessary to prepare. (B), (C), and (D) are all important, but unlikely without the commitment of the executive management team.

Avoiding the pitfalls of social media

It feels as though everyone is on social media. Professional associations, personal pages, business reviews, and more are the many ways that people can stay connected in today's world. This poses a few interesting issues for employers to address:

- ✔ **Decreased productivity:** Statistics abound about how many workers peruse social media while on the clock. It's safe to say that regardless of the size of your employer, someone is surfing social media on company time. Limiting the use of mobile devices or company equipment to access social media while at work is appropriate for employers. Ways to do so include allowing it only while employees are on break and prohibiting mobile device use completely while driving a company vehicle or for company business. Consider best practices when crafting these prohibitions and make sure that they're a business necessity and compliant with laws against discrimination.

- ✔ **Protected concerted activity:** An interesting twist in the evolution of social media is the National Labor Relations Board's (NLRB) position that an employee has a right to express her dissatisfaction with working conditions through social media. Another word for the NLRB term *concerted* is *collective*. Any time a group of employees is together — whether face-to-face or online — they have the right to discuss wages, hours, and other protected topics granted by the National Labor Relations Act (NLRA) for purposes of considering union organizing.

- ✔ **Privacy:** Social media is an effective tool for many business applications, such as recruiting, marketing, and building the employer brand. The decision to use social media in these capacities should be thoroughly evaluated to ensure that your company's practices don't violate the privacy rights of affected individuals. You also want to take care to avoid having to defend the use of candidate data that is protected, such as gender and family status. Although not illegal per se to know this information, you'll need to be able to show that you didn't use it to make your hiring decision.

- ✔ **Trade secrets and confidential information:** A business has the right to protect trade secrets and other competitive data, but doing so in a highly digitally connected age may be difficult. Think of protecting confidential information on social media by reverting to its antithesis — the power of the pen. Have strong *nonsolicitation agreements* (a signed contract prohibiting employees from approaching existing clients) signed by affected employees to protect customer lists. Write and enforce policies regarding the ownership rights of company social media pages, with specific information about privacy settings. Use confidentiality agreements to define clearly what are considered to be trade secrets, and communicate to affected workers that the company will aggressively pursue legal remedies for failing to comply.

What type of data is generally included in a confidentiality agreement?

(A) Dates of employment

(B) Definition of property not to be disclosed

(C) An agreement to not solicit competitors upon employee separation

(D) The proper storage methods of confidential data

The correct answer is (B). A *confidentiality agreement* defines the types of property that must be kept private, including trade secret and customer lists. Dates of employment (A) won't be included, but the term dates of the contract would be identified. (C) is an element of a nonsolicitation/noncompete agreement, and (D) isn't a general item of a confidentiality agreement.

Exam objective 09 asks specifically for knowledge about policies and procedures to direct employee use of email, social media, and websites, so do some research to see how yours and other employers are handling these issues. Regardless of the specific social media conundrums, the exam objective appears to be directing you to a comprehensive email and social media policy that protects both the employer and employee rights — in other words, managing the risks.

Note that social media issues in employment continue to emerge. Wise employers (and their HR counsel) must stay up-to-date on court interpretation of existing law pertaining to social media use in the workplace. Check out this blog (www.socialmediaemploymentlawblog.com/) to stay up-to-date on all things social media.

Completing common reports and tools

As with all of the other functional areas of human resources, risk management has a fair share of paperwork. These reports and tools are very useful in demonstrating compliance with safety laws, such as the safety audit and safety training matrix. Other reports assist employers in making decisions about risk, such as workers compensation reports and data reports from their human resource information system. Read on for more information about these useful options.

Safety audits

Safety audits differ from hazard assessments in that they're used to evaluate compliance with safety programs rather than identify hazards. Even though hazard identification may certainly be a byproduct, their primary focus is to evaluate whether the controls established in the safety planning process are firmly rooted in place. Depending on the need, a safety audit can be conducted by visual walkthroughs, data collection, drills, or stressing the system to see what works and what doesn't. Check out www.oshatrain.org/pdf/audit1.pdf for an excellent example of a safety audit.

Workers' compensation reports

Keeping track of workers' compensation claims should be a monthly activity. Doing so requires that HR professionals are familiar with the workers' compensation laws in their states. The compensation reports help track the accrued versus paid amounts on open claims and allow you to manage the accruals where possible by working with the administrator. Compensation reports are useful to trigger status checks on injured workers still off work. This gives you the opportunity to engage in one of the exam objectives by building return-to-work programs such as modified duty. By doing so, the employee returning to work in a limited capacity is paid through regular payroll rather than through the workers' compensation insurance, lowering the overall claim costs. Because workers' compensation insurance is experience rated, doing so is an effective way to keep insurance costs down long term.

Safety training matrix

Depending on the industry from which you practice, safety training can be a mixed bag. For purposes of exam prep, objectives 06 and 08 ask you to communicate and train the workforce on security, business continuity, and disaster recovery plans, which assumes that these plans have been written using a needs assessment specific to your place of work.

A *training matrix* is a spreadsheet that compiles all of the required safety training in one place. Figure 12-2 gives you an example of one such matrix that can be modified on several levels to account for the who, what, where, when, and how often aspects of safety training. It can also help employers demonstrate a commitment to compliance.

2015 Smith Brothers, Inc.			Spring	Spring	Fall	Fall	2 Yr Expiration	Fall
Training Resource		Who	Who	Local Fire Department	Train the Trainer	Who	Consultant	Who
Employee#	Name	Accident Investigation/ Prevention Signs And Tags	IIPP plans- disaster, emergency	Fire Extinguisher	Forklift	(SDS) Hazcom Training & Fall Protection	Supervisor Harassment Training	Employee Harassment Training
1	Samantha Jones	–	–			–	–	–
2	Archie Martin	–	–					
3	Emma Russell					–		
4	Stan Smith	–	–			–	–	
5	Ethan Taylor	–				–	–	

Figure 12-2: A sample safety training matrix.

© John Wiley & Sons, Inc.

Another option is to utilize your human resource information system (HRIS) to track dates and send reminders to management that safety training is coming due. Managing it from the time of hire and though the tenure of the employees is a streamlined way to keep track and run reports.

Using the Internet for More Resources

With a solid study plan in place you can use the Internet to great effect in preparing for the RM section of these exams. Be creative. Remember that RM is not just about workplace safety and health risks, but it's also about data protection and financial security measures. Here are a couple of websites to get you started.

Federal Accounting Standards Advisory Board

Managing financial risks can be supported by employing the Generally Accepted Accounting Principles (GAAP) in the workplace. Found at www.fasab.gov, the advisory board has links to other websites and the complete standards of best practices. Use this website to help understand accepted ways to record financials and establish controls to reduce financial risks in reporting.

Trends in HR information systems

A 2014 Workforce report identified that employers are spending more on HR technology than ever before (www.workforce.com/articles/ 20692-special-report-hrms-vendors- say-hey-you-get-onto-my-cloud). This report describes the systems being useful for regular operations such as payroll and benefits. The exams more than likely will continue to address this trend by asking you to understand how to best apply technology on the job. Other trends to prepare for mention by the Workforce report include the need to move HR systems into the cloud. *Cloud computing* is an electronic storage solution that houses information on the Internet. RM activities impacted by this process include data security and data retrieval — issues that exist for paper storage but must also be accounted for in the digital era.

Department of Homeland Security

The Department of Homeland Security (DHS) is an excellent source of information, both personally and professionally. You can find information on how to prepare businesses for emergencies.

If you're taking the SPHR, pay special attention on how to conduct a *business impact analysis (BIA)*, which can help you quantify for management the financial impact of a disaster. Impacts to analyze include lost sales and income, regulatory fines, and contractual hiccups that may arise due to disasters. You can use a helpful questionnaire in worksheet format to conduct a BIA at your place of work in order to add the experience component that is so prevalent in these exams. Find this worksheet and more at www.dhs.gov; note that it will redirect you as necessary to FEMA to access some of these tools. You can also access them directly at www.fema.gov.

Part IV

Employing Your Knowledge: Practice Exams

Five ways to maximize the use of practice tests

- ✔ Test your knowledge with PHR and SPHR exam quality questions.
- ✔ Prepare yourself for exam day conditions through test taking.
- ✔ Discover how experience translates into exam questions.
- ✔ Assess your exam readiness both before and after your study efforts.
- ✔ Interpret correct answers and explanations for more learning.

Exam survivors universally recommend that you take multiple practice exams before the big event. But doing so can be tough to know which simulations to spend your dollars on. Find answers to this conundrum online by reading a free online article at www.dummies.com/extras/phrsphrexam on low-cost and free practice resources. You can also take practice exams at www.dummies.com/go/phrsphrexam.

In this part . . .

✔ Employ the practice-makes-perfect principle by immersing yourself in practice tests with exam-style questions weighted as you'll see them on test day.

✔ Interpret answers when you run up against *best* versus *right* options and discover how to set aside frustration and break down the question and answer options effectively.

✔ Get to know exam answer logic and figure out why an answer is correct to enhance retention for future use.

✔ Feel the mind numbness of answering 175 questions in one sitting, so you can prepare you mind and body for exam day conditions.

Chapter 13

Facing the Challenge: PHR Practice Exam I

. . . .

Any study material worth your dollars must include practice exams. Taking a test is, after all, the whole point of all of your efforts!

If you're a PHR candidate, remember that your exam is written from the perspective of operational activities. Get ready to see 175 exam-quality items about how the work of business and human resources gets done. Set aside three hours for the test included here, and limit all potential distractions such as your phone or the Internet. Chapter 2 gives you a lot more advice on how to best use the prep resource of practice exams.

Use the bubble sheet that I include here to fill in the correct answers. You can mark the questions that you want to review after you complete the test.

Don't forget, online you can find another PHR exam to supplement your efforts at www.dummies.com/go/phrsphrexam. The more exams you take, the better prepared you will be. Be mindful that the following exam is just one of the many you should prepare to take before the big day. Good luck!

1. Ⓐ Ⓑ Ⓒ Ⓓ
2. Ⓐ Ⓑ Ⓒ Ⓓ
3. Ⓐ Ⓑ Ⓒ Ⓓ
4. Ⓐ Ⓑ Ⓒ Ⓓ
5. Ⓐ Ⓑ Ⓒ Ⓓ
6. Ⓐ Ⓑ Ⓒ Ⓓ
7. Ⓐ Ⓑ Ⓒ Ⓓ
8. Ⓐ Ⓑ Ⓒ Ⓓ
9. Ⓐ Ⓑ Ⓒ Ⓓ
10. Ⓐ Ⓑ Ⓒ Ⓓ
11. Ⓐ Ⓑ Ⓒ Ⓓ
12. Ⓐ Ⓑ Ⓒ Ⓓ
13. Ⓐ Ⓑ Ⓒ Ⓓ
14. Ⓐ Ⓑ Ⓒ Ⓓ
15. Ⓐ Ⓑ Ⓒ Ⓓ
16. Ⓐ Ⓑ Ⓒ Ⓓ
17. Ⓐ Ⓑ Ⓒ Ⓓ
18. Ⓐ Ⓑ Ⓒ Ⓓ
19. Ⓐ Ⓑ Ⓒ Ⓓ
20. Ⓐ Ⓑ Ⓒ Ⓓ
21. Ⓐ Ⓑ Ⓒ Ⓓ
22. Ⓐ Ⓑ Ⓒ Ⓓ
23. Ⓐ Ⓑ Ⓒ Ⓓ
24. Ⓐ Ⓑ Ⓒ Ⓓ
25. Ⓐ Ⓑ Ⓒ Ⓓ
26. Ⓐ Ⓑ Ⓒ Ⓓ
27. Ⓐ Ⓑ Ⓒ Ⓓ
28. Ⓐ Ⓑ Ⓒ Ⓓ
29. Ⓐ Ⓑ Ⓒ Ⓓ
30. Ⓐ Ⓑ Ⓒ Ⓓ
31. Ⓐ Ⓑ Ⓒ Ⓓ
32. Ⓐ Ⓑ Ⓒ Ⓓ
33. Ⓐ Ⓑ Ⓒ Ⓓ
34. Ⓐ Ⓑ Ⓒ Ⓓ
35. Ⓐ Ⓑ Ⓒ Ⓓ

36. Ⓐ Ⓑ Ⓒ Ⓓ
37. Ⓐ Ⓑ Ⓒ Ⓓ
38. Ⓐ Ⓑ Ⓒ Ⓓ
39. Ⓐ Ⓑ Ⓒ Ⓓ
40. Ⓐ Ⓑ Ⓒ Ⓓ
41. Ⓐ Ⓑ Ⓒ Ⓓ
42. Ⓐ Ⓑ Ⓒ Ⓓ
43. Ⓐ Ⓑ Ⓒ Ⓓ
44. Ⓐ Ⓑ Ⓒ Ⓓ
45. Ⓐ Ⓑ Ⓒ Ⓓ
46. Ⓐ Ⓑ Ⓒ Ⓓ
47. Ⓐ Ⓑ Ⓒ Ⓓ
48. Ⓐ Ⓑ Ⓒ Ⓓ
49. Ⓐ Ⓑ Ⓒ Ⓓ
50. Ⓐ Ⓑ Ⓒ Ⓓ
51. Ⓐ Ⓑ Ⓒ Ⓓ
52. Ⓐ Ⓑ Ⓒ Ⓓ
53. Ⓐ Ⓑ Ⓒ Ⓓ
54. Ⓐ Ⓑ Ⓒ Ⓓ
55. Ⓐ Ⓑ Ⓒ Ⓓ
56. Ⓐ Ⓑ Ⓒ Ⓓ
57. Ⓐ Ⓑ Ⓒ Ⓓ
58. Ⓐ Ⓑ Ⓒ Ⓓ
59. Ⓐ Ⓑ Ⓒ Ⓓ
60. Ⓐ Ⓑ Ⓒ Ⓓ
61. Ⓐ Ⓑ Ⓒ Ⓓ
62. Ⓐ Ⓑ Ⓒ Ⓓ
63. Ⓐ Ⓑ Ⓒ Ⓓ
64. Ⓐ Ⓑ Ⓒ Ⓓ
65. Ⓐ Ⓑ Ⓒ Ⓓ
66. Ⓐ Ⓑ Ⓒ Ⓓ
67. Ⓐ Ⓑ Ⓒ Ⓓ
68. Ⓐ Ⓑ Ⓒ Ⓓ
69. Ⓐ Ⓑ Ⓒ Ⓓ
70. Ⓐ Ⓑ Ⓒ Ⓓ

71. Ⓐ Ⓑ Ⓒ Ⓓ
72. Ⓐ Ⓑ Ⓒ Ⓓ
73. Ⓐ Ⓑ Ⓒ Ⓓ
74. Ⓐ Ⓑ Ⓒ Ⓓ
75. Ⓐ Ⓑ Ⓒ Ⓓ
76. Ⓐ Ⓑ Ⓒ Ⓓ
77. Ⓐ Ⓑ Ⓒ Ⓓ
78. Ⓐ Ⓑ Ⓒ Ⓓ
79. Ⓐ Ⓑ Ⓒ Ⓓ
80. Ⓐ Ⓑ Ⓒ Ⓓ
81. Ⓐ Ⓑ Ⓒ Ⓓ
82. Ⓐ Ⓑ Ⓒ Ⓓ
83. Ⓐ Ⓑ Ⓒ Ⓓ
84. Ⓐ Ⓑ Ⓒ Ⓓ
85. Ⓐ Ⓑ Ⓒ Ⓓ
86. Ⓐ Ⓑ Ⓒ Ⓓ
87. Ⓐ Ⓑ Ⓒ Ⓓ
88. Ⓐ Ⓑ Ⓒ Ⓓ
89. Ⓐ Ⓑ Ⓒ Ⓓ
90. Ⓐ Ⓑ Ⓒ Ⓓ
91. Ⓐ Ⓑ Ⓒ Ⓓ
92. Ⓐ Ⓑ Ⓒ Ⓓ
93. Ⓐ Ⓑ Ⓒ Ⓓ
94. Ⓐ Ⓑ Ⓒ Ⓓ
95. Ⓐ Ⓑ Ⓒ Ⓓ
96. Ⓐ Ⓑ Ⓒ Ⓓ
97. Ⓐ Ⓑ Ⓒ Ⓓ
98. Ⓐ Ⓑ Ⓒ Ⓓ
99. Ⓐ Ⓑ Ⓒ Ⓓ
100. Ⓐ Ⓑ Ⓒ Ⓓ
101. Ⓐ Ⓑ Ⓒ Ⓓ
102. Ⓐ Ⓑ Ⓒ Ⓓ
103. Ⓐ Ⓑ Ⓒ Ⓓ
104. Ⓐ Ⓑ Ⓒ Ⓓ
105. Ⓐ Ⓑ Ⓒ Ⓓ

106. Ⓐ Ⓑ Ⓒ Ⓓ
107. Ⓐ Ⓑ Ⓒ Ⓓ
108. Ⓐ Ⓑ Ⓒ Ⓓ
109. Ⓐ Ⓑ Ⓒ Ⓓ
110. Ⓐ Ⓑ Ⓒ Ⓓ
111. Ⓐ Ⓑ Ⓒ Ⓓ
112. Ⓐ Ⓑ Ⓒ Ⓓ
113. Ⓐ Ⓑ Ⓒ Ⓓ
114. Ⓐ Ⓑ Ⓒ Ⓓ
115. Ⓐ Ⓑ Ⓒ Ⓓ
116. Ⓐ Ⓑ Ⓒ Ⓓ
117. Ⓐ Ⓑ Ⓒ Ⓓ
118. Ⓐ Ⓑ Ⓒ Ⓓ
119. Ⓐ Ⓑ Ⓒ Ⓓ
120. Ⓐ Ⓑ Ⓒ Ⓓ
121. Ⓐ Ⓑ Ⓒ Ⓓ
122. Ⓐ Ⓑ Ⓒ Ⓓ
123. Ⓐ Ⓑ Ⓒ Ⓓ
124. Ⓐ Ⓑ Ⓒ Ⓓ
125. Ⓐ Ⓑ Ⓒ Ⓓ
126. Ⓐ Ⓑ Ⓒ Ⓓ
127. Ⓐ Ⓑ Ⓒ Ⓓ
128. Ⓐ Ⓑ Ⓒ Ⓓ
129. Ⓐ Ⓑ Ⓒ Ⓓ
130. Ⓐ Ⓑ Ⓒ Ⓓ
131. Ⓐ Ⓑ Ⓒ Ⓓ
132. Ⓐ Ⓑ Ⓒ Ⓓ
133. Ⓐ Ⓑ Ⓒ Ⓓ
134. Ⓐ Ⓑ Ⓒ Ⓓ
135. Ⓐ Ⓑ Ⓒ Ⓓ
136. Ⓐ Ⓑ Ⓒ Ⓓ
137. Ⓐ Ⓑ Ⓒ Ⓓ
138. Ⓐ Ⓑ Ⓒ Ⓓ
139. Ⓐ Ⓑ Ⓒ Ⓓ
140. Ⓐ Ⓑ Ⓒ Ⓓ

141. Ⓐ Ⓑ Ⓒ Ⓓ
142. Ⓐ Ⓑ Ⓒ Ⓓ
143. Ⓐ Ⓑ Ⓒ Ⓓ
144. Ⓐ Ⓑ Ⓒ Ⓓ
145. Ⓐ Ⓑ Ⓒ Ⓓ
146. Ⓐ Ⓑ Ⓒ Ⓓ
147. Ⓐ Ⓑ Ⓒ Ⓓ
148. Ⓐ Ⓑ Ⓒ Ⓓ
149. Ⓐ Ⓑ Ⓒ Ⓓ
150. Ⓐ Ⓑ Ⓒ Ⓓ
151. Ⓐ Ⓑ Ⓒ Ⓓ
152. Ⓐ Ⓑ Ⓒ Ⓓ
153. Ⓐ Ⓑ Ⓒ Ⓓ
154. Ⓐ Ⓑ Ⓒ Ⓓ
155. Ⓐ Ⓑ Ⓒ Ⓓ
156. Ⓐ Ⓑ Ⓒ Ⓓ
157. Ⓐ Ⓑ Ⓒ Ⓓ
158. Ⓐ Ⓑ Ⓒ Ⓓ
159. Ⓐ Ⓑ Ⓒ Ⓓ
160. Ⓐ Ⓑ Ⓒ Ⓓ
161. Ⓐ Ⓑ Ⓒ Ⓓ
162. Ⓐ Ⓑ Ⓒ Ⓓ
163. Ⓐ Ⓑ Ⓒ Ⓓ
164. Ⓐ Ⓑ Ⓒ Ⓓ
165. Ⓐ Ⓑ Ⓒ Ⓓ
166. Ⓐ Ⓑ Ⓒ Ⓓ
167. Ⓐ Ⓑ Ⓒ Ⓓ
168. Ⓐ Ⓑ Ⓒ Ⓓ
169. Ⓐ Ⓑ Ⓒ Ⓓ
170. Ⓐ Ⓑ Ⓒ Ⓓ
171. Ⓐ Ⓑ Ⓒ Ⓓ
172. Ⓐ Ⓑ Ⓒ Ⓓ
173. Ⓐ Ⓑ Ⓒ Ⓓ
174. Ⓐ Ⓑ Ⓒ Ⓓ
175. Ⓐ Ⓑ Ⓒ Ⓓ

1. Which of the following documents is used in a post-hire activity?

    (A) Completing Form I-9

    (B) Completing Form W-4

    (C) Coordinating relocation

    (D) All of the above

2. Which of the following would be an unfair labor practice?

    (A) Moving the work to a different plant with no union

    (B) Asking employees if they will vote for or against the union

    (C) Lecturing to employees how historical corruption caused problems with unions

    (D) Threatening to fire supervisors if they show support for the union

3. Which of the following is NOT an affirmative defense for a company being sued for quid pro quo sexual harassment?

    (A) Demonstrating that the employer exercised reasonable care to prevent unlawful behavior

    (B) Demonstrating that the employer promptly corrected unlawful behavior

    (C) Demonstrating that the employee failed to take advantage of any preventive or corrective opportunities provided by the employer

    (D) Demonstrating that the accused employee wasn't a supervisor

4. Jim accepts a contingent offer of employment from a new company and consequently gives notice. The employer eventually rescinds the offer after his drug screen came back positive for marijuana. Which of the common law doctrines did this employer violate?

    (A) Promissory estoppel

    (B) Duty of good faith and fair dealing

    (C) Fraudulent misrepresentation

    (D) None

5. A marketing function that reflects the concept of putting the right product, in the right place for the right promotion at the right _____.

    (A) Price

    (B) Power

    (C) Practice

    (D) Percentage

6. Mary Jones is a full-time employee who has worked for a nationwide car manufacturer for more than 15 years. She needs time off of work to care for her child, who has recently been diagnosed with asthma. Which of the following steps should you take FIRST?

    (A) Notify her supervisor that she will be off of work.

    (B) Verify her eligibility for FMLA.

    (C) Call a staffing agency to find a replacement for her to train before she's off.

    (D) Request medical certification from her child's doctor.

7. Lori is a recruiter for a large marketing firm based out of New York City with multiple branches across the United States. Working out of the corporate offices is considered a career advantage, and she is determined to find a quality candidate. Which of the following recruiting activities should she do first?

   (A) Create an internal job posting.

   (B) Call a staffing agency with locations in multiple US locations.

   (C) Research online recruiting resources.

   (D) Get the job posted on the company's website.

8. Which of the following decisions by an HR professional is the most ethical?

   (A) Allowing an employee to work a second job based on need, even though policy prohibits moonlighting

   (B) Staying with an occupational clinic because it sends her tickets to sporting events

   (C) Attending professional development meetings with subordinates

   (D) Giving preferred treatment to employees who are nice to her

9. The process of becoming part of an organizational team is called what?

   (A) Assimilation

   (B) Cultural integration

   (C) Onboarding

   (D) Affiliation

10. Jannah is a supervisor at ABC Speech Pathology with 14 direct reports. These employees are known as her what?

    (A) Management responsibility

    (B) Span of control

    (C) Management scope

    (D) Organizational structure

11. Data recall, confidential customer information, and the protection of digital assets must be reviewed according to which element of a PEST analysis?

    (A) Political

    (B) Economic

    (C) Social

    (D) Technological

12. Videoing an employee telling about his employment experience and then posting the video on the company recruitment website is an example of which of the following?

    (A) Recruiting

    (B) Documentation

    (C) Establishing the employer brand

    (D) Communicating the company culture

13. An employment arrangement in which an employee may quit at any time and the employer may terminate at any time is defined by which common law doctrine?

    (A) Employment at will

    (B) Respondeat superior

    (C) Implied contract

    (D) Employment relationship

14. Which of these tools would best capture the reasons that employees leave an organization?

    (A) Employee satisfaction surveys

    (B) Exit interviews

    (C) Turnover reports

    (D) Labor market analysis

15. A group composed of members of the same race or the same heritage would be attributed as being what?

    (A) Homogeneous

    (B) Heterogeneous

    (C) Patriot

    (D) Fellows

16. An employee refused to go out on a date with her supervisor and was fired by him as a result. This is known as what type of harassment?

    (A) Unlawful

    (B) Discriminatory

    (C) Quid pro quo

    (D) Hostile

17. Which of the following visas may be extended to religious workers?

    (A) R-1

    (B) O-1

    (C) L-1A

    (D) P-1

18. A mass layoff of more than 500 employees would trigger which of the following acts protecting workers?

    (A) The Consolidated Omnibus Budget Reconciliation Act

    (B) The Health Insurance Portability and Accountability Act

    (C) The Workforce Adjustment and Retraining Notification Act

    (D) All of the above

19. Which of the following has had the most growth in online media recruiting?

    (A) Video branding

    (B) Mobile apps

    (C) Virtual interviewing

    (D) Personal networks

20. Which of the following most accurately describes at-will employment?

   (A) The employer may terminate an employee at any time, for any reason.

   (B) The employee may quit without giving notice.

   (C) The employee serves at the will of the employer.

   (D) Both the employer and the employee can separate at any time without cause.

21. Conducting a pre-employment drug screen is most useful to prevent what?

   (A) Negligent hiring

   (B) Workplace violence

   (C) Injuries

   (D) All of the above

22. Why should a private-sector employer hire interns?

   (A) It's a great way to get free work done.

   (B) It's useful to prequalify potential candidates.

   (C) It invests in the communities in which the employer does business.

   (D) It's the right thing to do.

23. Which landmark case found that a seemingly neutral pre-employment test could result in unlawful discrimination if it has an adverse impact against a protected class group?

   (A) Griggs vs. Duke Power

   (B) The UGESPs

   (C) McDonnell Douglas vs. Green

   (D) Albermarle Paper vs. Moody

24. If an employee is found to be the victim of unlawful discrimination, he or she may be entitled to back pay under which landmark court decision?

   (A) Griggs vs. Duke Power

   (B) The UGESPs

   (C) McDonnell Douglas vs. Green

   (D) Albermarle Paper vs. Moody

25. Conducting employee exit interviews by a third party is most useful for which of the following?

   (A) Controlling the high emotions associated with separations

   (B) Obtaining honest feedback

   (C) Protecting the employer from a wrongful termination claim

   (D) Utilizing external resources to keep HR focused on operations

26. The Age Discrimination in Employment Act protects individuals over the age of what?

   (A) 40

   (B) 50

   (C) 63

   (D) All of the above

27. Which of the following activities are often outsourced to an external agency?

    (A) Payroll

    (B) Hiring

    (C) COBRA administration

    (D) All of the above

28. Consistent branding and the use of videos are combined for successful what?

    (A) Social media recruiting

    (B) Employee retention

    (C) Job satisfaction

    (D) Communicating benefits

29. Which of the following is an alternative staffing method?

    (A) Direct hires

    (B) Online recruiting

    (C) Job sharing

    (D) Temporary workers

30. How are ideas shared in a Socratic seminar?

    (A) Through adherence to an agenda

    (B) By the use of questions and answers

    (C) Through classroom lecture

    (D) As a fishbowl

31. If the passive method of teaching focuses on the instructor, the _____ method focuses on the learner.

    (A) Active

    (B) Engaged

    (C) Participative

    (D) Managed

32. Which of the following is an example of on-the-job training?

    (A) Vestibule

    (B) Lecture

    (C) Simulation

    (D) Job rotation

33. Banquet-style seating is most effective for which of the following training formats?

    (A) Films

    (B) Lectures

    (C) Manuals

    (D) Group discussions

34. An employee self-assessment is useful when _____.

    (A) There are problems with teamwork.

    (B) The employee is new.

    (C) The job criteria aren't well established.

    (D) An employer wants to compare employees to each other.

35. The presence of more than 50 percent of women in the workforce population is an indication of what?

    (A) The need for flexible work arrangements

    (B) The need for employment practice liability insurance (EPLI)

    (C) The likelihood of a sexual harassment lawsuit

    (D) The need for a dating policy

36. Conducting a needs assessment occurs at which stage of the ADDIE model?

    (A) Analyze

    (B) Design

    (C) Develop

    (D) Implement

37. The marketing department has been asked to create visual representations of SOPs to be used during the on-boarding process of new hires. This is an example of which stage of the ADDIE model of instructional design?

    (A) Analyze

    (B) Design

    (C) Develop

    (D) Implement

38. Visual learners are best served through which style of training?

    (A) Lecture

    (B) Hands-on work

    (C) On the job

    (D) Handouts

39. A customer service representative isn't keeping up with the required call volume. For which of the following causes would training NOT be a solution?

    (A) He is unfamiliar with the products.

    (B) His headset is faulty.

    (C) He has only been on the job for 30 days.

    (D) The company installed a new ERP system.

40. When a job is designed to allow employees to apply multiple skill sets on the job, this job is likely high on what?

    (A) Task identity

    (B) Functional loading

    (C) Skill variety

    (D) Task significance

41. Statements that describe the measurable outcomes of training are known as what?

    (A) Goals

    (B) Interventions

    (C) Targets

    (D) Objectives

42. Maintaining the confidentiality of customer information is a function of what holistic risk management system?

    (A) Enterprise risk management

    (B) A response to a technological fail

    (C) The establishment of a firewall

    (D) The protection of human assets

43. It was discovered that an employee was able to siphon off cash from sales because she was responsible for both collecting the money and creating deposits. This failure is due to a lack of what?

    (A) Training

    (B) Documentation

    (C) Standard operating procedures

    (D) Internal controls

44. An emergency response plan is a required element of what safety compliance effort?

    (A) A fire prevention plan

    (B) The protection of information assets

    (C) The establishment of IIPPs

    (D) The identification of financial risks

45. Which of the following is the most important step in the implementation of an Injury and Illness Prevention Program?

    (A) Hazard abatement procedures

    (B) Management leadership and commitment

    (C) Worker participation

    (D) Program evaluation

46. Which of the following statements is true regarding state-run OSH programs?

    (A) State programs aren't allowed under OSH.

    (B) State programs are able to operate independently of the federal standards.

    (C) State programs must exceed federal program standards.

    (D) State programs must meet federal program standards.

47. An employee called OSHA to report a safety hazard that the employer had failed to address, resulting in a worksite inspection and fines. The employer found out and quietly demoted the worker. This is an example of which unlawful employment action?

    (A) Discrimination

    (B) Harassment

    (C) Wrongful discipline

    (D) Retaliation

48. Which statement regarding the FMLA is false?

    (A) FMLA leave focuses on wage replacement and job protection.

    (B) FMLA provides 12 work weeks of leave for eligible workers.

    (C) The certification requirements for leave are the same for all requests, including military.

    (D) An eligible employee is one who has worked 1,250 hours in the preceding 12-month period.

49. Employers are required to provide reasonable break time to nursing mothers for up to how many years after the child's birth?

    (A) None

    (B) One

    (C) Two

    (D) Three

50. Which of the following acts amended the FLSA to further define compensable time?

    (A) Davis-Bacon

    (B) McNamara-O'Hara

    (C) Portal-to-Portal

    (D) Equal Pay

51. _____ is/are the amount of money an employee will make on an hourly or salaried basis.

    (A) Minimum wage

    (B) Total compensation

    (C) Base pay

    (D) Incentives

52. Merit pay increases are what type of compensation?

    (A) Base

    (B) Total

    (C) Performance

    (D) Entitlement

53. Shift premiums are a type of what?

    (A) Pay differential

    (B) Hazard pay

    (C) Benefit

    (D) Entitlement

54. The CCPA _____ the amount of wages that can be garnished against an employee.

    (A) Prohibits

    (B) Doesn't address

    (C) Limits

    (D) Defines

55. If an employer is issuing evidence of past health insurance, to an exiting employee, it is most likely complying with which law?

    (A) COBRA

    (B) Title VII

    (C) HIPAA

    (D) PPACA

56. If an employee is motivated by a high-level desire to achieve, which pay strategy is most likely to work?

    (A) Annual increases

    (B) Robust benefits

    (C) Variable pay

    (D) Group incentives

57. What pay practice is most nearly the opposite of base pay?

    (A) Piecework

    (B) Holiday pay

    (C) Benefits

    (D) Perquisites

58. In which of the following examples is there an experience rating to determine cost?

    (A) Unemployment claims

    (B) Workers' compensation

    (C) Company car insurance

    (D) All of the above

59. A pension plan that guarantees a set amount of benefits at the time of retirement is what kind of plan?

    (A) Cash balance

    (B) Contributory plan

    (C) Defined benefit

    (D) Defined contribution

60. Generally a retirement plan may require that an employee be at least _____ years of age and have at least _____ year(s) of service before participating in a plan.

    (A) 18, one

    (B) 21, one

    (C) 18, two

    (D) 21, two

61. In selecting a payroll vendor, which of the following activities should you complete first?

    (A) Gain executive approval.

    (B) Gather an RFP.

    (C) Conduct a needs assessment.

    (D) Request a trial.

62. If an employer's social media policy violates the right of an employee to engage in coordinated discussion about wages or working conditions, what kind of a charge may be filed?

    (A) Discrimination

    (B) ULP

    (C) Harassment

    (D) Whistleblower

63. What do union organizers do?

    (A) They assist union members in negotiating the CBA.

    (B) They serve as employer ambassadors to the union.

    (C) They're employees sponsored by a union who helps workers organize.

    (D) They serve as employee ambassadors to the union.

64. If an applicant intentionally applies for a job at a non-union shop specifically to begin an organizing drive, he is said to be engaged in what practice?

    (A) Salting

    (B) Featherbedding

    (C) Double breasting

    (D) Alter ego

65. The decline in union membership has been attributed to what?

    (A) Rights granted by varying national and state standards

    (B) Improved working conditions

    (C) Modernization of tools and equipment

    (D) All of the above

66. Brown bag lunches, word of mouth, and company intranet are all forms of what?

    (A) Training

    (B) Communicating with employees

    (C) Providing informal feedback

    (D) Reporting company information

67. An employee may quit at any time, and for any reason, similar to which of the following?

    (A) Doctrine of free will

    (B) Doctrine of Lord Acton

    (C) Statutory exceptions

    (D) At-will employment

68. In which type of sexual harassment may the employer not establish an affirmative defense?

    (A) Quid pro quo with a tangible injury

    (B) Hostile environment

    (C) Vicarious liability

    (D) Workplace violence

69. A tangible employment action may be demonstrated by which of the following?

    (A) Documented in employment records

    (B) Subject to review by higher ups

    (C) An official act of the company

    (D) All of the above

70. Which court case decided that same sex harassment is actionable under (anti-harassment) laws?

    (A) Medina Rene vs. MGM Grand Hotel

    (B) Burlington Industries vs. Ellerth

    (C) Oncale vs. Sundowner Offshore Services

    (D) Faragher vs. City of Boca Raton

71. Which agency is responsible for enforcing the standards related to unfair labor practices?

    (A) EEOC

    (B) NLRA

    (C) NLRB

    (D) DOL

72. Which act first defined a list of unfair labor practices by employers?

    (A) Labor-Management Relations Act (Taft-Hartley)

    (B) National Labor Relations Act (Wagner)

    (C) Labor-Management Reporting and Disclosure Act (Landrum-Griffith)

    (D) Railway Labor Act

73. If a union fails to properly hold a local leadership election every three years, which act is the union violating?

    (A) Labor-Management Relations Act (Taft-Hartley)

    (B) National Labor Relations Act (Wagner Act)

    (C) Labor-Management Reporting and Disclosure Act (Landrum Griffin Act)

    (D) Railway Labor Act

74. When President Ronald Reagan ordered striking air traffic controllers back to work, he was acting with authority granted by which of the following acts?

    (A) Labor-Management Relations Act (Taft-Hartley Act)

    (B) National Labor Relations Act (Wagner Act)

    (C) Labor-Management Reporting and Disclosure Act (Landrum-Griffith)

    (D) Railway Labor Act

75. Striking workers that seek higher wages or shorter working hours is engaged in what type of lawful strike?

    (A) Protest

    (B) Picketing

    (C) Unfair labor practices

    (D) Economic

76. Which of the following statements is true regarding unfair labor practice strikers?

    (A) They may be permanently replaced while on strike.

    (B) They are entitled to their jobs back after the strike has ended.

    (C) The striking workers are engaged in a ULP.

    (D) They cannot have their jobs back if it discharges another worker.

77. HazMat United has a policy that requires employees to clock out at the end of their shift prior to changing out of their hazardous material suits back into civilian clothing. Which of the following labor laws is the company violating?

    (A) Occupational Safety and Health Act

    (B) Service Contract Act

    (C) The Portal-to-Portal Act

    (D) None. This employer practice is legal.

78. Which element of a Human Capital Management Plan involves developing the necessary workforce and practices to achieve an organization's mission, vision, and values?

    (A) Strategic direction

    (B) Goal setting

    (C) Project implementation

    (D) Sustainability

79. Electromation, Inc. was a small, non-union company with 200 employees experiencing financial difficulties. It decided to form committees in response to a change to employee bonuses and other employee concerns regarding polices, favoritism, and communication. Although these committees consisted of both employees and management, management had the final say on who was seated. Which of the following is one of the reasons the National Labor Relations Board rules that this was an unlawful, company-dominated union?

    (A) Managers were on the committee.

    (B) The committees included discussions about conditions of employment.

    (C) Compensation committees without union representation are unlawful.

    (D) It wasn't recognized as a formal union.

80. Employees at Natural Bee Organics have to work on Saturdays because they are behind in production. The supervisor promises that if they catch up, they can go back to their regular schedules. This is an example of what type of operant conditioning?

    (A) Punishment

    (B) Extinction

    (C) Positive reinforcement

    (D) Negative reinforcement

81. Place the following in the order of importance as it relates to managing risk for an employer:

    A. Safety hazards

    B. Disaster preparedness planning

    C. Customer confidentiality procedures

    D. Workplace violence policy

    (A) C, A, D, B

    (B) D, A, C, B

    (C) B, C, D, A

    (D) A, C, B, D

82. In which of the following examples does a positive correlation exist?

    (A) The longer employees are with a company, the less attendance problems they have.

    (B) Workplace harassment increases the likelihood of employee depression.

    (C) In the absence of random drug screening, employee drug use increases.

    (D) Positive coaching efforts result in decreased turnover.

83. Which of the following types of graphs best identify the status of employees when succession planning?

    (A) Pareto chart

    (B) Forced distribution

    (C) Ranking

    (D) Fishbone diagram

84. Decentralized decision-making is more likely to occur in which of the following organizational structures?

    (A) Functional

    (B) Organizational

    (C) Product-based

    (D) Hierarchical

85. A retail distributor was suffering from a process that took the company too long to hire, particularly during the seasonal peaks associated with holidays. Which of the following should you recommend?

    (A) Continuous recruitment of salespeople

    (B) A human capital management plan

    (C) Promotions from within

    (D) The use of staffing agencies

86. Walling Dairy has agreed to co-brand its milk products with a famous cookie brand. This is an example of which of the following?

    (A) Alliance

    (B) Joint venture

    (C) Merger

    (D) Divestiture

87. Job expansion and divestitures are examples of what type of organizational activity?

    (A) Restructuring

    (B) Downsizing

    (C) Mergers

    (D) Acquisition

88. What should occur prior to writing an organization's mission, vision, and values (MVV) statements?

    (A) Establish the company's budget.

    (B) Gain management buy-in to the process.

    (C) Conduct an environmental scan.

    (D) Evaluate the corporate strategy.

89. Engagement is to the employee life cycle what the employee's _____ is to the company.

    (A) Job

    (B) Responsibility

    (C) Impact

    (D) Performance

90. James, an employee at your company, was recently told that he must continue to work the Saturday/Sunday shift even though his co-worker Sally will be working a preferred shift as an accommodation of her disability. James sues for reverse discrimination. What is the most likely outcome of his claim?

    (A) James wins his suit because he is the victim of reverse discrimination under the ADA.

    (B) James loses his lawsuit because he isn't a qualified individual with a disability.

    (C) James's lawsuit is thrown out because charges of reverse discrimination are prohibited.

    (D) The employer changes James's shift to settle the dispute without having to go to court

91. If an employment test is found to not predict what the employer thought it was going to predict, it may low on what type of validity?

    (A) Content validity

    (B) Criterion-related validity

    (C) Face validity

    (D) Discriminant validity

92. Which of the following is one of the five disciplines of Peter Senge's learning organization?

    (A) Systems thinking

    (B) Drive for results

    (C) Strategic planning

    (D) Employee training

93. Using dimensions to identify the requirements of the job that are supported by anchor statements of behavior will best be transferred to which type of performance evaluation?

    (A) BARS

    (B) Narrative

    (C) Comparison

    (D) Ranking

94. The school of medicine for which you work has partnered with a national university to create a leadership development program. Which of these outcomes might this program serve?

    (A) Initiating a companywide patient care program

    (B) Building a motivated and engaged workforce

    (C) Identifying the technical skills required for physicians

    (D) All of the above

95. Erica's Corner Café employs servers that are considered tipped employees under the FLSA. She pays them a base salary of $2.13 an hour and allows them to keep all of their tips. Some employees make below the federal minimum wage. Which of the following statements is true?

    (A) Erica may be violating their rights under the FLSA if their base pay plus tips doesn't meet the minimum wage standard.

    (B) Erica may be violating the FLSA because the base pay is too low, regardless of tip earnings.

    (C) Erica should be paying a base pay of the federal minimum wage of $7.25 per hour, plus overtime.

    (D) There is nothing wrong with the café claiming a tip credit against its minimum wage obligation.

96. How are incentives a type of variable pay?

    (A) They are part of a total compensation package.

    (B) They are based on individual or organizational performance.

    (C) Incentives aren't calculated as part of base pay.

    (D) They are not guaranteed.

97. Which of the following is the best reason an employer may choose to pay below-market rates for a certain position?

    (A) The competitors are paying below-market rates.

    (B) The job is only worth a below-market rate.

    (C) The rates are in-line with the company budget.

    (D) There is an abundance of talent for the position.

98. The company you work for would like you to recommend a gainsharing plan that rewards the manufacturing workers when they exceed productivity requirements. Which program should you recommend?

    (A) Improshare

    (B) Profit sharing

    (C) An ESOP

    (D) An ESPP

99. An employee has been called back to military status, but has an unresolved employment dispute with his employer. His attorney may request the arbitrator to _____ the statute until he returns from duty.

    (A) Toll

    (B) Dismiss

    (C) Dispute

    (D) Interrupt

100. The executive management team at Harbor Marina needs to know how long it will take for the value of a training activity to be equal to the cost. Which of the following approaches should the HR professional use?

    (A) Cost-benefit analysis

    (B) Return on investment

    (C) Break-even analysis

    (D) Training investment factors

101. Which of the following is an example of a key performance indicator (KPI) in a sales department?

    (A) Employee attendance

    (B) Sales growth

    (C) Sales commissions

    (D) Number of injuries

102. Hazel Billings has been working for the company for the last 12 months. She is still struggling to acclimate to the organization. She feels alienated from her work group, often eating lunch alone. As such, she begins calling out sick to work. In which of Maslow's hierarchical stages of needs is Hazel?

    (A) Physiological

    (B) Safety

    (C) Social

    (D) Esteem

103. Why should an employer have a return-to-work program?

    (A) To reduce the overall cost of workplace injuries

    (B) To comply with OSHA

    (C) To avoid the lost productivity of injured workers

    (D) To do the right thing

104. An employee puts money in a vending machine, expecting to receive a soda. When the soda is not forthcoming, he pushes the button again with much greater force. This is an example of which of the following theories of motivation?

    (A) Hierarchy of needs

    (B) Achievement, affiliation, and power

    (C) Theory X and Theory Y

    (D) Operant conditioning

105. Bruchacek Manufacturing is a Californian fabricator of custom steel products. The company has one German vendor for specialty fans that recently was unable to deliver a shipment due to extreme hailstorms off the coast. This is an example of which of the following SWOT elements?

    (A) Strengths

    (B) Weaknesses

    (C) Opportunities

    (D) Threats

106. The Society of Executive Management publicly criticized a member of the SEC for suggesting that publicly traded companies with profits more than $2 million should be mandated to report their executive compensation packages. The Society's goal is to stop a bill that would make this information part of the public record. This is an example of which of the following activities?

    (A) Appropriating

    (B) Lobbying

    (C) Conferencing

    (D) Petitioning

107. A Catholic church placed a job ad for a new secretary with a requirement that the new hire must be Catholic. A Protestant woman applied and was denied. She filed a charge of unlawful discrimination based on her religion. Which of the following statements is true?

    (A) The woman was correct. It's unlawful to make a hiring decision based on a protected class characteristic.

    (B) The church was correct. In this case, the applicant's religion was a bona fide occupational qualification.

    (C) The church was correct, because it is exempt from Title VII.

    (D) There isn't enough information, because it is unclear whether she was otherwise qualified for the job.

108. Keeping an employee's personnel file up-to-date is most likely in response to which of the following?

    (A) Attorneys recommend doing so.

    (B) It allows you to demonstrate compliance with labor law.

    (C) If it isn't documented, it never happened.

    (D) It gives supervisors the ability to terminate an employee for cause.

109. Why would you use a staffing agency to fulfill key positions within your organization?

    (A) It allows you to prequalify workers on the job.

    (B) It establishes the agency as the employer of record.

    (C) It's a necessary strategy in order for you to focus on other company core competencies.

    (D) It's less expensive than direct recruiting.

110. GrandMart LLC is being sued for multiple charges of unlawful discrimination and begins to analyze the political climate in the states where it operates to see where there may be favorable court conditions toward business. This practice is known as what?

    (A) Predictive analysis

    (B) Court selection

    (C) Scanning the environment

    (D) Forum shopping

111. Which of the following was not originally identified for protection under Title VII of the Civil Rights Act of 1964?

    (A) Age

    (B) Sexual orientation

    (C) Gender

    (D) All of the above

112. For which group may a written AAP be required?

    (A) Companies with a court-ordered mandate

    (B) Construction companies under contract with the federal government

    (C) Supply and service contractors to the federal government

    (D) All of the above

113. Freddy's Family Farmacy is a locally grown, holistic distributor of prescription and over-the-counter medications. The owners recently asked you to line up a polygraph exam for prospective employees as part of the hiring process. What act would you violate if you comply?

    (A) The Privacy Act of 1974

    (B) The Employee Polygraph Protection Act of 1988

    (C) The Fair Credit Reporting Act

    (D) None. Lie detector tests aren't illegal if used under these circumstances.

114. The company you work for has recently decided that it must lay off an entire management tier as part of a recent merger. The executive team asks you for recommendations on how to reward the departing employees for years of service. Which strategy would be best?

    (A) Offer outplacement services.

    (B) Design severance agreements.

    (C) Educate them on any available unemployment benefits.

    (D) Offer to cover their COBRA insurance for an extended period of time.

115. To what does the natural disaster exception apply?

    (A) Exclusion from WARN requirements

    (B) Exclusion from Title VII compliance

    (C) Coverage for work-related injuries if the result of the natural disaster

    (D) None of the above

116. Which of the following activities is the most acceptable in the storage of Form I-9?

    (A) Electronic copy stored on a shared drive

    (B) Scanned documents, then the shredding of the original

    (C) At an offsite storage location with limited access

    (D) Paper storage with the employee's personnel file

117. Jasmine Jones, a manager at your organization, was recently diagnosed with severe asthma. She may qualify for what?

    (A) Job protection under the ADA

    (B) Wage replacement under FMLA

    (C) Health certification under HIPAA

    (D) Paid family leave

118. What technique or tool should you use to expose a potential employee to a typical day on the job for which he or she is applying?

    (A) Job description

    (B) Job analysis

    (C) Job shadowing

    (D) Peer interview

119. Why should a company use a professional employer organization (PEO)?

    (A) To reduce the risks associated with being the employer of record

    (B) To eliminate the costs associated with employee benefits

    (C) To avoid having to pay for workers' compensation

    (D) To streamline management processes

120. If an employee believes she has been discriminated against based on her race, which of the following statements is true?

    (A) The employee must file a charge with the EEOC before she can file a lawsuit against her employer.

    (B) The employee should hire an attorney to help her navigate the court system.

    (C) The employee has one year to file a claim.

    (D) The employee should first attempt to resolve the dispute with her employer.

121. Which strategy may be used if an organization finds that it needs to downsize?

    (A) Work furloughs

    (B) Layoffs

    (C) Reductions in force

    (D) All of the above

122. Geography, technological, and education are examples of which of the following?

    (A) Forces affecting the competitive landscape

    (B) SWOT audit sources

    (C) Segments of the labor market

    (D) Internal departments

123. What is an ethnocentric staffing strategy?

    (A) Filling key international openings with parent-country nationals

    (B) Filling key international openings without regard to home country

    (C) Using host-country nationals to fill key management positions

    (D) Using host-country nationals or regional nationals to fill key positions

124. In the _____phase of training evaluation, participants are immediately asked questions about their thoughts on the training.

    (A) Reaction

    (B) Learning

    (C) Behavior

    (D) Results

125. In the _____phase of training evaluation, participants are evaluated based on the amount of knowledge that has been transferred to the job.

    (A) Reaction

    (B) Learning

    (C) Behavior

    (D) Results

126. In the _____phase of training evaluation, participants are evaluated based on how the employees apply the training to their jobs.

    (A) Reaction

    (B) Learning

    (C) Behavior

    (D) Results

127. A negatively accelerated learning curve is characterized by which of the following?

    (A) Early growth that slows over time

    (B) Slow beginning with gradual increases

    (C) A combined up-and-down demonstration of performance

    (D) Erratic performance that slowly improves

128. A positively accelerated learning curve is characterized by which of the following?

    (A) Early growth that slows over time

    (B) Slow beginning with gradual increases

    (C) A combined up-and-down demonstration of performance

    (D) Erratic performance that slowly improves

129. An S-shaped learning curve is characterized by which of the following?

    (A) Early growth that slows over time

    (B) Slow beginning with gradual increases

    (C) A combined up-and-down demonstration of performance

    (D) Erratic performance that slowly improves

130. The management team at Rowdy Mfg. wants you to design training that allows the new hires to work on production equipment, but without disrupting the production output. What type of training should you recommend?

    (A) On the job

    (B) Vestibule

    (C) Classroom simulation

    (D) Offsite

131. An employee at Clara's Toes shoe store has the skills to be a superstar, but she seems to lack motivation. Which of the following training strategies should be engaged?

    (A) Discipline

    (B) Job shadowing

    (C) Coaching

    (D) Simulation

132. The company you work for is struggling with a quality issue that it thinks is the result of lack of training and outdated equipment. Which of the following tools would be best to help the company brainstorm about the issue?

    (A) Fishbone

    (B) Pareto chart

    (C) Stratification chart

    (D) Histogram

133. The auto parts store you work for distributes 1,000 products per day, of which angry customers reject approximately 195 because of poor packaging. These customers are threatening to stop business with you. This defect is representative of which of the following quality phenomenon?

    (A) Vendor weaknesses

    (B) Pareto rule

    (C) Lack of quality assurance

    (D) The Peter Principle

134. Grant Packaging LLC has a flat line structure with very little opportunities for advancement. What strategy would BEST retain a high-potential employee worker?

    (A) Offering her more challenging work

    (B) Paying her a higher salary

    (C) Fast-tracking her into an executive role

    (D) Allowing her additional time off

135. Taylor Turkeys has its busiest time of year coming up in three months and needs to design a training program that gets a temporary workforce up and running as quickly as possible. Which of the following training evaluations would best serve this purpose?

    (A) Reaction evaluation

    (B) Behavior evaluation

    (C) Pilot program

    (D) Summative evaluation

136. Tanya is the HR manager tasked with a strategic initiative to make the performance-feedback system more meaningful and effective. Which of the following activities should she do first?

    (A) Compare the current program to external benchmarks.

    (B) Interview the executives to find out what they want.

    (C) Train the evaluators on how to conduct a review.

    (D) Interview both the employees and managers to find out what they need.

137. Hearing executives say, "Women won't stay long at a company because they will have to leave for family reasons" is evidence that there is a need for what type of training?

    (A) Education on work/life balance

    (B) Diversity training

    (C) Teaching of the leave benefits that the company offers

    (D) Better new hire on-boarding

138. Defining what is confidential and identifying how long it must remain so are two objectives to writing what?

    (A) An arbitration agreement

    (B) A noncompete agreement

    (C) A nondisclosure agreement

    (D) A policy to comply with the FCRA

139. In which scenario is a random drug screen the best solution?

    (A) When compelled to random drug screen by law

    (B) Before an employee returns to work after an injury

    (C) When there is reasonable suspicion that someone is under the influence

    (D) To test all employees for drug use on a regular basis

140. Which of the following statements is true regarding workers' compensation?

    (A) Workers' compensation isn't required for federal employees.

    (B) Workers' compensation is within the scope of individual states.

    (C) Workers' compensation is the result of a common law doctrine.

    (D) OSHA requires workers' compensation.

141. For every dollar spent on an injury and illness prevention plan, employers can expect a _____ time return on that investment.

    (A) two-

    (B) four-

    (C) six-

    (D) eight-

142. In an effort to eliminate workplace hazards, jobs with the highest injury and illness rates would benefit most from which of the following safety intervention strategies?

    (A) A job hazard analysis

    (B) A hired safety consultant

    (C) Lockout/tag-out procedures

    (D) Outsourced employees

143. Management at Arbini Winery is in the process of updating its risk management plans and efforts. The management needs to decide what to do about the potential liability in unlawful discrimination claims. In which of the following solutions does the employer decide to transfer the risk?

    (A) The company purchases EPLI.

    (B) The company prohibits unlawful discrimination through policy and training.

    (C) The company develops investigative steps should a claim of discrimination be reported.

    (D) The employer decides that it's unlikely that these types of claims will occur and tables it for the next fiscal year.

144. Two supervisors completed work for the day and began to change out of their uniforms. A friendly argument began but quickly escalated, resulting in one employee stabbing the other in the leg, causing an injury that required stitches. Which statement is true?

    (A) The injury isn't recordable because it was just horseplay gone awry.

    (B) The injury isn't recordable because it wasn't work related.

    (C) The injury is recordable, because it was work related and required treatment beyond first aid.

    (D) The injury is recordable because it escalated into an act of workplace violence.

145. Jobs in which employees come into contact with hazardous materials should include what safety precautions?

    (A) Hires who have experience working with the material

    (B) Very close supervision by management

    (C) The use of PPE

    (D) All of the above

146. According to the FLSA, an employee's work week is a fixed and regular recurring period of _____ hours.

    (A) 40

    (B) 56

    (C) 160

    (D) 168

147. An employee must be ____ years of age to work in most non-farm jobs, and ____ years of age to work in hazardous, non-farm jobs.

    (A) 12, 14

    (B) 14, 16

    (C) 16, 18

    (D) Children under 18 may never work in hazardous non-farm jobs.

148. The bank you work for has partnered with the local university to offer a front-line supervision course for any employee that wants to attend. The classes are held every Saturday morning from 8 a.m. to noon. Which statement is true?

    (A) The time is considered compensable under the FLSA.

    (B) The time is considered compensable under the Portal-to-Portal Act.

    (C) The time is compensable because the employer established the program.

    (D) The time is not compensable because attendance is voluntary and not directly related to an employee's work.

149. An employer established a training program to be delivered after hours and, although voluntary, implied that Chris's position at work would be enhanced should he attend. What did the employer violate?

    (A) The employee's rights under Title VII

    (B) The compensable time requirements of the Portal-to-Portal Act

    (C) The overtime requirements of the FLSA

    (D) Nothing. The program was voluntary and not required as a condition of employment.

150. Which of the following is a characteristic of a top-hat plan?

    (A) It establishes a baseline for organizational productivity.

    (B) The employee completely funds it.

    (C) It may allow executives to defer compensation into the next year.

    (D) It allows employees to own company stock.

151. When a new job is created and the wage range established, what activity was most likely completed?

    (A) Job analysis

    (B) Job pricing

    (C) Job ranking

    (D) Point factoring

152. The labor market had an abundance of service technicians in years past, allowing your company to pay below-market rates. Now that the skill set is in high demand, you are being forced to pay more for the same talent. What is most likely occurring?

    (A) Pay compression

    (B) Green-circled employees

    (C) Red-circled employees

    (D) COLAs have not kept up.

153. Using the scenario in the previous question, what strategy should you recommend to your employer going forward?

    (A) Regularly audit the market and match pay rates for all employees, not just new hires.

    (B) Give pay raises to all green-circled employees.

    (C) Freeze pay increases for red-circled employees.

    (D) Offer COLAs annually on a go-forward basis.

154. A company offers equity compensation to new employees. In which stage of the life cycle is this organization?

    (A) Infancy

    (B) Growth

    (C) Maturity

    (D) Decline

155. Workers' compensation insurance is to _____ as retirement plans are to _____.

    (A) Required, desired

    (B) Obligated, generous

    (C) State run, national

    (D) Compliance, optional

156. If the CEO's pay is 354 times that of the average worker within your company, which problem do you have?

    (A) Ethical

    (B) Internal equity

    (C) Discriminatory

    (D) Illegal

157. The most general cause of employee dissatisfaction with pay is what?

    (A) That the supervisors are unfair in their ratings.

    (B) Employees think that they are worth more.

    (C) A negative perception occurs in the fairness of outcomes.

    (D) The job is not paid what it is worth.

158. Which of the following statements is true about vesting?

    (A) Employees are immediately vested in their own contributions.

    (B) Employees must wait to access all funds until they have met the vesting requirements.

    (C) Employees must be 100 percent vested after two years in a plan.

    (D) Employees may be 20 percent vested after three years of service in the plan

159. For which of the following positions does compensation outsourcing make the most sense?

    (A) Executives

    (B) Sales staff

    (C) Piece rate workers

    (D) Exempt level employees

160. Open enrollment support, summary plan description creation, and COBRA administration are all examples of what?

    (A) HR generalist responsibilities

    (B) Functions of a large HR department

    (C) Responsibilities of an insurance broker

    (D) Potential outsourced functions

161. The company you work for, Health Systems Management, Inc., has a blanket policy that prohibits any employee from speaking negatively about the employer on social media. This policy may be unlawful based on which of the following?

    (A) It may violate an employee's right to engage in protected concerted activity under the NLRA.

    (B) It's a violation of an employee's right to freedom of speech.

    (C) It violates an employee's right to privacy.

    (D) It's only unlawful if it isn't consistently applied.

162. A large retail store has a social media policy that, in part, urges employees to develop a healthy suspicion of other employees or customers who try to trick them out of confidential information. Which statement is true?

    (A) The policy may be discriminatory.

    (B) The policy violates an employee's right to privacy.

    (C) The policy may create a hostile work environment.

    (D) The policy is lawful.

163. A construction company fired five workers after they appeared in a YouTube video to complain about the potential handling of hazardous materials without proper training. These employees were illegal immigrants, and the company was non-union. Which of the following statements is true?

    (A) The employees have no rights under the NLRB because they were illegally in the United States.

    (B) The employees had no rights under the NLRB because the company was non-union at the time.

    (C) The employees had every right to the claim, because the complaint was about safety.

    (D) The employees had every right to complain, because social media policies that prohibit negative press are valid.

164. Which of the following techniques would be most effective in avoiding union organizing?

    (A) Having an open-door policy

    (B) Prohibiting leaflet distribution on company premises

    (C) Fostering an open, inclusive work environment

    (D) Offering higher pay rates

165. An HR manager in Arizona fired an employee in New Mexico whom she had never met based on the reports of the employee's direct supervisor. She was unaware that this supervisor had a history of treating African-American employees differently than others. The company may be liable for unlawful discrimination under which doctrine?

 (A) Respondeat superior

 (B) Constructive discharge

 (C) EO 11246

 (D) Cat's paw

166. In arbitration law, it is generally impermissible for a decision maker to communicate with a party to a disagreement when the other party is absent. This is known as what?

 (A) Toll

 (B) Ex parte

 (C) In absentia

 (D) Precedent

167. Which statement is best when giving an employment reference of a past employee who was terminated for excessive absenteeism?

 (A) The employee missed five days in three months.

 (B) The employee was terminated for excessive absenteeism.

 (C) The employee missed too much work.

 (D) The employee had an attendance problem.

168. An employee was terminated because she was talking with her co-workers about trying to get pregnant. The employer told her that she was separating under the at-will doctrine of employment. To challenge this separation in court which of the following exemptions to at-will employment most likely will the employee use?

 (A) Contract

 (B) Statutory

 (C) Public policy

 (D) Duty of good faith and fair dealing

169. A supervisor changed an employee's schedule, forced him to commute to a farther location than usual, and otherwise made his working conditions unpleasant in the hopes that the employee would quit, which of course he eventually did. What charges did he file against the company?

 (A) Discrimination

 (B) Harassment

 (C) Constructive discharge

 (D) Respondeat superior

170. Of the following answer choices, which represents the best example of the main purpose of employment policies?

 (A) Complying with labor law

 (B) Changing the behavior of employees

 (C) Establishing standard operating procedures

 (D) Improving employee performance

171. Select the option that best demonstrates an employer's commitment to true performance management.

    (A) Accountability to company policy

    (B) Annual performance reviews that aren't late

    (C) Systems for regular formal and informal communication

    (D) A commitment to hiring right the first time

172. Employee engagement is best demonstrated through which of the following individual behaviors?

    (A) Zero tardies

    (B) Regular attendance at meetings

    (C) A demonstrated desire to learn

    (D) A feeling of job security

173. One of your superstar employees just gave notice and is leaving for the competition. When asked his reason for leaving, he stated that although he loved the work and the company, the travel schedule was affecting his ability to be home with his family. Which strategy would have most likely resulted in preventing this from happening with similar employees?

    (A) A formal system to complain about working conditions

    (B) Regular employee surveys

    (C) Annual performance reviews

    (D) Job rotation between otherwise qualified employees

174. The primary difference between a performance improvement plan (PIP) and discipline is what?

    (A) A PIP is more legally defensible.

    (B) A PIP is focused on success rather than termination.

    (C) Employees are more accepting of a PIP.

    (D) Discipline provides documentation.

175. Behavior management is a science, and therefore it can be both observed and _____.

    (A) Corrected

    (B) Measured

    (C) Changed

    (D) Modified

Chapter 14

Answers and Explanations to PHR Practice Exam I

. . . .

All right, one test down. You may want to take a moment before scoring your exam to focus on the areas that you felt gave you a bit of trouble. Write down what topics or question format felt tricky or the content that you had never seen before in your studies. Do so quickly, without regard for grammar or formatting so you can refer back to it after you score the test to see if your gut feeling or concerns are accurate.

After you complete your scoring, you can convert the numbers into a percentage by dividing the number of correct answers by the total number of items. Say for example that you missed 20 questions. Your score would be an 89 percent (155 correct items divided by 175 items).

Refer to Chapter 3 for more tips and tricks on how to handle the question format and what to do if you have to guess an answer on exam day.

1. **(D)** Post-hire activities are those that are done after an offer has been made and accepted and often have legal implications. Answer (D) is correct, because all of the options are completed once an employee had been hired.

   Form I-9 (A) must be completed no later than 72 hours after an employee's first day of work. (B) is a required payroll document that is only necessary if the candidate begins work for wages. (C) shouldn't begin until the individual has accepted an offer of employment.

2. **(B)** (B) is the correct answer because it violates Section 8 of the National Labor Relations Act (Wagner Act).

   (A) is incorrect because companies can do it for economic reasons. (C) is incorrect because it's called a *captive audience meeting* and is protected if done on company time. (D) is incorrect because supervisors can be fired if they show support for a union. They must take a company position as a supervisor or risk being fired.

3. **(D)** (D) is correct. Supervisory status will rarely be used (although recent Supreme Court rulings may change this). (A), (B), and (C) are all acceptable affirmative defenses established by case precedent.

4. **(D)** In this case, the employer was well within its right to rescind the conditional job offer of employment based upon an employee's pre-employment drug screen results, making (D) the correct answer.

   The other answers are all examples of common law doctrines. *Promissory estoppel* (A) would have occurred if the employer promised something and the individual acted on that promise. The *duty of good faith and fair dealing* (B) would have been compromised if the employer had acted in an unfair manner, and *fraudulent misrepresentation* (C) would have occurred, for example if the employer had given false information to entice the employee to leave his current position.

5. **(A)** (A) is correct. Often referred to as the 4 Ps of marketing — product, place, promotion, and price — are decisions that must be made regarding a company product or service. The other answers aren't part of the 4 Ps of marketing.

6. **(B)** (B) is correct. By verifying that Mary is eligible for Family Medical Leave Act (FMLA), you're ensuring that her rights are protected and that you comply with the standard if required. After you have verified her eligibility, you may request medical certification from her physician and work with the supervisor to determine replacement needs and sources.

7. **(A)** The correct answer is (A). Promoting from within capitalizes on the resources already expended in an earlier recruiting effort, and the question stem states that working at corporate is an attractive option. (B), (C), and (D) are all good efforts, but not the best answer to this scenario.

8. **(C)** The correct answer is (C). Attending professional development activities with subordinates isn't unethical. Answers (B) and (D) are clearly inappropriate, and (A), although compassionate, isn't appropriate when considering ethical behavior.

9. **(A)** The correct answer is (A). *Assimilating* to the company is what is known as becoming part of a team and the group dynamics.

   Cultural integration (B) may occur as the result of a merger or acquisition, whereas *onboarding* (C) is a step to getting the new hire acquainted with the job. *Affiliation* (D) is a term associated with the need theory of motivation.

10. **(B)** (B) is correct. *Span of control* refers to the number of employees a manager directly supervises. (A) and (C) refer to much more than just direct reports, and (D) is a visual representation of the organizational hierarchy.

11. **(D)** The correct answer is (D). Technological factors, such as the ability to recall data and protection of assets, must be reviewed as part of a thorough PEST analysis. The political (A), economic (B), and social (C) landscapes don't address the items in the question.

12. **(C)** (C) is the correct answer. *Employer branding* serves to tell the public about why people should come and work for the organization. Establishing the employer brand is the broader scope of two of the other answers — (A) and (D). Videoing and then posting the video doesn't serve as a compliance document (B).

13. **(A)** The correct answer is (A), *employment at will,* which allows either party to terminate the employment relationship at any time and for any reason.

   (B) is another common law doctrine, dealing with the employer being responsible for the actions of its employees. (C) is an exception to the at-will doctrine, and the *employment relationship* (D) exists when both parties agree to work with each other.

14. **(B)** In the correct answer, (B), employee reasons for leaving are captured prior to their last day of work in *exit interviews.*

   Employee satisfaction surveys (A) are designed to measure employee opinions before they make a decision to leave. *Turnover reports* (C) are designed to identify what positions are unfilled, and a *labor market analysis* (D) is too broad in scope to capture specific information about why people choose to leave a specific employer.

15. **(A)** A *homogeneous* group (A) includes people who share the same background or heritage. (B) is the opposite. (C) is a devoted citizen, and (D) is the recognition of academic merit.

16. **(C)** The correct answer is (C). *Quid pro quo* harassment occurs when a supervisor requires a romantic or sexual behavior in exchange for something else, such as not being fired.

   (A) and (B) aren't the correct terms, although the harassment certainly may be found to be unlawful and discriminatory. (D) is another type of harassment in which an employee's working conditions are altered due to abuse based on a protected class characteristic.

17. **(A)** The correct answer is (A). An *R-1* is a non-immigrant visa that may be extended to religious workers to be in the United States for up to five years. (B) is for workers with extraordinary abilities, (C) is a visa for executives, and (D) may be extended to athletes or entertainers.

18. **(D)** Separation of employment is a trigger for multiple worker protection acts, including all listed here, which makes (D) correct.

    COBRA (A) allows separated workers to continue to purchase healthcare. HIPAA (B) allows them to get future coverage despite pre-existing conditions. WARN (C) requires notice because the layoff affects more than 99 workers.

19. **(B)** The explosion of mobile job apps within the last testing window makes (B) the correct answer.

    Also increasing, but at a slower pace, includes the use of videos for the employer brand (A) and virtual interviewing (C) for out-of-town candidates or pre-screening. (D) has been growing at a more steady pace since its birth several years ago.

20. **(D)** At-will employment is a common law doctrine that allows either party to employment to separate at any time, and for any reason, making answer (D) the best answer.

21. **(D)** Many benefits to pre-employment drug screening include a defense against a negligent hiring claim (A), the prevention of potential violence on the job (B), and workplace injuries (C), making (D) the correct answer.

22. **(B)** (B) is correct. Using student interns is an excellent source of hiring for companies that allow both the candidate and the employer to qualify each other for the position.

    (A) could get the employer in trouble if not properly managed, and both (C) and (D), although correct, aren't the focus of student internships.

23. **(A)** The correct answer is (A), which found that a high school diploma requirement was excluding African Americans. (B) requires that all employment tests be valid predictors of behavior. (C) places the burden on an employer to show why it failed to hire someone who was otherwise qualified. In (D), an employee who had been the subject of unlawful discrimination may be eligible for back pay.

24. **(D)** The correct answer is (D). *Albermarle Paper vs. Moody* found that an employee who had been the subject of unlawful discrimination may be eligible for back pay.

    In (A), a high school diploma requirement excludes African Americans, making it discriminatory. (B) requires that all employment tests be valid predictors of behavior. (C) places the burden on an employer to show why it failed to hire someone who was otherwise qualified.

25. **(B)** The correct answer is (B). Using a third party to conduct the exit interview allows the exiting employee to provide more honest, meaningful feedback as to why he or she is leaving.

    It may not have an impact on how an employee feels about the separation (A), and it won't protect an employer from a charge of wrongful termination (C). (D) may be necessary to the busy HR professional, but it's not the best answer.

26. **(D)** The correct answer is (D). The Age Discrimination in Employment Act applies to all individuals older than the age of 40.

27. **(D)** The correct answer is (D). Outsourcing is a very useful way to accomplish many of the functions of HR in the absence of a robust HR department. Activities include processing payroll (A), hiring (B), and complying with COBRA (C).

28. **(A)** (A) is correct. Successful social media use in recruiting has a consistent message communicated via the brand, and videos are one way to do that. The employer brand isn't used for retention (B) or satisfaction efforts (C), nor does it help communicate the benefits (D).

29. **(C)** The correct answer (C) highlights an alternative to traditional staffing sources, such as direct hires (A) and temporary workers (D) and the use of Internet to find talent (B).

30. **(B)** In a *Socratic seminar*, conclusions are drawn and ideas shared through questions and answers, so (B) is correct.

    An agenda (A), classroom lecture (C), or room set up such as fishbowl (D), aren't key factors to this instructional method.

31. **(A)** Answer (A) is the best answer because active teaching addresses the needs of the training participant. The active method of teaching results in engaged (B) and participative (C) attendees. (D) is an answer distractor and doesn't apply.

32. **(D)** The correct answer is (D) because on-the-job training occurs in real time at the workstations.

    Meanwhile, off-the-job training pulls employees out of the environment in which they will eventually apply their knowledge. In *vestibule training* (A), work is simulated at a different location from where the work would normally be done. A *lecture* (B) is a method used in a classroom setting, and *simulation training* (C) is training that mimics actual conditions of the job but is not done where the work is regularly completed.

33. **(D)** (D) is correct. *Banquet-style seating* helps facilitate training that requires discussion because it has already organized them into groups. Films (A) and lectures (B) are best facilitated using theater-style seating, and the use of manuals (C) or other hands-on activities are best served by a traditional classroom setup.

34. **(B)** The best answer to this question is (B). New employees should be asked to conduct a self-assessment after the first 90 days of employment in order to help facilitate the constructive feedback that is often necessary to get them up to speed. An employee assessment isn't the best way to address teamwork issues (A), because most employees won't point the finger at themselves. (C) won't be served by an assessment of the employee's behavior, a similar reason as to why (D) also isn't correct.

35. **(A)** The correct answer is (A). *Flexible work arrangements* can help retain key workers of both sexes, allowing for better work/life balance. EPLI insurance (B) and a dating policy (D) aren't the direct result of women in the workplace. The question doesn't adequately predict a sexual harassment lawsuit (C).

36. **(A)** (A) is correct. The *analysis* stage of the instructional design model of ADDIE is a function of data collection to assess the need.

    The *design* stage (B) is concerned with designing training around tasks and participants. The *development* (C) of training is where the collateral materials to be used in the training are created, and *implementation* phase (D) occurs after you're ready to begin the sessions.

37. **(C)** The correct answer is (C) because the development stage of ADDIE is when training material is created or *developed*.

    The *design* stage (B) is concerned with designing training around tasks and participants. The *analysis* stage (A) occurs when the needs to be addressed through training are identified. After documents have been developed, they can be implemented (D).

38. **(D)** Visual learners learn by seeing the material in print or graphic form, making (D) the correct answer. Lectures (A) work well for auditory learners, whereas tactile learners are best served through hands-on (B) or on-the-job training (C).

39. **(B)** Training won't solve a problem with tools or equipment, so (B) is correct. Training may have impact on being unfamiliar with the products (A), being a new hire (C), or becoming proficient with software programs (D).

40. **(C)** The correct answer is skill variety (C), which allows employees to apply more than one talent to a position.

    (A) is the ability to identify how the employee's task contributes to the final product. *Horizontal loading* (B) refers to assigning tasks that share similar skill sets. Task significance is an intrinsic motivator when the job has a larger purpose or meaning (D).

41. **(D)** (D) is correct. In instructional design, the objectives to learning should be clearly defined prior to the development of training. In training design, objectives state the outcomes that will shape the learning content and final effectiveness evaluations.

    Goals (A) tend to be stated on operational level tricking down from the strategic plan. Interventions are also linked to business strategy used to fill the gap between actual and desired state (B). (C) is a generic term used both at a strategic and operational level.

42. **(A)** Enterprise Risk Management (ERM) is a system to address all aspects of organizational risk, including protecting the confidentiality of customer information, which makes (A) correct.

    Responding to a technological fail (B) and establishing firewalls (C) are aspects of the system. The protection of human assets (D) doesn't address information, but rather the physical well-being of employees.

43. **(D)** Establishing internal controls helps avoid potential conflicts such as the one described in the question, making (D) the correct answer. In this case, separating the functions so that the responsibilities are shared would prevent something like this from happening, whereas (A), (B), and (C) serve only to prohibit it.

44. **(C)** The correct answer is (C). Injury and illness prevention plans (IIPPs) are designed to communicate information to employees about workplace hazards. Many of these plans share elements whereas others, such as fire prevention plans (A), are specific to the hazard. It isn't an element of protecting information or financial assets as in (B) and (D).

45. **(B)** The correct answer is (B). Without leadership and management commitment, a company's IIPP will struggle to allocate resources to abate hazards (A), engage workers (C), or evaluate program outcomes (D).

46. **(D)** State-run programs must meet the federal safety standards established by the Occupational Safety and Health Act and Administration, making (D) the correct answer.

47. **(D)** Retaliation occurs when an employer punishes a worker for exercising a right under the law — in this case, the right to blow the whistle — making (D) the correct answer.

    Discrimination (A) occurs when an employee is unlawfully treated based on a protected class characteristic. Harassment (B) may be present if the employee is forced to endure taunting or abusive conduct from coworkers or supervisors. In (C), a claim of wrongful discipline may have merit, however, it's secondary to the correct answer.

48. **(A)** The correct answer is (A). The Family Medical Leave Act (FMLA) provides unpaid, job protected leave to eligible employees.

49. **(B)** The correct answer is (B). The Patient Protection and Affordable Care Act amended the Fair Labor Standards Act in 2010 requiring employers to accommodate nursing mothers' need to express breast milk for a year following the birth of a child.

50. **(C)** The correct answer is (C). The Portal-to-Portal Act amended the FLSA in 1947 to clarify what was compensable time. One of the primary outcomes was that regular commute time — from one portal or doorway to another — wasn't compensable under the FLSA.

    Davis-Bacon (A) required prevailing wages for public works projects. McNamara-O'Hara (B) addressed minimums for service workers. The Equal Pay Act (D) addressed disparity in pay between men and women doing the same jobs.

51. **(C)** (C) is the correct answer. *Base pay* is the amount of money an employee receives as the result of performing work.

    Minimum wage (A) is set by law, total compensation (B) includes variable pay and benefits, and incentives (D) are a type of variable pay based on performance.

52. **(C)** The correct answer is (C). *Performance-based pay* is earned based on effort.

    Base pay (A) is paid as part of the work agreement, and total compensation (B) includes all facets of remuneration. Entitlement pay (D) is based on years of service or cost of living increases; an employee is entitled to the increase because she works there.

53. **(A)** The correct answer is (A). Shift premiums are considered a pay differential, because they're different from the regular hourly rate.

    Hazard pay (B) is also a type of pay differential, paying a higher premium for difficult or dangerous work. A benefit (C) is generally a part of an overall compensation plan, and entitlement (D) is a compensation philosophy.

54. **(C)** The Consumer Credit Protection Act limits the amount of pay that can be garnished on a weekly basis, thus answer (C) is correct.

55. **(C)** The correct answer is (C). The Health Insurance Portability and Accountability Act (HIPAA) prohibits the exclusion of pre-existing conditions when an employee had previous coverage of said condition.

    The Consolidated Omnibus Budget Reconciliation Act (COBRA) (A) is the right for employees to continue to purchase the employer plan when there is a qualifying event. Title VII (B) is part of the Civil Rights Act of 1964 that prohibits discrimination in employment and doesn't govern health insurance. Future coverage of pre-existing health conditions isn't the focus of the Patient Protection and Affordable Care Act (PPACA) (D).

56. **(C)** Because *variable pay* is based on individual and/or organizational performance, (C) is the best answer. Annual increases (A) and benefits (B) don't directly reward achievement, and group incentives (D) reward team rather than personal effort.

57. **(A)** The correct answer is (A). The opposite of base pay is pay based on merit. (B), (C), and (D) aren't performance driven.

58. **(D)** In all of the answers, an experience factor is generated based on claims experience, making (D) the correct answer.

59. **(C)** The correct answer is (C). A *defined benefit plan* guarantees an employee a set amount of money at the time of retirement, usually as a monthly payment.

    A *cash balance plan* (A) is a retirement program where employers deposit a percentage of the employee's pay into a retirement account, and the employee isn't required to contribute. A *contributory plan* (B) is one in which a percentage of earnings are deposited into a retirement account. A *defined contribution* (D) doesn't define the benefit, but rather it defines the amount an employee/employee may contribute to the plan, such as a 401k.

60. **(B)** The correct answer is (B). The Employee Retirement Income Security Act (ERISA) established that a plan may require an employee be at least 21 years of age with at least one year of service before being eligible to participate.

61. **(C)** The correct answer is (C). *Conducting needs assessment* helps identify what the company's need is in managing payroll.

    After it has been completed, you can then write a Request for Proposal (RFP) (B) that addresses the needs, request a trial run (D) of selected software, and then present executives with options to approve (A).

62. **(B)** The correct answer is (B). The National Labor Relations Board (NLRB) may file an Unfair Labor Practice (ULP) charge against the employer if its social media policy is too broad. The question doesn't discuss any discriminatory elements such as protected class conditions (A), nor does it describe a situation of sexual or hostile workplace harassment (C). A *whistleblower* (D) is someone who reports a company for corrupt or unsafe business practices.

63. **(C)** The correct answer is (C). Union organizers are sponsored and trained by unions to travel and help workers organize. With the AFL-CIO, they select their union organizing training participants from union members or elected union representatives; others are from college campuses or community groups.

    A bargaining agent assists members with the collective bargaining agreement (CBA) (A), and union stewards serve as employee ambassadors to the union (D). Any person with decision-making authority may act on behalf of the employer when bargaining (B).

64. **(A)** The term *salting* refers to the process of padding the applicant pool with those in sympathy with union aims, making (A) the correct answer.

Featherbedding (B) is the hiring of more workers than is necessary to perform a job. *Double breasting* (C) refers to a common owner of two businesses, one of which is union. The *alter ego doctrine* (D) is a term used to describe an employer who is trying to dodge its collective bargaining responsibilities by setting up another company with substantially the same operations.

65. **(D)** The correct answer is (D). Union issues such as safety and fair pay have been granted as rights by statute (A), while working conditions (B) and updated tools and equipment (C) have improved, making unions less necessary than in earlier times.

66. **(B)** The correct answer is (B). You can communicate with employees several different ways, and they include informal brown bag lunches in which employees voluntarily bring their lunches to a meeting, a company intranet where business issues and announcements are posted, and word of mouth, where supervisors and other employees are used to pass information among employees.

Word of mouth isn't a type of training, making (A) incorrect. Both (C) and (D) are types of information an employer would need a mode of communication for.

67. **(D)** *At-will employment* is the right for an employer to terminate or an employee to quit at any time for any reason, making answer (D) correct.

There is no such thing as the doctrine of free will (A). The doctrine of Lord Acton (B) refers to an author of freedom essays unrelated to employment issues. Statutory exceptions (C) are conditions under which a labor law or employment doctrine may not apply.

68. **(A)** The correct answer is (A). The Supreme Court established that in cases where an adverse employment action was made by a supervisor via quid pro quo harassment, an employer may not build an affirmative defense.

An example of a tangible injury includes denial of a promotion or wage, or a demotion. In the other three answer choices, an employer may have the opportunity to provide an affirmative defense demonstrating that they took all possible preventive efforts.

69. **(D)** The correct answer is (D). A tangible employment action, such as hiring, firing, and demoting, can only be caused by someone — such as a supervisor — acting on behalf of the employer. The EEOC states that this action can be demonstrated by documentation, higher-level review, and execution of the action, making (D) correct.

70. **(C)** The correct answer is (C). The Supreme Court found in *Oncale vs. Sundowner Offshore Services* that Title VII is violated anytime the work environment is permeated with hostile or discriminatory behavior that alters the work environment, regardless of sex.

71. **(C)** The correct answer is (C). The National Labor Relations Board (NLRB) is responsible for enforcing the standards set forth in the National Labor Relations Act (B). The Equal Employment Opportunity Commission (EEOC) (A) enforces Title VII, and the Department of Labor (D) is responsible for many other labor laws including safety and wage/hour.

72. **(B)** The correct answer is (B). The trifecta of labor law governs unions, and the National Labor Relations Act (NLRA) was the act that first defined unfair labor practices.

The Labor-Management Relations Act (LMRA) (A) followed, which protected employers from union abuses. The third act was the Labor-Management Reporting and Disclosure Act (LMRDA) (C), which established controls for unions in response to corrupt union practices against their members. The Railway Labor Act of 1926 (D) was a cooperative effort between labor unions and railway employers to minimize the impact that striking workers had on US transportation.

73. **(C)** The correct answer is (C). The Labor-Management Reporting Act (Landrum-Griffith) established rules for unions in an effort to protect members from corrupt practices. The National Labor Relations Act (Wagner) (B) gave employees the right to unionize, and the Labor-Management Relations Act (Taft-Hartley) (A) protected employers from union abuses. The Railway Labor Act (D) was one of the first efforts between unions and employers to find alternative dispute methods to strikes.

74. **(A)** The correct answer is (A). The Labor Management Relations Act sought to balance the power between unions and employers.

    The National Labor Relations Act (B) first granted union power in 1935. The Labor-Management Reporting and Disclosure Act (C), which established controls for unions in response to corrupt union practices against their members, also curbed union power. The Railway Labor Act (D) was collaboration between unions and railway employers to minimize the likelihood of strikes and thus avoid the disruptions to transportation they cause.

75. **(D)** The correct answer is (D). *Economic* strikers are those workers that are protesting conditions of employment such as wages or hours. *Picketing* (B) may be an activity used by strikers to communicate their dissatisfaction. Unfair labor practices strikers (C) are protesting unlawful acts by the employer. There is no such thing as a protest strike (A).

76. **(B)** The correct answer is (B). Absent serious misconduct on the part of the worker, unfair labor practice strikers are entitled to their jobs back, even if it means discharging a replacement worker.

77. **(C)** The correct answer is (C) because compensable time was first established as a concept under the Fair Labor Standards Act, and later clarified through the Portal-to-Portal Act.

    It requires that "preparatory and concluding activities" that are integral to the job function be paid. The OSH Act (A) communicates safety standards, whereas the Service Contract Act (B) requires affected employers pay prevailing wage and fringe benefits under certain conditions.

78. **(A)** Because HCMPs are used as a strategic planning tool to guide a company's responses to emerging workforce and organizational needs, the correct answer is (A). Goal setting (B) may be a tool used for plan implementation, and project implementation (C) is an activity described within the plan. Sustainability (D) is a corporate responsibility concept that helps organizations avoid resource depletion.

79. **(B)** The National Labor Relations Act (NLRA) guarantees workers the right to organize independent of their employer. Having managers appoint employees who were then allowed to discuss conditions of employment makes (B) the correct answer. Also, the committee could make recommendations that have job security and economic implications for current workers. These decisions, outside the normal collective bargaining domain, would violate NLRB rules.

    The presence of management on the committees and the committees themselves, (A) and (C), aren't unlawful; (D) is irrelevant, because all company committees don't have to be declared part of an official union.

80. **(D)** The correct answer is (D). *Negative reinforcement* occurs when something unpleasant is removed in response to employee behavior. *Positive reinforcement* (C) provides a reward when behavior occurs, for example, incentives for speeding up production.

    Punishment (A) would exist if the supervisor told the workers they would have to start working on Saturdays if production isn't caught up. *Extinction* (B) is similar to negative reinforcement; however, it refers to extinguishing the behavior, not removing the consequence.

81. **(D)** In the absence of an emergency, existing safety hazards (A) should be the first addressed. (C) describes action steps designed to protect confidentiality, and (B) includes communicated plans to use in the event of a disaster. (D) is last in this scenario because a policy won't directly protect a stakeholder, so (D) is correct.

82. **(B)** When two sets of data are strongly linked together, a high correlation is said to exist, referred to as a *co-relationship*. A *positive correlation* demonstrates that when one variable increases, the second variable also increases or if one variable decreases, the second likewise decreases, so (B) is correct. Answers (A), (C), and (D) are examples of negative correlations because when one variable increases, the other decreases.

83. **(B)** (B) is the correct answer. Similar to a bell curve, this activity identifies the top 25 percent of employees within a department, 50 percent of workers who can stay in their current position, and the bottom 25 percent of employees in need of intervention.

    A *Pareto chart* (A) and a *fishbone diagram* (D) are tools used in problem solving. (C) is a simpler version of forced distribution and isn't a chart.

84. **(C)** In a *product-based structure* (C), divisions are formed based on lines of products, customers, or geography.

    While lending itself to either centralized or decentralized, it's more likely to be decentralized than the traditional *functional* (A) or *hierarchical* (D) corporate structure. In (B), the term *organizational* is a distractor.

85. **(B)** (B) is correct. A *human capital management plan* is part of the strategic planning process in which talent needs are forecasted and addressed. Continuous recruitment (A) won't solve seasonal peaks, and making promotions from within (C) still leaves gaps. The use of staffing agencies (D) may be a solution, but only after the needs are predicted.

86. **(A)** The correct answer is (A). Also known as a *strategic alliance,* companies may choose to join brands to influence sales positively.

    (B) could be considered a type of alliance, but it typically joins two companies together to undertake new business. (C) occurs when a company merges larger scale operations and assets, whereas (D) is the elimination of a product or division.

87. **(A)** (A) is correct because it may include both expansion and reduction to address a strategic initiative. (B) is an example of reduction, whereas (C) and (D) are more about the joining of assets than simple restructures.

88. **(B)** The best answer to this question is (B). Having management committed to the process will help shape and influence a meaningful MVV.

    Establishing a budget (A) is a transactional activity that shouldn't influence the MVV. Scanning the environment (C) is helpful to collect data, but not in advance of management engagement. (D) is an evaluation step, usually occurring after the MVV is in place.

89. **(D)** Employee performance (D) is the correct answer because the engagement stage in the employee life cycle is related to the worker's performance management.

    (A) is communicated at the onboarding stage of the life cycle, as are responsibilities (B). Answer (C) isn't relevant.

90. **(C)** The correct answer is (C), because the amended version of the ADA prohibits reverse discrimination claims under the ADA. This answer makes the other answer choices irrelevant.

91. **(B)** The correct answer is (B). A test is said to be low in *criterion-related validity* if it doesn't predict the behaviors that an employer thought it was going to predict. (A) refers to the test being reflective of all relevant job responsibilities. (C) refers to the appearance of the successful prediction of outcomes. In (D), uncorrelated items stay uncorrelated.

92. **(A)** The correct answer is (A). *Systems thinking* refers to a holistic view of the interrelatedness of an organization.

    (B) and (C) aren't one of the five disciplines. (D) is a distractor, because a learning organization is not just about employee training; it's the science of how a company works.

93. **(A)** The Behaviorally Anchored Rating Scale (BARS) uses anchor statements to support job requirements, so (A) is the correct answer. (B) is descriptive, and both (C) and (D) use other employees to measure performance.

94. **(B)** The correct answer is (B). A *leadership development program* first serves the broader needs and desired outcomes of an organization. These programs typically are designed to serve narrower needs such as quality or job competencies for a specific role.

    (A) isn't the best answer simply because the focus of leadership development is not on one single outcome, but rather many. Technical skills for physicians is too narrow of a focus to be served by a leadership development program.

95. **(A)** The best answer is (A). Companies are allowed to claim a tip credit against the minimum wage earnings, provided they pay the difference when base pay plus tips to not meet the minimum wage standards.

96. **(B)** Because the focus on variable pay is performance, (B) is the best answer. The other answers, although true, aren't the best options for this question because they aren't critical to the existence of a variable pay system.

97. **(D)** The correct answer is (D). Employers have many reasons for paying below-market rates, but when evaluating compensation rates. They should first consider the abundance of talent.

    Regardless of what competitors are doing (A), job worth (B), or the budget requirements (C), the absence or abundance of talent drives results.

98. **(A)** The correct answer is (A). *Improshare* is a gainsharing plan that rewards efforts that exceed past production standards.

    Improshare is more narrowly focused than a profit-sharing plan (B). It also doesn't offer employee stock as in Employee Stock Ownership Plans (C) and Employee Stock Purchase Plans (D).

99. **(A)** A *toll* temporarily suspends the counting of time in a legal action for various reasons, making (A) the correct answer in this example.

    Dismissing the statute (B) would close out the case permanently from a legal perspective. The case is already in dispute, so (C) wouldn't make sense, and (D) is an answer distractor, a term that doesn't apply to the described situation.

100. **(C)** In this question, the key word is *equal*. Although all answers may provide the executive team members with the information they seek, (C) is the most specific; a *break-even analysis* will determine at what point total revenue equals total return.

    Answers (A), (B), and (D) speak to an overall return on the investment dollars, but are broader than the initial request.

101. **(B)** (B) is correct. *Sales growth* (B) is a key indicator of performance in a sales department. KPI helps a company measure progress toward organizational goals, is generally long term in nature, and must be adaptable to changing realities. These goals are most often established through the strategic planning process.

    Answers (A) and (D), although important, speak to operational issues that shouldn't be fluid. Answer (C) won't adequately capture the sales information necessary to determine whether a change of strategy is required.

102. **(C)** (C) is correct. Abraham Maslow stated that employees have needs at different stages that must be met in order for them to stay motivated. The *social stage* (C) speaks to the desire of individuals to belong to a workgroup, so it's the correct answer.

    Answers (A) and (B) refer to the most basic needs of individual's such as food, shelter, and safe working conditions. (D) is a higher level in the hierarchy, referencing that people are motivated by achievement and recognition.

103. **(A)** The correct answer is (A). A *return-to-work program* helps get injured workers back to work in a modified capacity and on payroll, rather than having their wages replaced through the insurance, thereby reducing the overall cost of the injury.

    OSHA doesn't require return-to-work programs, (B), and most productivity (C) isn't a primary goal of these programs. (D) isn't the best answer because it's subjective.

104. **(D)** The correct answer is (D), B.F. Skinner's *operant conditioning* is what happens to an employee when he executes one behavior and receives a consistent result, reinforcing the behavior and future expectation.

    (B) is McClelland's *three-factor theory of motivation*, identifying an employee needs to achieve, belong, and/or lead. In (C), McGregor addresses a manager's view of how employees are motivated. (A) is Maslow's *hierarchy of needs*.

105. **(D)** The correct answer is (D). Scanning the external environment for threats such as the supplier being unable to deliver product is an important part of the strategic planning process.

    An external scan also includes looking for opportunities (C). Answers (A) and (B) are examples of internal indicators. This information is used to put contingency plans in place during the strategic planning process.

106. **(B)** (B) is correct. *Lobbying* is the effort of a group to influence legislation.

    Appropriating (A) is the process of setting funds aside for a specific purpose. *Conferencing* (C) is the gathering together of individuals to discuss specific issues, and *petitioning* (D) is a formal plea to a lawmaker to make desired changes to existing or proposed laws.

107. **(B)** The correct answer is (B). Under very narrow circumstances, an employer may claim a protected class characteristic is a bona fide occupational qualification (BFOQ) and use it as a condition of employment.

    Answer (C) is incorrect because churches aren't exempt from Title VII, and both (A) and (D) are irrelevant as religion is a BFOQ.

108. **(B)** Compliance with labor law is the fundamental reason for maintaining a personnel file, making answer (B) the best choice in this scenario.

    (A), (C), and (D) are by-products of compliance helping to manage employer risk as recommended by attorneys. Managing risks include the employer having the documentation necessary to defend a wrongful termination charge.

109. **(C)** HR professionals must wear multiple hats, and outsourcing is an effective way to marshal resources. It allows you to focus on other areas of core competencies, making (C) the correct answer.

    Prequalifying workers (A) is part of the recruiting process, not the post-hire process, and (B) is irrelevant because there may be co-employment issues regardless. (D) isn't always true.

110. **(D)** The correct answer is (D), the practice of trying to get a trial held in a court that is more likely to produce a favorable outcome.

    Predictive analysis (A) is a data-mining process, and scanning the environment (C) is part of the strategic planning process. (B) is a generic term that can be applied to multiple behaviors.

111. **(D)** Although age, sexual orientation, and gender are currently granted protected class status, Title VII of the Civil Rights Act of 1964 originally prohibited discrimination based on race, ethnicity, national origin, and religion, making answer (D) correct.

112. **(D)** The correct answer is (D), all of the above. Companies with past discriminatory practices may be compelled by the court to have a written affirmative action plan (AAP). Construction companies and supply and service contractors may also be required to have written plans, depending upon the value of their contracts.

113. **(D)** The correct answer is (D), because the use of a polygraph in this example is an exception.

    (B) prohibits the use of lie detector tests with certain exceptions. One exception is the limited use in hiring of individuals with access to storage of or sale of controlled substances. Answers (A) and (C) don't address polygraphs.

114. **(B)** The correct answer is (B). Severance packages are often structured based on years of service.

    Outplacement services (A) and unemployment benefit counseling (C) are helpful, but they don't result in the requested outcome. (D) may be built into a severance agreement.

115. **(A)** The correct answer is (A). If a plant closing is due to a natural disaster, such as an earthquake or flood, otherwise obligated employers are exempt from the notification requirements of WARN. They aren't however exempt from discrimination laws (B) or worker's compensation (C).

116. **(B)** The best answer is (B). As long as other measures are taken to ensure the integrity, readability, and access of the records, the original documents can be destroyed after they're stored electronically. Storing Form I-9 on a shared drive doesn't adequately address confidentiality issues. (C) may inhibit presentation on demand, and (D), although acceptable, isn't recommended.

117. **(A)** Because breathing is considered a major life activity under the Americans with Disabilities Act (ADA), the correct answer is (A).

    FMLA (B) doesn't offer wage replacement, and HIPAA (C) will become necessary only if her employment is terminated. (D) doesn't exist at a national level.

118. **(C)** The best answer is (C), because an organization may use job shadowing to communicate both the positive and negative aspects of the job as part of the interview process.

    An organization does a *job analysis* (B) to identify the key tasks, duties, and responsibilities and then uses the job analysis to write job descriptions (A). A peer interview (D) could be used, but it's not the best answer.

119. **(A)** A PEO reduces exposure to the risks associated with being an employer, making (A) the correct answer.

    (B) and (C) are examples of those risks and are often built into the billing rate. Whether or not a PEO would have a positive effect on (D) is dependent upon many unique employer factors such as the total number of workers and labor burden.

120. **(D)** The correct answer is (D). The EEOC encourages employees to first address the issue with their employer prior to filing a formal complaint.

    In most cases, an employee must file a discrimination charge with the EEOC prior to filing a lawsuit, (A). (B) must be considered on a case-by-case basis. In (C), the employee has 180 days to file a charge with the EEOC.

121. **(D)** An organization can downsize in several ways, and it doesn't all have to be permanent, making (D) the correct answer.

122. **(C)** The correct answer is (C) because they're subsets of the labor market that may be used to identify targeted recruiting efforts.

    The forces referred to in answer (A) are competitive in nature, such as new entrants to the market or supplier power. SWOT audit sources (B) scan the external environments for threats and weaknesses. Internal departments (D) aren't catalogued or recorded by the question criteria.

123. **(A)** The correct answer is (A). An *ethnocentric staffing* strategy is one that uses home-country expatriates to staff global positions.

    (B) is a geocentric strategy, (C) is a polycentric strategy, and (D) is a regiocentric staffing policy.

124. **(A)** Donald Kirkpatrick described four methods of training evaluation. The correct answer is (A) because in *reaction evaluations,* participants are queried on their feelings about the training immediately afterward.

    In *learning evaluations* (B), the amount of knowledge is measured, often through a quiz. In *behavior evaluations* (C), employees are observed applying the newly acquired behaviors on the job. In *results evaluations* (D), the effects of the training are measured.

125. **(B)** Donald Kirkpatrick described four methods of training evaluation. The correct answer is (B) because what participants have learned is measured, often through a quiz.

    In *reaction evaluations* (A), participants are queried on their feelings about the training immediately afterward. In *behavior evaluations* (C), employees are observed applying the newly acquired behaviors on the job. In *results evaluations* (D), the effects of the training are measured.

126. **(C)** Donald Kirkpatrick described four methods of training evaluation. The correct answer is (C) because in behavior evaluations, employees are observed applying the newly acquired behaviors on the job.

    In *reaction evaluations* (A), participants are queried on their feelings about the training immediately afterward. In *learning evaluations* (B), the amount of knowledge is measured, often through a quiz. In *results evaluations* (D), the effects of the training are measured.

127. **(A)** The correct answer is (A). Employees learn and apply information from training at different paces. A *negatively accelerated learning curve* shows early performance that gradually declines over practice.

    A *positively accelerated learning curve* (B) is one in which early performance outcomes are low, but they gradually improve. An *S-shaped learning curve* (C) is characterized by a combined up-and-down graph of learning. (D) isn't an example of the formal types of learning curves.

128. **(B)** The correct answer is (B). Employees learn and apply information from training at different paces. A *positively accelerated learning curve* is one in which early performance outcomes are low, but they gradually improve.

    A *negatively accelerated learning curve* (A) shows early performance that gradually declines over practice. An *S-shaped learning curve* (C) is characterized by a combined up-and-down graph of learning. (D) isn't an example of the formal types of learning curves.

129. **(C)** The correct answer is (C). Employees learn and apply information from training at different paces. An *S-shaped learning curve* is characterized by a combined up-and-down graph of learning.

    A *negatively accelerated learning curve* (A) shows early performance that gradually declines over practice. A *positively accelerated learning curve* (B) is one in which early performance outcomes are low, but they gradually improve. (D) isn't an example of the formal types of learning curves.

130. **(B)** (B) is correct because in *vestibule training,* employees are removed from the main production line and trained on real equipment.

    On-the-job training (A) wouldn't solve the workflow issue, and classroom simulation (C) or offsite training (D) may not allow for equipment simulation.

131. **(C)** The correct answer is (C) because the employee is given the opportunity to work through her motivation issues and apply her talent.

    Discipline (A) is a form of training, but it may not lead to successful retention of said talent. (B) and (D) address her abilities, which isn't the training need.

132. **(A)** A *fishbone diagram* is a helpful problem-solving tool that captures common issues, such as man, material, or machines, which makes (A) the correct answer.

     A *Pareto chart* (B) graphically represents the 80/20 rule, which states that 20 percent of the defects cause 80 percent of the issues. A *stratification chart* (C) breaks down a problem in components. A *histogram* (D) seeks to find patterns of issues.

133. **(B)** The correct answer is (B). A *Pareto chart* graphically represents the 80/20 rule, which approximates that 20 percent of the defects cause 80 percent of the issues.

     Vendor weakness (A) is unknown without more information, as is a lack of quality assurance (C). The Peter Principle (D) states that employees are promoted up to their highest levels of inefficiencies, which doesn't apply here.

134. **(A)** (A) is correct. By offering your high potential employees more challenging work, it gives them the opportunity to use their talents.

     (B) and (D) can be replicated elsewhere and therefore don't serve a retention need. (C) isn't available, because it's a flat line structure with low opportunity for advancement.

135. **(C)** The correct answer is (C). Running a pilot program allows the training designers to evaluate the relevance of the content.

     Summative evaluations (D) occur after training and include (A) and (B).

136. **(D)** The correct answer is (D). Interviewing the employees and managers will give Tanya a good idea of what to do and what not to do in the design of performance management.

     (A) and (C) both are incorrect as first steps, although they may prove to be helpful further in the process. (B) would be redundant, because she already has executive direction in the form of the strategic initiative.

137. **(B)** The correct answer is (B). Stereotypes such as these that the executives have said may be present and unaccounted for in the workplace. Although careful navigation is recommended to avoid the appearance of discriminatory practices, serving to change the attitudes of the workforce will help.

     Answers (A), (C), and (D) don't adequately address the stereotype.

138. **(C)** In the correct answer, (C), a *nondisclosure agreement* binds an employee to protect confidential information for a period of time.

     An *arbitration agreement* (A) binds an employee to an alternative dispute resolution, whereas a *noncompete agreement* (B) requires an employee to not directly compete with the business should she leave. The examples aren't objectives of the Fair Credit Reporting Act (D).

139. **(A)** Random drug screening is advisable when required by law (such as for commercial drivers), making (A) the best answer.

     (B) is known as a return-to-work test and isn't unannounced. Reasonable suspicion testing (C) is used when a trained supervisor suspects an employee is under the influence, and *blanket testing* (D) is used to regularly test all employees.

140. **(B)** The correct answer is (B). Although public workers are entitled to workers' compensation benefits, state laws mostly govern private employers regarding coverage.

     Answers (A), (C), and (D) are false.

141. **(C)** The Occupational Safety and Health Administration (OSHA) estimates that an employer can expect a six times return on the investment of a single dollar into an IIPP, making (C) the correct answer.

142. **(A)** Employers who have high injury rates will more effectively eliminate hazards if they're properly identified, making (A) the correct answer.

     Hiring a safety consultant (B) or outsourcing the employees (D) doesn't eliminate the risk. Lockout/tag-out (C) may be an appropriate solution for some, but not all hazards.

143. **(A)** The correct answer is (A). Arbini Winery transfers the risk to the insurance company by purchasing Employment Practices Liability Insurance (ELPI).

   In (B) and (C), the company attempts to minimize or avoid the risk altogether. In (D), the company decides to accept the risk.

144. **(C)** The correct answer is (C). Because the injury occurred in the work environment while changing from uniforms which was a condition of employment, and the treatment received went beyond first aid, this injury is recordable.

   Answers (A), (B), and (D) are false statements.

145. **(C)** The correct is answer is (C). OSHA standards require that employers provide gear and training to workers that come into contact with hazardous conditions at work. It isn't always necessary to hire workers with experience (A), and close supervision by management isn't realistic (B).

146. **(D)** The correct answer is (D). The FLSA defines an employee's workweek as seven consecutive 24-hour periods.

147. **(C)** The option that answers both parts of the question is (C). According to the Fair Labor Standards Act, 16-year-olds may work in most non-hazardous jobs, whereas for jobs declared hazardous by the Secretary of Labor, the individual must be at least 18. Younger workers from the age of 12 to 15 are able to work on a limited basis under the FLSA.

148. **(D)** The correct answer is (D). The Portal-to-Portal Act has four factors to use when determining compensable time in attending training programs. These factors are

   1. Attendance is outside of regular working hours.

   2. Attendance is truly voluntary.

   3. The course or seminar isn't directly related to an employee's job.

   4. The employee doesn't produce any work as the result of attendance.

149. **(B)** The correct answer is (B). The Portal-to-Portal Act requires payment for time spent in training if an employee is led to believe that his work or status would be affected by not attending.

   Employee rights under Title VII (A) are related to protected class characteristics. The question doesn't give you enough information for answer (C) to be correct, because you don't know how many hours Chris worked that week, making (C) incorrect. (D) is simply false.

150. **(C)** A *top-hat plan* is a type of executive retirement plan, making (C) the correct answer.

   It isn't based on organizational performance (A). Depending on the type of plan offered, it may be funded completely by the employer, making (B) incorrect, and it isn't a part of stock ownership (D).

151. **(B)** The correct answer is (B). *Job pricing* occurs when a new job is created or an existing job is changed to establish wage ranges that are in-line with the market.

   Job analysis (A) is part of creating a job in general, and *job ranking* (C) compares the value of jobs to one another. *Point factoring* (D) is a method used to classify jobs on an organizational basis.

152. **(A)** *Pay compression* occurs when there is a small difference in pay between employees despite tenure, education, or skills, making (A) the correct answer.

   The question referred to the external labor market, not the internal pay scales, making (B) and (C) incorrect. Cost-of-living adjustments (D) aren't based on skill sets or the availability of talent.

153. **(A)** To avoid pay compression, you should recommend to your employer regular wage surveys to increase retention and ensure equity to market conditions, making (A) the correct answer.

    Pay raises (B), pay freezes (C), and cost-of-living adjustments (D) won't adequately address the avoidance of pay compression in the future.

154. **(A)** The correct answer is (A). Young companies often don't have the cash to pay top wages for talent, and as such, make good use of equity ownership as a recruiting and retention strategy.

    Companies in a growth stage (B) are more likely to focus on pay/benefits that improve retention of key workers. Companies in the maturity stage (C) are better positioned cash-wise to offer higher base wages without the need to sacrifice equity. Equity compensation when an organization is in decline (D) wouldn't be an attractive option for new employees.

155. **(D)** The correct answer is (D). Workers' compensation insurance is required by law, whereas retirement plans are voluntary, not regulated until they're offered.

156. **(B)** The best answer is (B). Issues of compensation equity focus on both the perceived and actual fairness of outcomes.

    Ethics in this case is a matter of debate depending on the job worth (A), and the question doesn't have enough information to determine whether the practice is either discriminatory (C) or illegal (D).

157. **(C)** The correct answer is (C). Perceptions of fairness, although not reality, often drive whether or not employees are satisfied with their pay.

    (A), (B), and (D) are all examples of fairness in outcomes based on job or self worth.

158. **(A)** The correct answer is (A). The Employee Retirement Income Security Act (ERISA) requires that employees be allowed immediate access to their own contributions, but does allow a vesting schedule for employer-contributed funds, depending upon the type of plan selected.

159. **(B)** The correct answer is (B). Sales commissions can be especially difficult to track and manage for large organizations, making the use of incentive compensation outsourcing a viable option.

    The board of directors or a compensation committee often determines executive compensation (A). *Piece rate pay* (C) is a measure tied to manufacturing productivity. *Exempt* (D) is an attribute of responsibilities more than pay practices.

160. **(D)** The correct answer is (D). Outsourcing compensation and benefits responsibilities is becoming increasingly more popular. Duties commonly outsourced include supporting open enrollment, creating summary plan descriptions (SPD), and complying with COBRA requirements.

161. **(A)** The correct answer is (A). The National Labor Relations Board (NLRB) considers the use of social media by employees to discuss wages and working conditions a concerted (coordinated) protected activity.

    It isn't a violation of an employee's freedom of speech (B), because employers can prohibit some discussion as it relates to trade secrets or other confidential information, nor is it a violation of their right to privacy (C). (D) is false.

162. **(D)** The correct answer is (D). The National Labor Relations Board (NLRB) found that cautioning employees about being tricked into divulging confidential information doesn't violate employee rights to engage in protected activity.

163. **(C)** Because the complaint was about safety conditions, answer (C) is correct. The construction company settled and offered back pay and reinstatement, of which all employees declined.

164. **(C)** Fostering an open, inclusive work environment that takes into account employee opinions and needs is the foundation of union avoidance strategies, making (C) the correct answer.

Although an open door policy (A) would help, it doesn't guarantee that policy is in practice, making it not as strong as (C). A prohibition against distributing leaflets (B) must be very broad to avoid an ULP charge, and offering higher pay rates (D) doesn't address the root cause of union organizing.

165. **(D)** The correct answer is (D). An employer may be liable for a subordinate's bias even if it's unaware of it under the cat's paw doctrine. As such, it's advised that HR conduct its own independent investigation prior to taking employment action.

Respondeat superior (A) is a common law doctrine that stands for the company being responsible for the actions of its supervisors. In constructive discharge, (B), an employee quit his job due to a hostile work environment. Executive order (EO) 11246 (C) is the benchmark presidential order prohibiting employment discrimination.

166. **(B)** Known as *ex parte,* it's generally impermissible for a party to a disagreement to be deprived its ability to defend its position, making (B) the correct answer.

A *toll* (A) means that the time on the statute of limitations has run out or has been suspended. *In absentia* (C) refers to a decision being made in the absence of a relevant party to a contract or dispute. A *precedent* (D) is set based on previous court decisions.

167. **(A)** Although many attorneys recommend only giving dates of employment, title, and salary history, the best defense against a claim of defamation is factual information. For this reason, answer (A) is the most suitable.

168. **(B)** The best answer is (B). The statutory exception to at-will employment protects employees from being terminated for a discriminatory reason as set forth in equal opportunity legislation.

A *contract exception* (A) occurs when there is a violation of an employment agreement. The *public policy exception* (C) suspends at-will employment for employees who refuse to break the law or for filing a workers' comp claim. The duty of good faith and fair dealing (D) excepts at-will employment when an employer terminates an employee for an unfair or unethical reason, such as wanting to avoid the payment of a sales commission.

169. **(C)** The correct answer is (C). In *constructive discharge,* a supervisor makes working conditions so hostile or unpleasant that the employee feels he or she has no other choice than to quit.

Discrimination (A) occurs when an employee is treated adversely based on a protected class condition. *Harassment* (B) exists when an employee is subjected to sexual or hostile working conditions. *Respondeat superior* (D) is a legal condition in which employers are held responsible for their employees' actions.

170. **(A)** The best answer is (A). Having a written policy that communicates standards of behavior is often an employer's effort at compliance with labor law.

A policy doesn't change employee behavior (B) directly or improve performance, nor is it the place for written standard operating procedures (SOP) (C). Employment policies (D) may provide general guidelines for employee behavior, but it's not the main purpose for having these policies.

171. **(C)** True performance management occurs on a regular basis both on the job and through formal reviews, making (C) the correct answer. The other options, although important facets to a total performance management system, are less important in the behavior management of people.

172. **(C)** The correct answer is (C). Employees who feel valued and engaged will have a desire to learn, both on the job and through more formal training programs.

    This leads to looking forward to being at work and on time (A), regular attendance at meetings (B), and a feeling of job security (D).

173. **(B)** In this example, answer (B) is most likely to have retained this employee.

    Having a crystal ball is impossible for employers; therefore, HR professionals need to have tools at their disposal to help address issues before employees leave. In this case, a survey of department employees may have identified the travel issue, allowing for creative problem solving and solution such as job rotation (D). An annual review (C) or complaint system (A) wouldn't have adequately addressed this issue.

174. **(B)** The correct answer is (B). A *performance improvement plan* gives employees tools and feedback that are geared toward successful behavior modification.

    A PIP and discipline both provide legally defensible documentation when done properly (A) and (D), and it isn't necessarily true that employees are more receptive to performance feedback via a PIP, as in (C).

175. **(B)** The best answer is (B). The ability to observe and measure behavior allows for intervention strategies to be developed, but doesn't in and of itself correct (A), change (C), or modify (D), the behavior.

Chapter 15

Using Your Skill Set: SPHR Practice Exam I

· ·

*L*ike a professional athlete, you can train all day, but the moment of truth is all about game day. Practice exams are one of the most important tools for studying, and this chapter includes 175 questions of exam level items to use as a dry run.

These questions are designed to be difficult, because the SPHR exam is for a senior HR leader. Be mindful of the time constraints of about a minute per question, but also be sure to be thoughtful about your answers.

You may want to use a blank piece of paper to log your answers so you can take the test more than once or use the following bubble answer sheet. Check out Chapter 2 for more ideas on how to use practice exams for maximum effect. You can also go online at www.dummies.com/go/phrsphrexam for an additional SPHR practice test.

1. Ⓐ Ⓑ Ⓒ Ⓓ   36. Ⓐ Ⓑ Ⓒ Ⓓ   71. Ⓐ Ⓑ Ⓒ Ⓓ   106. Ⓐ Ⓑ Ⓒ Ⓓ   141. Ⓐ Ⓑ Ⓒ Ⓓ
2. Ⓐ Ⓑ Ⓒ Ⓓ   37. Ⓐ Ⓑ Ⓒ Ⓓ   72. Ⓐ Ⓑ Ⓒ Ⓓ   107. Ⓐ Ⓑ Ⓒ Ⓓ   142. Ⓐ Ⓑ Ⓒ Ⓓ
3. Ⓐ Ⓑ Ⓒ Ⓓ   38. Ⓐ Ⓑ Ⓒ Ⓓ   73. Ⓐ Ⓑ Ⓒ Ⓓ   108. Ⓐ Ⓑ Ⓒ Ⓓ   143. Ⓐ Ⓑ Ⓒ Ⓓ
4. Ⓐ Ⓑ Ⓒ Ⓓ   39. Ⓐ Ⓑ Ⓒ Ⓓ   74. Ⓐ Ⓑ Ⓒ Ⓓ   109. Ⓐ Ⓑ Ⓒ Ⓓ   144. Ⓐ Ⓑ Ⓒ Ⓓ
5. Ⓐ Ⓑ Ⓒ Ⓓ   40. Ⓐ Ⓑ Ⓒ Ⓓ   75. Ⓐ Ⓑ Ⓒ Ⓓ   110. Ⓐ Ⓑ Ⓒ Ⓓ   145. Ⓐ Ⓑ Ⓒ Ⓓ
6. Ⓐ Ⓑ Ⓒ Ⓓ   41. Ⓐ Ⓑ Ⓒ Ⓓ   76. Ⓐ Ⓑ Ⓒ Ⓓ   111. Ⓐ Ⓑ Ⓒ Ⓓ   146. Ⓐ Ⓑ Ⓒ Ⓓ
7. Ⓐ Ⓑ Ⓒ Ⓓ   42. Ⓐ Ⓑ Ⓒ Ⓓ   77. Ⓐ Ⓑ Ⓒ Ⓓ   112. Ⓐ Ⓑ Ⓒ Ⓓ   147. Ⓐ Ⓑ Ⓒ Ⓓ
8. Ⓐ Ⓑ Ⓒ Ⓓ   43. Ⓐ Ⓑ Ⓒ Ⓓ   78. Ⓐ Ⓑ Ⓒ Ⓓ   113. Ⓐ Ⓑ Ⓒ Ⓓ   148. Ⓐ Ⓑ Ⓒ Ⓓ
9. Ⓐ Ⓑ Ⓒ Ⓓ   44. Ⓐ Ⓑ Ⓒ Ⓓ   79. Ⓐ Ⓑ Ⓒ Ⓓ   114. Ⓐ Ⓑ Ⓒ Ⓓ   149. Ⓐ Ⓑ Ⓒ Ⓓ
10. Ⓐ Ⓑ Ⓒ Ⓓ   45. Ⓐ Ⓑ Ⓒ Ⓓ   80. Ⓐ Ⓑ Ⓒ Ⓓ   115. Ⓐ Ⓑ Ⓒ Ⓓ   150. Ⓐ Ⓑ Ⓒ Ⓓ
11. Ⓐ Ⓑ Ⓒ Ⓓ   46. Ⓐ Ⓑ Ⓒ Ⓓ   81. Ⓐ Ⓑ Ⓒ Ⓓ   116. Ⓐ Ⓑ Ⓒ Ⓓ   151. Ⓐ Ⓑ Ⓒ Ⓓ
12. Ⓐ Ⓑ Ⓒ Ⓓ   47. Ⓐ Ⓑ Ⓒ Ⓓ   82. Ⓐ Ⓑ Ⓒ Ⓓ   117. Ⓐ Ⓑ Ⓒ Ⓓ   152. Ⓐ Ⓑ Ⓒ Ⓓ
13. Ⓐ Ⓑ Ⓒ Ⓓ   48. Ⓐ Ⓑ Ⓒ Ⓓ   83. Ⓐ Ⓑ Ⓒ Ⓓ   118. Ⓐ Ⓑ Ⓒ Ⓓ   153. Ⓐ Ⓑ Ⓒ Ⓓ
14. Ⓐ Ⓑ Ⓒ Ⓓ   49. Ⓐ Ⓑ Ⓒ Ⓓ   84. Ⓐ Ⓑ Ⓒ Ⓓ   119. Ⓐ Ⓑ Ⓒ Ⓓ   154. Ⓐ Ⓑ Ⓒ Ⓓ
15. Ⓐ Ⓑ Ⓒ Ⓓ   50. Ⓐ Ⓑ Ⓒ Ⓓ   85. Ⓐ Ⓑ Ⓒ Ⓓ   120. Ⓐ Ⓑ Ⓒ Ⓓ   155. Ⓐ Ⓑ Ⓒ Ⓓ
16. Ⓐ Ⓑ Ⓒ Ⓓ   51. Ⓐ Ⓑ Ⓒ Ⓓ   86. Ⓐ Ⓑ Ⓒ Ⓓ   121. Ⓐ Ⓑ Ⓒ Ⓓ   156. Ⓐ Ⓑ Ⓒ Ⓓ
17. Ⓐ Ⓑ Ⓒ Ⓓ   52. Ⓐ Ⓑ Ⓒ Ⓓ   87. Ⓐ Ⓑ Ⓒ Ⓓ   122. Ⓐ Ⓑ Ⓒ Ⓓ   157. Ⓐ Ⓑ Ⓒ Ⓓ
18. Ⓐ Ⓑ Ⓒ Ⓓ   53. Ⓐ Ⓑ Ⓒ Ⓓ   88. Ⓐ Ⓑ Ⓒ Ⓓ   123. Ⓐ Ⓑ Ⓒ Ⓓ   158. Ⓐ Ⓑ Ⓒ Ⓓ
19. Ⓐ Ⓑ Ⓒ Ⓓ   54. Ⓐ Ⓑ Ⓒ Ⓓ   89. Ⓐ Ⓑ Ⓒ Ⓓ   124. Ⓐ Ⓑ Ⓒ Ⓓ   159. Ⓐ Ⓑ Ⓒ Ⓓ
20. Ⓐ Ⓑ Ⓒ Ⓓ   55. Ⓐ Ⓑ Ⓒ Ⓓ   90. Ⓐ Ⓑ Ⓒ Ⓓ   125. Ⓐ Ⓑ Ⓒ Ⓓ   160. Ⓐ Ⓑ Ⓒ Ⓓ
21. Ⓐ Ⓑ Ⓒ Ⓓ   56. Ⓐ Ⓑ Ⓒ Ⓓ   91. Ⓐ Ⓑ Ⓒ Ⓓ   126. Ⓐ Ⓑ Ⓒ Ⓓ   161. Ⓐ Ⓑ Ⓒ Ⓓ
22. Ⓐ Ⓑ Ⓒ Ⓓ   57. Ⓐ Ⓑ Ⓒ Ⓓ   92. Ⓐ Ⓑ Ⓒ Ⓓ   127. Ⓐ Ⓑ Ⓒ Ⓓ   162. Ⓐ Ⓑ Ⓒ Ⓓ
23. Ⓐ Ⓑ Ⓒ Ⓓ   58. Ⓐ Ⓑ Ⓒ Ⓓ   93. Ⓐ Ⓑ Ⓒ Ⓓ   128. Ⓐ Ⓑ Ⓒ Ⓓ   163. Ⓐ Ⓑ Ⓒ Ⓓ
24. Ⓐ Ⓑ Ⓒ Ⓓ   59. Ⓐ Ⓑ Ⓒ Ⓓ   94. Ⓐ Ⓑ Ⓒ Ⓓ   129. Ⓐ Ⓑ Ⓒ Ⓓ   164. Ⓐ Ⓑ Ⓒ Ⓓ
25. Ⓐ Ⓑ Ⓒ Ⓓ   60. Ⓐ Ⓑ Ⓒ Ⓓ   95. Ⓐ Ⓑ Ⓒ Ⓓ   130. Ⓐ Ⓑ Ⓒ Ⓓ   165. Ⓐ Ⓑ Ⓒ Ⓓ
26. Ⓐ Ⓑ Ⓒ Ⓓ   61. Ⓐ Ⓑ Ⓒ Ⓓ   96. Ⓐ Ⓑ Ⓒ Ⓓ   131. Ⓐ Ⓑ Ⓒ Ⓓ   166. Ⓐ Ⓑ Ⓒ Ⓓ
27. Ⓐ Ⓑ Ⓒ Ⓓ   62. Ⓐ Ⓑ Ⓒ Ⓓ   97. Ⓐ Ⓑ Ⓒ Ⓓ   132. Ⓐ Ⓑ Ⓒ Ⓓ   167. Ⓐ Ⓑ Ⓒ Ⓓ
28. Ⓐ Ⓑ Ⓒ Ⓓ   63. Ⓐ Ⓑ Ⓒ Ⓓ   98. Ⓐ Ⓑ Ⓒ Ⓓ   133. Ⓐ Ⓑ Ⓒ Ⓓ   168. Ⓐ Ⓑ Ⓒ Ⓓ
29. Ⓐ Ⓑ Ⓒ Ⓓ   64. Ⓐ Ⓑ Ⓒ Ⓓ   99. Ⓐ Ⓑ Ⓒ Ⓓ   134. Ⓐ Ⓑ Ⓒ Ⓓ   169. Ⓐ Ⓑ Ⓒ Ⓓ
30. Ⓐ Ⓑ Ⓒ Ⓓ   65. Ⓐ Ⓑ Ⓒ Ⓓ   100. Ⓐ Ⓑ Ⓒ Ⓓ   135. Ⓐ Ⓑ Ⓒ Ⓓ   170. Ⓐ Ⓑ Ⓒ Ⓓ
31. Ⓐ Ⓑ Ⓒ Ⓓ   66. Ⓐ Ⓑ Ⓒ Ⓓ   101. Ⓐ Ⓑ Ⓒ Ⓓ   136. Ⓐ Ⓑ Ⓒ Ⓓ   171. Ⓐ Ⓑ Ⓒ Ⓓ
32. Ⓐ Ⓑ Ⓒ Ⓓ   67. Ⓐ Ⓑ Ⓒ Ⓓ   102. Ⓐ Ⓑ Ⓒ Ⓓ   137. Ⓐ Ⓑ Ⓒ Ⓓ   172. Ⓐ Ⓑ Ⓒ Ⓓ
33. Ⓐ Ⓑ Ⓒ Ⓓ   68. Ⓐ Ⓑ Ⓒ Ⓓ   103. Ⓐ Ⓑ Ⓒ Ⓓ   138. Ⓐ Ⓑ Ⓒ Ⓓ   173. Ⓐ Ⓑ Ⓒ Ⓓ
34. Ⓐ Ⓑ Ⓒ Ⓓ   69. Ⓐ Ⓑ Ⓒ Ⓓ   104. Ⓐ Ⓑ Ⓒ Ⓓ   139. Ⓐ Ⓑ Ⓒ Ⓓ   174. Ⓐ Ⓑ Ⓒ Ⓓ
35. Ⓐ Ⓑ Ⓒ Ⓓ   70. Ⓐ Ⓑ Ⓒ Ⓓ   105. Ⓐ Ⓑ Ⓒ Ⓓ   140. Ⓐ Ⓑ Ⓒ Ⓓ   175. Ⓐ Ⓑ Ⓒ Ⓓ

1. What is the median number of the following series of values?

    13, 13, 14, 16, 18, 21, 24

    (A) 13

    (B) 14

    (C) 16

    (D) 18

2. A company decides to video employee testimonials asking them why they love working for the business. These videos will be posted on the company intranet to use as a recruiting tool. They are engaged in which business practice?

    (A) Marketing

    (B) Sales

    (C) Branding

    (D) Social media

3. Tailgate training conducted by a supervisor is an example of what?

    (A) Downward communication

    (B) Upward communication

    (C) Cross-functional communication

    (D) Compliance training

4. An HR professional is using a staffing agency exclusively because it gives her tickets to major sporting events four times a year. This is an example of what?

    (A) A discriminatory practice

    (B) Unethical behavior

    (C) Illegal activity

    (D) Conflict of interest

5. An ice cream company that has vendor criteria for the humane treatment of dairy cows is practicing what?

    (A) Compliance with the FDA

    (B) Food safety standards

    (C) Social responsibility

    (D) Corporate governance

6. How is a nominal group technique different from a Delphi group?

    (A) Nominal groups never meet face-to-face, whereas Delphi members do.

    (B) Delphi groups never meet face-to-face, whereas nominal members do.

    (C) Delphi members share their findings together, whereas nominal groups keep their information private.

    (D) Nothing. Nominal is another term for Delphi.

7. If the recruiting department chooses to hire one internal sales rep for every five outside sales reps, this would MOST likely indicate that the department is using what kind of HR forecasting?

   (A) Estimate

   (B) Delphi technique

   (C) Rule of thumb

   (D) Statistical analysis

8. A company with a cost-leadership strategy will MOST likely engage in which of the following HR activities?

   (A) Recruit robustly for R & D personnel.

   (B) Have a long planning horizon.

   (C) Offer less training than their counterparts.

   (D) Promote from within.

9. What calculation will tell you when a training initiative will begin to pay off?

   (A) Cost-benefit analysis

   (B) Break-even analysis

   (C) Return on investment

   (D) All of the above

10. The amount of time a company will look forward when building a strategic plan is called what?

    (A) Scanning timeline

    (B) Future forecast

    (C) Projection schedule

    (D) Planning horizon

11. Which of the following is LEAST likely to occur as the result of downsizing?

    (A) Lower operating costs

    (B) Improved productivity

    (C) Lower employee morale

    (D) Layoffs

12. Calculate the turnover rate for a company with 500 employees that had 50 FTE separate over the course of one year.

    (A) 5%

    (B) 10%

    (C) 15%

    (D) 50%

13. MVF Producers has decided to move its operations to new city. It was able to find a warehouse location that had been the site of a previous distributor, but it's going to require some major capital improvements. Which of the following statements is TRUE?

    (A) This is a brownfield operation.

    (B) This is a greenfield operation.

    (C) The company will have to pay less in city taxes because it is making improvements.

    (D) The company will have to pay more in city taxes because it will need more infrastructure.

14. A manufacturer decides to offer its items for sale through a network of distributors. Which of the 4 Ps of marketing does this represent?

    (A) Product

    (B) Placement

    (C) Price

    (D) Promotion

15. The more employees a supervisor manages, the wider the _____?

    (A) span of control

    (B) sphere of influence

    (C) job responsibilities

    (D) pay gap

16. A system that is designed to integrate multiple business functions such as HR, product planning, and sales is called a what?

    (A) HRIS

    (B) ERP

    (C) HRMS

    (D) IMS

17. An HR manager develops a document that outlines the merit of transferring corporate training to an LMS. She included market data, a cost-benefit analysis, and a list of the relevant training topics that the system would deliver. She is presenting which of the following?

    (A) Business case

    (B) Business plan

    (C) Balanced scorecard

    (D) Training assessment

18. Which element of the strategic planning process involves determining threats in the external environment?

    (A) Planning

    (B) Implementation

    (C) Evaluation

    (D) Scanning

19. What is the purpose of a transition stay bonus?

    (A) To reward employees who aren't laid off as the result of a merger

    (B) To offset the financial pressure of a layoff for a pre-determined period of time

    (C) To reward longevity to exiting employees

    (D) To encourage workers in eliminated positions to remain for a period of time.

20. ABC Industries has decided to start a new business in a foreign country. In addition to the new building, the company will be adding hundreds of long-term jobs. This is known as what?

    (A) Joint venture

    (B) Enterprise risk management

    (C) Greenfield investment

    (D) Corporate task

21. The DOD is the primary customer of defense contractors. This is an example of which of Porter's five forces?

    (A) Buyer power

    (B) Supplier power

    (C) Threat of new entrants

    (D) Rivalry

22. Buyer and supplier power are examples of what type of strategic force that affects a company's ability to compete?

    (A) Internal

    (B) Driving

    (C) Critical

    (D) External

23. What number in the following sequence is the mode?

    4 3 5 4 4 3 2

    (A) 4

    (B) 3

    (C) 5

    (D) 2

24. What is the average number of the following series of values?

    4 3 5 4 4 3 2

    (A) 4.25

    (B) 3.57

    (C) 4.17

    (D) 2

25. In which of the following ways might a company save money through a merger?

    (A) The elimination of duplicate jobs

    (B) Shared marketing materials

    (C) Co-branding

    (D) The merging of budgets

26. Outsourcing the recruiting function of human resources BEST serves which organization?

    (A) A small start-up

    (B) A company in a growth phase

    (C) An established company with a robust recruiting budget

    (D) A nonprofit organization

27. Which of the following is correlated to high employee morale?

    (A) A small number of temporary staffers

    (B) A well used employee suggestion system

    (C) High number of employee referrals

    (D) Low injury rates

28. Corporate America, Inc. is seeking to expand into the Pacific Rim starting with an outpost in Japan. The company wants to staff this location with the MOST qualified talent. This is an example of which type of staffing strategy?

    (A) Ethnocentric

    (B) Geocentric

    (C) Polycentric

    (D) Country-neutral

29. What is a host-country national?

    (A) Employees that are hired for jobs in their own country

    (B) Employees working outside of their home country

    (C) Employees that are from neither the host or home country

    (D) None of the above

30. What is another term for a parent-country national?

    (A) Inpatriate

    (B) Expatriate

    (C) Local national

    (D) Patriots

31. Which of the following activities is a strategy for managing a company that must downsize?

    (A) Attrition

    (B) Hiring freezes

    (C) Early retirement buyouts

    (D) All of the above

32. A new hire received a TNC email from the USCIS. What does he need to do next?

    (A) Provide approved documentation within 72 hours.

    (B) Contact the employer for a Further Action Notice.

    (C) Contact USCIS to contest the notification.

    (D) Visit the necessary offices to correct documentation.

33. The fundamental factor of the Uniform Guidelines on Employee Selection Procedures is that all tests must be what?

    (A) Job related

    (B) Nondiscriminatory

    (C) Predictive of success

    (D) Legally defensible

34. What option would be the MOST effective at measuring an applicant's aptitude for mathematical reasoning?

    (A) A high school diploma

    (B) An online general math test

    (C) Interview questions that ask applicants to solve equations

    (D) A paper-and-pencil test that asks math questions of the type likely to be found on the job

35. Which of the following statements about the ADA is TRUE?

    (A) The ADA requires essential functions of the job to be identified.

    (B) The ADA applies to employers with 25 or more employees.

    (C) The Office of Disability Employment Policy enforces the ADA standards.

    (D) Any person with a disability is entitled to accommodation under the ADA.

36. Which of the following statements is TRUE if an employer asks a female applicant in an interview "how many children do you have?"

    (A) The employer has discriminated against the applicant based on her family status.

    (B) The employer has violated gender discrimination laws.

    (C) The question is only a problem if the employer doesn't also ask men the same question.

    (D) The employer has not technically violated antidiscrimination laws, but the question may be evidence of intent to discriminate.

37. "This job requires that you like working with people. Do you like working with people?" This interview question is an example of what interviewer error?

    (A) Leading question

    (B) Snap judgment error

    (C) Negative emphasis

    (D) Halo effect

38. Saving money and travel costs while still being effective techniques are advantages to which of the following recruiting methods?

    (A) Virtual interviewing

    (B) College recruiting

    (C) Job fairs

    (D) Online advertising

39. Working at a popular fast-food chain is less attractive now that the chain's food has been linked to overprocessing their menu items. This is an example of what?

    (A) Employer brand

    (B) Product perception

    (C) Marketing efforts

    (D) Unethical business practices

40. Which of the following groups is required to complete an EEO-1 report?

    (A) All private employers

    (B) All public employers

    (C) Private employers with more than 100 employees

    (D) The EEO-1 report is voluntary for employers.

41. A school-to-work transition program is what type of training?

    (A) On-the-job training

    (B) Cooperative training

    (C) Classroom-based training

    (D) Apprenticeships

42. Blended learning is a mix of traditional classroom training and what?

    (A) On-the-job features

    (B) Simulations

    (C) Vestibules

    (D) Online classes

43. If an HR specialist wishes to take three months off to teach career skills at inner city schools, which program should you recommend?

    (A) A leave of absence

    (B) A sabbatical leave

    (C) A layoff

    (D) A voluntary resignation with option to rehire

44. A supervisor within your organization gave all of his employees a 3 on a scale of 5 in his performance reviews. Which error did he MOST likely commit?

    (A) Halo

    (B) Horn

    (C) Central tendency

    (D) Bias

45. Which of the following is an example of synchronous training?

    (A) Face-to-face classroom

    (B) Video conferencing

    (C) Team projects

    (D) All of the above

46. A continuing education strategy for an employee is part of what kind of planning?

    (A) Succession

    (B) Strategic

    (C) Workforce

    (D) Career

47. A student who is able to access online training via videos and discussion boards is engaged in what kind of learning?

    (A) Asynchronous

    (B) Synchronous

    (C) Distance

    (D) Independent

48. Which of the following indicators of employee job satisfaction is present when a retail store clerk is allowed to issue refunds of up to $100 without management approval?

    (A) Job enrichment

    (B) Self-direction

    (C) Autonomy

    (D) Job enlargement

49. Which of the following BEST represents task significance as a job satisfier?

    (A) The level of importance of the job

    (B) The degree to which a job has impact on others

    (C) The amount of authority a worker has in their position

    (D) All of the above

50. What does the vertical axis of the learning curve represent?

    (A) Experience

    (B) Education

    (C) Learning

    (D) Time lapse

51. The system designed to develop, implement, and measure employee performance is called what?

    (A) Human resource development

    (B) Performance appraisal

    (C) Feedback

    (D) Performance management

52. Which demographic does flexible scheduling BEST serve?

    (A) Older workers

    (B) Employees with families

    (C) Women

    (D) All of the above

53. Which of the following is NOT a goal of a performance review?

    (A) Discussing past performance

    (B) Disciplining the employee

    (C) Discussing future performance through development needs/wants

    (D) Tying performance to pay increases

54. A learning management system is BEST described as what?

    (A) A learning portal

    (B) Training receptacle

    (C) Company intranet

    (D) Human resource information system

55. An employee's desire to be well respected by others is an example of which of Maslow's levels on his hierarchy of needs?

    (A) Physiological

    (B) Self-esteem

    (C) Belonging

    (D) Self-actualization

56. An employee believes that he is the master of his own destiny. He very likely has a high what?

    (A) Opinion of his talents

    (B) Level of confidence

    (C) Internal locus of control

    (D) Context

57. A group of forklift drivers who had been with a company for five years recently discovered that their salary rates are only 5% higher than the newly hired. HR explains that it's because the market rates have substantially increased due to the shortage of qualified workers. What has occurred?

    (A) Pay disparity

    (B) Age discrimination

    (C) Pay compression

    (D) Broadbanding

58. Executive perquisites are generally _____ items.

    (A) noncash

    (B) taxable

    (C) transportation-related

    (D) deferred compensation

59. The Lilly Ledbetter Act established that the time period be 180 days for filing a charge of pay discrimination must be what?

    (A) Begin on the initial day the wage discrimination occurs.

    (B) Renew every time an employee is paid.

    (C) Begin on the employee's last day of work for wages.

    (D) Begin on the employee's first day of work.

60. A worker who sets her own hours, works for multiple customers, and has a business license is MOST likely a what?

    (A) Exempt employee

    (B) Non-exempt employee

    (C) Independent contractor

    (D) Business owner

61. A company that has a wide range of employee benefits needs should consider which of the following benefits packages?

    (A) The lowest priced

    (B) The option with the best ratio of cost to benefits

    (C) A cafeteria plan

    (D) A cash incentive to not take the company plan

62. A company is experiencing issues with employee attendance on Mondays and Fridays. Which pay-for-performance strategy is MOST likely to help with this problem?

    (A) Make a component of pay-for-performance tied to attendance.

    (B) Discipline employees who violate the attendance policy.

    (C) Reduce the team-based incentive for groups with less than perfect attendance.

    (D) Eliminate gainsharing as a possible option until overall attendance improves.

63. Which of the following is one of the primary reasons the FLSA was passed?

    (A) To provide employees with safe work

    (B) To discourage employers from requiring or abusing overtime

    (C) To streamline timecard reporting

    (D) To regulate payroll taxes through paycheck deductions

64. An employer requiring employees to sign nondisclosure agreements in order to prevent them from disclosing their pay rates does not have a high degree of what?

    (A) Ethics

    (B) Pay equity

    (C) Pay openness

    (D) Pay honesty

65. A severance benefit that gives an executive two to four times her annual salary in the event of termination is also known as a what?

    (A) Golden boot

    (B) Retirement proposal

    (C) Golden handcuffs

    (D) Golden parachute

66. A company wishing to share ownership with employees to encourage accountability should use which of the following bonus plans?

    (A) Stock options

    (B) Annual bonuses

    (C) Performance incentives

    (D) Perquisites

67. Which of the following benefits is voluntary?

    (A) Workers' compensation

    (B) Retirement

    (C) Social security

    (D) Disability

68. What is an advantage for employers that utilize lump-sum increases?

    (A) LSIs do not increase overtime costs.

    (B) LSIs can accelerate base wage progression.

    (C) LSIs are easier to track than hourly increases.

    (D) LSIs can increase pension payments.

69. Which of the following types of drug/alcohol screening is both reliable and legally defensible?

    (A) Urine

    (B) Hair

    (C) Breath

    (D) Blood

70. Which strategy would BEST protect worker and customer privacy?

    (A) Appointing a chief privacy officer

    (B) Limiting access to electronic and paper documents

    (C) Training employees on proper use of information

    (D) Having employees and vendors sign confidentiality agreements

71. An employee in good standing who has worked for a company for 20 years may not be separated under the employment at-will doctrine for what reason?

    (A) Public policy exception

    (B) Duty of good faith and fair dealing

    (C) Statutory rights

    (D) Implied employment contract

72. The duty to bargain in good faith is required of which party?

    (A) The employer

    (B) The union

    (C) The employee

    (D) Both the employer and the union

73. In the *NLRB vs. Weingarten,* what was the outcome?

    (A) The Supreme Court ruled that union members had a right to representation in a disciplinary session.

    (B) The Supreme Court held that no union presence was required at meetings that are designed to only investigate employee wrongdoing.

    (C) The Supreme Court ruled that all employees — union or otherwise — are entitled to representation at disciplinary and investigatory meetings.

    (D) The Supreme Court found that Weingarten had done nothing wrong.

74. During a union campaign, a supervisor told his employees that they were not allowed to talk about the union organizing during work, even though they are allowed to talk about other non-work related items. This is an example of what ULP from the TIPS doctrine?

    (A) Threatening

    (B) Interfering

    (C) Spying

    (D) Promise

75. In a case filed with the EEOC, it was described that a disabled worker was repeatedly called "retarded" by management and eventually terminated as a result of his disability. Which of the following did the EEOC eventually find?

    (A) Discriminatory treatment

    (B) Wrongful termination

    (C) Violation of the ADA

    (D) All of the above

76. Which of the following tools is BEST for an employee that needs an easy reminder of product codes when entering orders into the system?

    (A) Standard operating procedure

    (B) Reference guide

    (C) Policy

    (D) Work rule

77. How can HR BEST support a positive organizational climate?

    (A) Hiring the MOST qualified works for the job

    (B) Surveying employees to gain input on needs

    (C) Avoiding unnecessary policies, procedures, and rules

    (D) Implementing executive coaching activities

78. A company picnic sign posted on top of an exit safety sign is an example of what OSHA violation?

    (A) Serious

    (B) Willful

    (C) De minimus

    (D) Other than serious

79. An employer who wishes to avoid a claim of negligent hiring should conduct which of the following?

    (A) A background check on applicants

    (B) Reference checking of potential workers

    (C) School records check to verify education

    (D) All of the above

80. An employer with _____ or fewer employees does not have to keep injury and illness records.

    (A) three

    (B) five

    (C) ten

    (D) fifteen

81. Which of the following positions is considered an HR generalist?

    (A) Safety technician

    (B) LOA coordinator

    (C) HR manager

    (D) Forklift trainer

82. An employee at an insurance brokerage house is a cancer survivor. As a result, she is a strong believer in the products and services that the company offers, especially its survivor benefits and cancer insurance. She is highly invested in her clients. Which of Hofstede's dimensions exists?

    (A) Degree of identification

    (B) Degree of acceptance

    (C) Employee versus work orientation

    (D) Local versus professional orientation

83. Licensing and certification regulations of jobs may be linked to which of the following outcomes?

    (A) Slower economic recovery

    (B) Difficulties finding jobs

    (C) Higher pay rates

    (D) All of the above

84. Which statistical analysis would be MOST useful to calculate the need for employees if sales increase by a set dollar amount?

    (A) Regression analysis

    (B) Staffing ratios

    (C) Simulation models

    (D) Productivity ratios

85. A large dairy organization has a dedicated team that closely follows BEST business practices in quality assurance. Team members must have advanced degrees in dairy or quality, analyze processes, make recommendations, and implement solutions. This team is MOST likely a what?

    (A) Lean team

    (B) Community of experts

    (C) Community of practice

    (D) Center of excellence

86. The MOST important feature to the theory of economic valuation is what?

    (A) Individual preferences and choices

    (B) Market value of a nontangible item

    (C) Supply and demand

    (D) Cost to build

87. A company that uses a corporate code of conduct that includes rules for nonsegregation, fair pay, and global human rights MOST likely has adopted which of the following?

    (A) Nondiscriminatory treatment practices

    (B) Title VII of the Civil Rights Act

    (C) The Global Sullivan Principles

    (D) A greenfield operation

88. What is the relationship between the FMLA and the ADA?

    (A) Both require all employers to offer job-protected leave to affected employees.

    (B) Both govern leave laws for pregnant workers.

    (C) Neither prohibits discrimination based on race or ethnicity.

    (D) Both offer wage replacement for displaced workers.

89. An employee was passed over for a promotion because she had exercised her leave rights under the Family Medical Leave Act. What is the BEST example of the employer's unlawful act?

    (A) Retaliation

    (B) Interference

    (C) Discrimination

    (D) Harassment

90. An organization expanding into the Middle East is offering highly competitive salaries for employees who are willing to transfer for a period of three years. Based on the requirements of the foreign country, single women and homosexuals aren't eligible for transfer. What statement is TRUE?

    (A) Based on American labor law, this company is in danger of an unlawful discrimination lawsuit.

    (B) This company practice is correct, because American labor law does not apply in other countries.

    (C) Congress allowed for a foreign business exception in which American discrimination laws are suspended if compliance would violate foreign country laws.

    (D) This company should not do business in this region due to violations of civil rights.

91. Which statement is TRUE regarding partial public workers such as those paid through Medicaid to care for disabled family members?

    (A) They are still required to join the union.

    (B) They are not considered government workers.

    (C) They may only opt out of paying for purely political union activities.

    (D) They do not have to pay union dues.

92. A person who has "an ear to the people" is known as what?

    (A) Advocate

    (B) Steward

    (C) Ombudsman

    (D) Arbitrator

93. Of the following, which should be the FIRST response in an organizational crisis?

    (A) Protecting a company's financial assets

    (B) Responding to media inquiries

    (C) Communicating to stakeholders' status of response

    (D) Reporting to regulatory agencies

94. Reducing expenses and protecting company financial assets are the outcomes of which of the following risk management activities?

    (A) Establishing corporate credit policies and objectives

    (B) Providing oversight of departmental expenses

    (C) Establishing an employee code of conduct

    (D) Managing the company budget

95. A medical diagnosis is MOST likely a legitimate request for which HR documentation?

    (A) A listing of employee medications for purposes of complying with the company substance abuse program

    (B) Documenting history of workers' compensation claims

    (C) Certifying leave for a family emergency.

    (D) Requesting a doctor's certification for ADA LOA of more than three days

96. According to Bennis, which of the following elements is the LEAST important for visionary leadership?

    (A) A passion for their work

    (B) A focus on the bottom line

    (C) The ability to embrace errors

    (D) Willingness to take risks

97. Which answer is MOST reflective of a collaborative work environment?

    (A) Knowledge workers create and manual workers execute.

    (B) Information flows downward from the executive team.

    (C) Each teammate makes knowledge contributions and participates in decision-making.

    (D) Access to confidential information is restricted.

98. According to Mintzberg, mentor, disseminator, and spokesperson are examples of which management role?

    (A) Interpersonal

    (B) Decisional

    (C) Informational

    (D) Leader

99. Which of the following BEST contributes the success of an organization that is entering a new competitive market?

    (A) The presence of a strategic plan

    (B) Executive competencies

    (C) HRM policies that align with the corporate mission, vision, and values

    (D) The existence of relevant and up-to-date SOPs

100. Shared basic assumptions are BEST described as what?

    (A) Tribal knowledge

    (B) Brain drain

    (C) Cultural forces

    (D) Shared responsibilities

101. A culture of problem solving is a characteristic of what?

    (A) Quality programs

    (B) Learning organization

    (C) Good management

    (D) Employee intelligence

102. Although succession plans are necessary for all types of businesses, which of the following options would the *lack* of a succession plan have the MOST negative impact?

    (A) Small, family-owned businesses

    (B) Publicly traded corporations

    (C) Multinational corporations

    (D) Joint venture

103. Organizational development activities should focus first and foremost on what?

    (A) Financial realities

    (B) Employee development

    (C) Management development

    (D) Respect and inclusion

104. When change occurs in an organization, resistant employees often increase the old, undesirable behaviors. Why does this happen?

    (A) All employees fear change.

    (B) The company may not have communicated the expectations properly.

    (C) The employees have been conditioned (or rewarded) to behave a certain way.

    (D) The company did not hire the right people with the right attitudes.

105. An employee is required to work around a hot furnace that heats tools up above 500 degrees. When he puts on safety gloves, he can handle the hot tools without getting burned. This is an example of which of the following types of reinforcement?

    (A) Negative reinforcement

    (B) Positive reinforcement

    (C) Conditioning

    (D) Safety reinforcement

106. Which of the following measures the amount of employee performance improvement as the result of an organizational intervention?

(A) Utility analysis

(B) Cost-benefit analysis

(C) Return on investment

(D) Economic value add

107. Measuring the alignment of nonfinancial performance measurements with a company's strategic plan is BEST reported using which of the following tools?

(A) Quarterly reports

(B) Annual budget

(C) Balanced scorecard

(D) Profit and loss statement

108. Calculate the pay and benefits cost as a percentage of operating expense using this information:

Total number of employees: 30

Annual revenue: $90,000,000

Annual operating expenses: $3,600,000

Total pay and benefits cost: $1,300,000

(A) 20%

(B) 24%

(C) 36%

(D) 38%

109. A company with a decentralized approach to organizational structure is MOST likely to have which of the following?

(A) Foreign subsidiaries

(B) Flat-line structures

(C) Strategic business units

(D) A board of directors

110. You have been tasked with utilizing the Delphi technique to forecast business in the coming fiscal year. What are you MOST likely going to be doing?

(A) Interviewing management and employees

(B) Facilitating information gathering meetings

(C) Developing a series of questionnaires

(D) All of the above

111. An employer investigating a claim of harassment before terminating an employee and a company collecting financial data to use in a divestiture are examples of which of the following processes?

    (A) Legal

    (B) Ethical

    (C) Due diligence

    (D) Disclosure

112. The parent company of a foreign business must have what percent of control in order for it to be considered a subsidiary?

    (A) More than 25 percent

    (B) More than 50 percent

    (C) More than 75 percent

    (D) 100 percent

113. A gap analysis is MOST similar to which of the following terms?

    (A) Needs assessment

    (B) Core competencies

    (C) Training needs

    (D) Strategic plan

114. MartPro General is a retail giant that has such buying power that suppliers have no choice but to agree to the company's terms. This isn't the case for MartPro's smaller competitors. What is said to exist?

    (A) Monopoly

    (B) Monopsony

    (C) An unfair business practice

    (D) Discrimination

115. Which of the following statements about corporate social responsibility is TRUE?

    (A) American labor law requires social responsibility.

    (B) Ethical leadership creates profit.

    (C) Considering all stakeholder needs creates value.

    (D) Social responsibility has the MOST impact on the global landscape.

116. Strategy is to change as mission statements are to what?

    (A) Fluidity

    (B) Consistency

    (C) Necessary

    (D) Evolving

117. The HR manager of a multinational corporation has been tasked with developing a global training program that creates a shared corporate culture. She begins by surveying top management members at all locations to ask their opinions on what factors would contribute to this outcome. She is engaged in which of the following practices?

    (A) Communicating from the top down

    (B) Conducting an occupational assessment

    (C) Measuring corporate cultural intelligence

    (D) Conducting a needs assessment

118. Which of the following is MOST important critical competency when selecting virtual team members?

    (A) Independent

    (B) Technically proficient

    (C) Cost sensitive

    (D) Shared time zones

119. A candidate for an open IT position has successfully completed the first interview. She is now being asked to participate in a series of tests, which includes handling mock troubleshooting calls, coaching others on IT issues, and taking a programming quiz. She is MOST likely going where?

    (A) To a staffing agency

    (B) To a PEO

    (C) To an assessment center

    (D) To an occupational clinic

120. Marvin, a Latino VP at an elementary school, was arrested after being accused of inappropriately touching students. While out on bail, the school board decided to place him on administrative leave without pay, which subsequently led to his dismissal. Ultimately the courts found that inappropriate conduct had in fact occurred. Because he had been placed on leave prior to being found guilty, Marvin filed a charge of discrimination with the EEOC. Which of the following is the MOST likely outcome?

    (A) The school board's decision was nondiscriminatory, because the decision to suspend was based on the underlying conduct, not on the arrest.

    (B) The school board's decision was nondiscriminatory because there was no disparate impact.

    (C) The school board's decision was found to be discriminatory, because employers may not base decisions on arrest records.

    (D) The school board's decision was discriminatory, because it did result in disparate impact based on national origin.

121. The company you work for is planning a large reduction in force beginning in January. You suggest to the executive team that the company host job fairs, résumé writing workshops, and career counseling for those losing their jobs. These activities are examples of what HR activity?

    (A) Compassionate leadership

    (B) Legal compliance with WARN

    (C) Outplacement services

    (D) Recruiting

122. In the wake of September 11, 2001, many companies pulled together a group of HR professionals and executives to make quick decisions about how the terrorist attacks would affect their employees. Decisions were made about generous leave policies for the day and communicating critical information to employees. What kind of meetings and solutions occurred?

    (A) A rapid response

    (B) Ad hoc

    (C) Emergency response

    (D) Disaster recovery

123. What is the balance of probabilities in civil law?

    (A) It is the level of likelihood that a party to a dispute committed a crime.

    (B) It is when the burden of proof is upon the accused.

    (C) It is the concept that it's more likely than not that the accused caused harm.

    (D) It is when the burden of proof is upon the complainant.

124. Which of the following statements about gender identity discrimination is TRUE?

    (A) Federal law protects an individual's gender at birth.

    (B) Federal law has not yet been broadened to prohibit employment discrimination against LGBT people.

    (C) LGBT charges filed with the EEOC outpaced charges of discrimination based on race.

    (D) Gender identity discrimination is prohibited under Title VII of the Civil Rights Act.

125. Dial Corp. used a physical strength test to screen applicants for their entry-level workforce. Prior to using the strength test, 46 percent of the new hires were women. After its implementation, the hiring rate dropped to 15 percent. In addition, more than 90 percent of male applicants passed the test whereas less than 40 percent of female applicants were successful. What was the MOST likely findings of the EEOC?

    (A) That adverse impact against women had occurred.

    (B) The physical strength tests weren't job related.

    (C) The tests were appropriate because they simulated the job.

    (D) Dial intentionally discriminated against women.

126. A retail store offered Laura a position as a night sales clerk contingent upon her passing a urinalysis screen for drugs. Laura informed management that she could not produce urine because she had end stage of renal disease. The drug testing offered alternative drug screening methods if requested by the company. The company refused and Laura wasn't hired. What did the store violate?

    (A) The Family Medical Leave Act

    (B) Title VII of the Civil Rights Act of 1964

    (C) The Americans with Disabilities Act

    (D) None because blood or hair screening violates privacy laws

127. What is the BEST way to avoid a defamation lawsuit when giving employee references?

    (A) Have a policy that doesn't verify employment of past employees.

    (B) Don't allow management to give personal references.

    (C) Only verify employment with truthful information.

    (D) Give separating employees a document with final pay rate, dates of employment, and reason for termination to show future employers.

128. The purpose of the back-pay remedies of the OFCCP are to do what?

    (A) Punish an employer for unequal pay practices.

    (B) Recover damages if an employee is harmed by pay discrimination.

    (C) Make workers "whole" from discrimination.

    (D) Pay interest on lost wages.

129. High inter-rater reliability can be shown when?

    (A) Multiple interviewers reach the same or similar conclusion about an applicant.

    (B) A single interviewer reaches the same conclusion about an applicant over multiple interviews.

    (C) A test predicts a different outcome over a period of time.

    (D) The person hired has successful performance on the job.

130. Who is the employer of record in a PEO that conducts all of the administrative elements of HR, such as recruiting, processing payroll, and recordkeeping?

    (A) The business is where the work is done.

    (B) The employees are independent contractors.

    (C) The PEO is the employer of record.

    (D) It's a joint employment agreement.

131. You notice that an employee attending training does not take notes, focusing instead on what the trainer is saying. Which training technique will be MOST effective for him?

    (A) Auditory recording of the class

    (B) Graphs and charts that show pictures of the content

    (C) Hands-on training that allows him to practice

    (D) On-the-job showcase of the training techniques

132. A company in the maturity stage of the business life cycle is MOST likely to employ which employee development activity?

    (A) Technical training

    (B) Mentorships

    (C) Lifelong learning opportunities

    (D) Work-life balance

133. Which statement is TRUE about the development of high potential employees?

    (A) High potential employees will find a way to increase their own job satisfaction.

    (B) Every department has at least one high potential employee.

    (C) Having natural gifts is not enough to make high potential employees worth an investment.

    (D) High potential employees are usually supervisors or managers.

134. An insurance company that begins to offer human resource consulting and risk management consulting services is establishing itself as a what?

    (A) Preferred provider organization

    (B) Professional employer organization

    (C) Business process outsource service

    (D) Enterprise risk manager

135. What strategy would MOST benefit an organization for employees who have reached a career plateau?

    (A) Make a change into another department to learn new skills.

    (B) Find work at another company in a similar field.

    (C) Go back to school to improve their education.

    (D) Take a sabbatical to re-energize.

136. What should you do for a supervisor who is modeling the negative behaviors of his manager?

    (A) Discipline or demote him.

    (B) Coach the manager.

    (C) Assign the supervisor another mentor.

    (D) Offer development classes for the supervisor.

137. Psychological tests are high on what type of validity?

    (A) Content

    (B) Construct

    (C) Reliability

    (D) Predictive value

138. A 360-degree review is MOST useful when _____.

    (A) The position supports multiple departments.

    (B) The employee cannot be counted on to give himself a fair self-rating.

    (C) There is a performance deficiency.

    (D) The supervisor is perceived as being unfair.

139. Of the proposed training room configuration, which is the LEAST likely to encourage discussion?

    (A) Modular

    (B) Circular

    (C) Classroom

    (D) Conference

140. Why would employers choose vestibule training?

    (A) If they are limited on the space available for training

    (B) If they want to avoid the overproduction of inventory

    (C) If time constraints drive the training efforts

    (D) If they do not have a dedicated trainer

141. In forced distribution, supervisors may be required to do what?

    (A) Distribute 100 percent of their employees into three categories: 10 percent superstars, 80 percent at benchmark, 10 percent needing improvement

    (B) Rate the employees against each other on a curve

    (C) Eliminate the bottom 10 percent of their employees each year

    (D) All of the above

142. What is the first step in designing a performance-feedback process?

    (A) Analyzing the job

    (B) Aligning it to the mission

    (C) Developing the measurables

    (D) Observing employees

143. An employee refused to fill out a 360-degree assessment on his peers, feeling that it is "outside of his pay grade." What is MOST likely the problem?

    (A) The employee has low morale.

    (B) The employee does not know what is expected of him.

    (C) The employee has not accepted the process as meaningful or relevant.

    (D) The employee is not being properly supervised.

144. An employer has just completed a reduction in force and the tasks that were the responsibility of two employees has now become the tasks of one. This is an example of what?

    (A) Job enrichment

    (B) Job enlargement

    (C) Autonomy

    (D) Doing more with less

145. An employee has reported being bored in his job. His position has been adjusted to take on new responsibilities for which he will have to develop new skills that should make the job more interesting and challenging. This is known as what?

    (A) Job enrichment

    (B) Job enlargement

    (C) Job rotation

    (D) Mentoring

146. Which of the following is the BEST example of how learning occurs in a high context culture?

    (A) Learning is focused on productivity outcomes.

    (B) Learning occurs by following SOPs.

    (C) Learning occurs through on-the-job training and modeling.

    (D) Learning is focused on the technical aspects of the position.

147. If a supervisor is giving feedback to an employee about her productivity outputs, she is MOST likely measuring what?

    (A) Traits

    (B) Behaviors

    (C) Results

    (D) Characteristics

148. A manager has communicated to his production line supervisors that they must get their labor-to-sales ratio at or below 11% by the end of the fiscal year. Which of the following does this BEST represent?

    (A) Performance measure

    (B) Performance objective

    (C) SMART goal

    (D) Team objective

149. An employee is unable to pay his utility bill at home due to his low wages, and the strain is showing on the job. His supervisor tells him that if he would just learn to be a team player, others would respond more favorably to him and he could begin to apply for the higher-paying, supervisory positions. This strategy is not likely to work because the employee is at what level of Maslow's hierarchy of needs?

    (A) Psychological

    (B) Physiological

    (C) Esteem

    (D) Safety

150. The company you work for places heavy emphasis on tasks, duties, and responsibilities. What kind of culture is said to exist?

    (A) Transactional

    (B) Low context

    (C) High context

    (D) Managerial

151. A company with varying degree of employee diversity such as age, gender, and family status should consider offering what type of employee benefit plan?

    (A) PTO programs

    (B) Cafeteria plans

    (C) Flexible spending accounts

    (D) Cash-in-lieu of benefits

152. Which of the following is one challenge of pay-for-performance systems?

    (A) Employees may reject the criteria used to measure performance.

    (B) Pay for performance can only be adopted for management or executives.

    (C) Employees don't care how their performance impacts pay.

    (D) Pay-for-performance programs are very difficult to calculate.

153. How can a company resolve a long-term issue of pay compression?

    (A) Freeze raises for red-circled employees.

    (B) Regularly collect market wage data on all positions.

    (C) Terminate workers who are paid above the pay range.

    (D) Bump supervisors so the spread between supervisors and employees is greater.

154. What of the following is an example of collusion under the Sherman Antitrust Act?

    (A) A group of competitors agreeing to not offer free shipping for online merchandise.

    (B) A group of construction companies deciding who will submit the winning bid in exchange for subcontracts.

    (C) A group of hospitals in Connecticut getting together to fix the pay rates of healthcare industry workers.

    (D) All of the above are prohibited examples of collusion.

155. Your employer wants you to visually correlate employee work experience and skill development with pay increases. Which approach should you use?

    (A) Offer seniority-based pay.

    (B) Plot a maturity curve.

    (C) Review cost-of-living adjustments.

    (D) Recommend a pay-for-performance system.

156. Which of the following is TRUE of executive top-hat retirement plans?

    (A) They are funded entirely by the employer.

    (B) They are funded entirely by the employee via deferred compensation.

    (C) They must be the same plans as those offered to employees.

    (D) They are taxable at the time the money is paid in rather than when distributed.

157. Executive pay based on performance criteria that is approved by a board of directors allows companies to do what?

    (A) Include discretionary bonuses to the total reward package.

    (B) Gain a neutral perspective on what should be measured.

    (C) Deduct executive compensation in excess of $1 million.

    (D) Hold executives accountable to performance outcomes.

158. Variable pay is to voluntary what minimum wage is to what?

    (A) Performance

    (B) Deliberate

    (C) Discretionary

    (D) Compelled

159. The marketing manager's annual salary is $82,000. The range for this position is low $31.30, mid $47.91, and high $59.58. What is this employee's compa-ratio?

    (A) 55%

    (B) 74%

    (C) 82%

    (D) 121%

160. Breaking jobs down into compensable factors and then assigning weights to these factors is part of which job evaluation method?

    (A) Ranking

    (B) Classification

    (C) Point

    (D) Benchmarking

161. An employer may listen to employee phone conversations provided that what occurs or has occurred?

    (A) The employee provides signed permission.

    (B) The employer stops listening if it realizes the call is personal.

    (C) The employer notifies the employee and customers that all calls will be monitored.

    (D) All of the above

162. Which activity should be completed prior to the establishment of a peer review panel for discipline?

    (A) Have panel members sign a confidentiality agreement.

    (B) Hold a vote with the employees to select this dispute method.

    (C) Conduct a wage survey to determine how much extra pay the panelists should receive.

    (D) Select a neutral arbitrator to lead the team.

163. An employee was suspended for being found smoking in the bathroom. It was his first offense, and he appealed to the union because the punishment seemed unduly harsh. What is MOST likely driving his attitude?

    (A) Favoritism

    (B) Procedural justice

    (C) Distributive justice

    (D) Discrimination

164. A progressive discipline policy runs the risk of negating which of the following common law doctrines?

    (A) Employment at will

    (B) Respondeat superior

    (C) Duty of good faith and fair dealing

    (D) Rights granted by statute

165. One example of transferring organizational risk of wrongful termination or sexual harassment lawsuits is for HR to recommend what?

    (A) The employer provides annual supervisor training.

    (B) The company adopts a policy of zero tolerance for harassment.

    (C) The HR manager researches and recommends the purchase of EPLI insurance.

    (D) The company regularly investigates claims of harassment and only terminates for cause.

166. A union member recommended to his co-workers that he decertify the union because of lack of support from the union's elected officials. A union representative subsequently threatened that the employee was going to lose his job if he continued to try and get the union decertified. This is a violation of which of the following acts?

    (A) The National Labor Relations Act (Wagner Act)

    (B) The Labor-Management Reporting and Disclosure Act (Landrum Griffin Act)

    (C) The Labor-Management Relations Act (Taft-Hartley Act)

    (D) The Railway Labor Act

167. What is one of the primary purposes of the National Labor Relations Act?

    (A) To protect members from their union

    (B) To protect companies from union ULPs

    (C) To encourage collective bargaining

    (D) To regulate union activity

168. Having an open door policy will help in which of the following HR activities?

    (A) Training and development

    (B) Union avoidance

    (C) Productivity improvements

    (D) Improved job satisfaction

169. Union-avoidance strategies should fundamentally focus on activities that do what?

    (A) Educate workers on why unions are bad.

    (B) Weed out bad management.

    (C) Increase pay and benefits for workers.

    (D) Decrease employee dissatisfaction.

170. Which of the following statements is TRUE of employee handbooks?

    (A) A handbook protects employees from unfair business practices.

    (B) The law requires a handbook.

    (C) A handbook helps employers comply with various labor laws.

    (D) All of the above

171. Which of the following influencers has the MOST effect on an organizational climate?

    (A) Managers

    (B) Executives

    (C) Employees

    (D) Human resources

172. A legally binding method for solving disagreements between an employee and his employer is the definition of which of the following?

    (A) Mediation

    (B) Grievance proceedings

    (C) Arbitration

    (D) Alternative dispute resolutions

173. There has been a sharp decline in a previously productive employee's performance as the result of his divorce. Which of the following intervention strategies should HR recommend?

    (A) Documentation of performance to ensure consistent application of the discipline policy

    (B) Referral to the company EAP

    (C) Additional time off with pay until the issue is finalized

    (D) A layoff so he can collect unemployment while dealing with the divorce

174. Which of the following is an employee right if he is suspected of using illegal drugs on the job?

    (A) Protection under the ADA

    (B) Confidentiality

    (C) Time off to seek rehabilitation

    (D) Job protection if he successfully completes treatment

175. Which scenario is LEAST likely to be covered under workers' compensation insurance?

    (A) An injury at work due to employee intoxication

    (B) A mental stress claim due to supervisor harassment

    (C) An injury from a car accident while conducting company banking

    (D) All of the above would be covered.

Chapter 16

Answers and Explanations to SPHR Practice Exam I

Now it's time to see how you did. This chapter allows you to keep score, but it also provides you with a justification of the correct answer and explanations of the incorrect choices.

You may want to convert your score into a traditional percentage. You can easily do it by dividing the total number of correct answers by the total number of questions. For example, say that you missed 25 questions. Your score would be an 86 percent (150 divided by 175).

If you're an SPHR candidate, consider also taking the PHR exam included in Chapter 13. You really need a strong foundation, and taking practice exams can ensure that you're doing as much as you can to build your knowledge. You can also check out www.dummies.com/go/phrsphrexam for an additional practice PHR and SPHR exam.

1. **(C)** The correct answer is (C). The *median* number is the one that is found in the middle. To find it, count the total number of units and add 1. Divide this number by 2 and then find the answer by counting up. In this case, there are seven units — 7 + 1 is 8. 8 divided by 2 is 4. 16 is the fourth number on the list and therefore is the median.

2. **(C)** The employer *brand* is how a company presents itself to the public, employees, future employees, and customers, making (C) the correct answer.

   The company often uses social media (D) to accomplish it. *Marketing* (A) is the operational function of identifying what the public wants and getting the word out about a company's product and services. The *sales function* (B) is responsible for selling the goods or services indirectly through distributors or directly to the consumer.

3. **(A)** Organizational communication that flows down from management is called *downward communication*, making (A) the correct answer.

   Upward communication (B) is when information flows up the organizational hierarchy, just as through a suggestion system. *Cross-functional communication* (C) exists when multiple departments work together or have support responsibilities. *Compliance training* (D) is a specific type of training, not a form of communication (D).

4. **(D)** The correct answer is (D). HR professionals are expected to refrain from using their position for material or financial gain. When this occurs, the competing interests of the employee and the company create a *conflict of interest*.

   Her action isn't a discriminatory practice (A), which is an action taken based on a protected class status, nor is it necessarily an illegal activity (C). The decision could be an unethical behavior (B), but it's also dependent upon intent, making (D) the best answer to this question.

5. **(C)** The best answer is (C). *Social responsibility* practices focus company efforts on practices that do no harm or that positively affect the customers and communities where they live and work.

   The FDA is focused on food safety standards, more so than treatment of animals (A), (B). *Corporate governance* (D) is the balancing of needs of the stakeholders affected by business practices.

6. **(B)** The correct answer is (B). The primary difference between a nominal group and Delphi group is that participants in a Delphi group never meet, whereas nominal groups do.

7. **(C)** The correct answer is (C). A *rule of thumb* is a general principle adopted when forecasting staffing needs.

   An *estimate* (A) is a rough calculation used to make decisions, often based on historical and other statistical data (D). The *Delphi technique* (B) is a decision-making activity that involves participants that never meet to come to a group consensus.

8. **(D)** The correct answer is (D). An organization with a *cost-leadership strategy* is focused on building a stable workforce, which requires training (C) and promoting from within.

   (A) is a characteristic of a company with a differentiation strategy, not cost-leadership. A long planning horizon (B) is the amount of time a company looks ahead in its planning process and may not be the best strategy to support cost leadership.

9. **(B)** The best answer is (B). A *break-even analysis* is used to calculate when an effort will begin to make money or the break-even point at which time the activity's results have paid for the initial investment.

   Cost-benefit analysis (A) and *return on investment* (C) are used to calculate the return and benefit when compared to the initial investment.

10. **(D)** A *planning horizon* is how far into the future that a company will look at when strategic planning, making (D) the correct answer.

    Often, it's a one-, three-, or five-year view. A scanning timeline (A), future forecast (B), and projection schedule (D) are false terms for this forecasting activity.

11. **(B)** The correct answer is (B). *Downsizing* is a strategy for companies that need to realign their workforce through employee separations and job restructuring. The loss of employees often results in lower productivity for a period of time, not higher.

    It may lower short-term operating costs (A), it's accomplished by layoffs (D), and there is low morale in the employees that survive the cuts (C).

12. **(B)** The correct answer is (B). You calculate the turnover rate by dividing the total number of separations by the total number of employees.

13. **(A)** The correct answer is (A). A *brownfield operation* is one that reuses land or buildings for business, contrasted with *greenfield* (B), which is a new location where no building had previously existed. There is not enough information in the question to determine if their tax burden will be impacted (C) and (D).

14. **(B)** The placement of products refers to how the products will be offered to the consumer, making (B) the correct answer.

    The *product* (A) refers to what items or services will be sold, *price* (C) is the amount a customer will pay for a product, and *promotion* (D) is how the items will be marketed.

15. **(A)** *Span of control* refers to the number of employees, functions, or processes of which a manager is responsible, making (A) the correct answer.

    Sphere of influence (B) isn't the correct term for the definition in the example. Job responsibilities (C) and pay levels (D) aren't solely reliant upon the number of direct or indirect reports.

16. **(B)** The correct answer is (B). *Enterprise resource planning (ERP)* is a software platform designed to integrate many functions of business.

    Human resources information system (HRIS) (A) and human resources management systems (HRMS) (C) are more focused on the life cycle of the employee, from recruiting to separation. An information management system (IMS) (D) is a form of organizing the storage and retrieval of information.

17. **(A)** The correct answer is (A). A *business case* is the activity of putting together a proposal for a business activity that includes the scope, cost, and benefit.

    A *business plan* (B) is a company document that reviews the purpose of the organization and its goals and plans on how to achieve those goals. The *balanced scorecard* (C) is a set of business metrics that measures objectives, and a *training assessment* (D) measures the effectiveness of a training program.

18. **(D)** The correct answer is (D). *Scanning* involves a review of the external threats and opportunities as well as other forces, such as competition that may have an impact on a company's success within the strategic plan period.

    Scanning is a function of the *planning* process (A). *Implementation* (B) involves applying the elements of the plan to operations, and the *evaluation* stage (C) involves measuring whether or not the plan is working.

19. **(D)** The correct answer is (D). A *transition stay bonus* is used to help organizations that are closing facilities or eliminating jobs. It's a method of offering a financial incentive to employees to stay on until the process is complete.

    It isn't generally used as a recognition or reward (A) and (C), nor to offer wage replacement to displaced workers (B).

20. **(C)** The correct answer is (C). A *greenfield investment* exists when a company builds a new facility in a new location.

    A *joint venture* (A) is a partnership between two or more organizations. *Enterprise risk management* (B) is addressing the financial and operational risks of doing business. A *corporate task* (D) is a generic term for many of the activities associated with the day-to-day tasks of work.

21. **(A)** The correct answer is (A). *Buyer power* is increased when there is a low number of consumers compared to suppliers of goods or services — the buyer is able to bargain for better pricing or favorable treatment.

    Supplier power (B) is increased when there are a lot of buyers, but few providers. The *threat of new entrants* (C) refers to new competitors to a market, and *rivalry* (D) refers to the overall competitive landscape of an industry or product.

22. **(D)** The correct answer is (D). Michael Porter's five forces included *external* components, such as the level of both buyer and suppler power.

    Internal (A) forces affecting an organization's ability to compete include the presence of key people. Driving (B) and critical (C) aren't the correct terms for these strategic forces.

23. **(A)** The value that occurs most frequently in a series of numbers is called the *mode;* therefore, (A) is the correct answer.

24. **(B)** The correct answer is (B). You find the average of a set of numbers by adding all of the numbers and then dividing the total by the number of values. In this case, it's $25/7$, equaling 3.57.

25. **(A)** The best answer is (A). A common side effect of a merger is redundancy in support functions such as accounting or human resources. For this reason it becomes necessary to eliminate roles that are redundant.

    A shared (B) or unified (C) brand in options and the merging of budgets in (D) don't directly have an impact on cost savings.

26. **(B)** The correct answer is (B). A company in a growth phase may need access to talent fairly quickly and may not have the dedicated HR resources for the time-consuming task of hiring multiples such as (C) or (D). A small start-up (A) may not have the finances to pay for outsourced services.

27. **(C)** The best answer is (C). If employees are happy with their boss and company, they're more likely to refer qualified individuals from their personal network for open jobs.

    A small number of temporary staffers doesn't directly influence employee morale (A), nor is a suggestion system (B) a strong measure of employee satisfaction levels. Injury rates (D) are better correlated to a company's safety programs than to the company climate.

28. **(B)** The correct answer is (B). A *geocentric* staffing strategy seeks to hire the most qualified talent for key positions, regardless of nationality.

    Ethnocentric (A) fills key positions with parent-country nationals. In (C), the company would use Japanese talent to fill key positions at the outpost and American talent at corporate headquarters. Answer (D) is a distractor because there is no such staffing strategy.

29. **(A)** The correct answer is (A). *Host-country nationals* are employees working in the country of their birth.

    Employees working outside of their country of origin (B) are known as *expatriates,* and *third-country nationals* (C) are employees that aren't from either the home or host country.

30. **(B)** If corporate headquarters are in the same country as an employee's birth, and this employee is working at a global site, the employee is known as an *expatriate* or a *parent-country national,* which makes (B) correct.

    Inpatriates (A) are actually out of their *patria* (fatherland). *Local nationals* (C) are those employees that work in their home country. A *patriot* (D) is one who passionately defends his country, not a term that applies to global staffing strategies.

31. **(D)** The correct answer is (D). Companies that decide to downsize may do so by not replacing employees who quit or retire, known as *natural attrition,* freezing all hiring for current openings and offering early retirement buyouts to reduce employee headcount.

32. **(B)** The correct answer is (B). A *tentative nonconfirmation (TNC) email* will be sent to an employer and new employee if there is a record mismatch on Form I-9 documents. The employee should receive and review a Further Action Notice from the employer and make a decision about what to do to correct the findings. New hires have 72 hours to provide required documentation to employers (A) to complete Form I-9/eVerify. The employee shouldn't contact the USCIS (C) or visit the necessary offices for correction (D) until he knows what further action to take.

33. **(A)** The correct answer is (A). The *Uniform Guidelines on Employee Selection Procedures (UGESP)* require that any pre-employment requirement be linked to the required knowledge, skills, and abilities of the job.

    Doing so ensures that the tests are nondiscriminatory (B) predictors of success (C) on the job that will increase the likelihood of being legally defensible (D).

34. **(D)** The correct answer is (D). The closer pre-employment tests match the job, the more likely they are to be an effective predictor of future performance success. The UGESP require that pre-employment tests are job related.

    A high school diploma (A), online general math test (B), and interview questions (C) aren't the most reflective of the type of work to be done on the job.

35. **(A)** The correct answer is (A). The Americans with Disabilities Act (ADA) doesn't require that employers have written job descriptions. However, it does require that the essential functions of the job are identified and documented. Written job descriptions that exist prior to a charge of employment discrimination can be used to demonstrate compliance with the standards.

36. **(D)** The correct answer is (D). Technically, the employer hasn't done anything wrong by simply asking the question as in (A) and (B); however, if the employer uses the information to make a hiring decision, it will have unlawfully discriminated based on a protected class status. In addition, the EEOC has found that asking these types of questions may be used as evidence of intent to discriminate. For this reason, employers should avoid asking questions about protected class status in interviews of either men or women (C).

37. **(A)** (A) is correct. This is an example of a leading question, in which the interviewer *leads* the applicant down the path of the correct answer.

   A *snap judgment error* (B) occurs when the interviewer jumps to a conclusion about an applicant without probing for further information. *Negative emphasis* (C) occurs when the interviewer places more decision-making weight on a negative aspect of an applicant. The *halo effect* (D) is the opposite; the interviewer places heavy emphasis on a candidates positive traits.

38. **(A)** (A) is correct. The Internet has opened a host of lower cost recruiting options such as virtual interviewing. A first interview using an online program such as Skype allows for a quasi face-to-face interview without the investment of a full travel commitment.

   College recruiting (B) and job fairs (C) often require onsite efforts. Online advertising isn't characterized by its cost savings (D).

39. **(A)** The correct answer is (A). The image of the employer within the community can drive recruiting efforts. People don't want to work for companies that have a negative image or that are perceived to have a poor reputation within the community.

   Product perception (B) and marketing efforts (C) both relate directly to the company's products or services more so than company reputation. This scenario isn't an example of an unethical business practice (D).

40. **(C)** The correct answer is (C). Employers with more than 100 employees excluding state and local governments and primary and secondary school systems, institutions of higher education, Indian tribes, and tax-exempt private membership clubs other than labor organizations generally must file the EEO-1 report.

41. **(B)** The correct answer is (B). *Cooperative training* occurs when schools align their curriculum and activities with practical, real-world scenarios of work.

   On-the-job training (A) is learning that happens on the job. *Classroom-based training* (C) happens in a formal classroom setting, not necessarily in partnership with a vocation. An *apprenticeship* (D) is a paid position in which the person learns while on the job.

42. **(D)** *Blended learning* is growing because it utilizes both traditional classroom time and virtual or online options, making (D) the correct option.

   On-the-job training (A) is paid training that occurs while doing the actual work. *Simulations* (B) are practice runs of the work off the line or by using examples. *Vestibule training* (C) is a production training method that uses simulation techniques off the line.

43. **(B)** The correct answer is (B). *Unpaid sabbaticals* are underutilized tools that can help employers retain key employees who wish to develop or apply their skill set toward socially or personally rewarding activities. Used often in the academic world, they're becoming a more popular option in the business community as well.

   Formal sabbatical leave as a benefit is paid, whereas leaves of absence (A) are generally unpaid. (C) and (D) are more a form of company downsizing.

44. **(C)** The correct answer is (C). Rating all employees right down the middle is a strategy often used by supervisors who wish to avoid conflict, or by new supervisors who haven't had adequate time to assess employee performance. This strategy is an error because it doesn't accurately distinguish between employee work behaviors.

   In the *halo effect* error (A), the rater places heavier value on an employees positive characteristics, and the *horn* effect (B) is just the opposite. All of these rater errors are a form of rater bias (D).

45. **(D)** (D) is correct. Any method of training that occurs in real time — instructor-based or teams — is *synchronous* learning.

46. **(D)** The correct answer is (D). There are several options to creating a successful career plan. These options include formal and informal education opportunities, on-the-job training, and new job responsibilities.

    Succession plans (A) are used by organizations to develop employees while planning for replacement of key positions. *Strategic plans* (B) are a tool used by companies to manage threats and maximize opportunities. *Workforce planning* (C) evaluates the current skillset of the workforce and compares it to future needs to fill in any possible gaps.

47. **(A)** (A) is correct. *Asynchronous learning* occurs when students are able to access the training material at their own pace. It doesn't require logging in at the same time as the instructor or participating in real-time discussions like *synchronous training* (B).

    The participant not being at the same location as the instructor characterizes *distance learning* (C), and *independent learning* (D) isn't a formal term of the different types of learning methods.

48. **(C)** *Autonomy* is a job satisfier because employees are granted the authority to act in certain situations, making (C) the correct answer. One advantage of autonomy is that trusting the employees often results in ownership over the outcomes.

    Job enrichment (A) involves an expansion of job responsibilities, not necessarily an expansion of employee judgment or decision-making. *Self-direction* (B) isn't the proper term for job satisfiers, and in *job enlargement* (D), work tasks are added to an employee's existing job.

49. **(B)** The correct answer is (B). *Task significance* is measured by the impact the work has on the lives of others. Examples include working with the ill or in a socially responsible position. Employees with high levels of task significance report higher levels of job satisfaction and are less likely to leave their work.

    Job importance within the organization (A) is similar, but it's not the primary characteristic of task significance. Authority doesn't play an important role (C).

50. **(C)** The correct answer is (C). A *learning curve* is a graphical representation of the rate of learning and its impact on outputs.

    It doesn't represent the experience (A) or education level (B) of participants, nor is it representative of a time lapse (D).

51. **(D)** The correct answer is (D). A *performance-management system* is the framework from which performance feedback is given.

    Human resource development (A) is the name for the functional area of human resources. Activities include training, development, discipline, and formal appraisals. A performance appraisal (B) is a feedback (C) tool for use within the system.

52. **(D)** The correct answer is (D). Job sharing, phased retirement, and working from home are all flexible-scheduling options that may serve a broad demographic in a workforce made up of a highly diverse group of individual needs.

53. **(B)** The correct answer is (B). Although a *performance review* is designed to communicate both positive and negative information about past performance, it isn't a tool for discipline. Employees should have a basic understanding of their performance status prior to being given a formal appraisal.

54. **(A)** (A) is correct. A *learning portal* is a place where training participants are able to access training program materials and track progress.

    (B) isn't a training term. A company intranet (C) and HRI system (D) are both vehicles for accessing training rather than a build-out of learning content.

55. **(C)** The correct answer is (C). Maslow described a hierarchy of needs that serves to drive employee behavior.

    After the lower needs of physiological (A) or safety is met, the higher needs declare themselves. Being respected by peers creates a sense of belonging, which in turn serves as a motivator. This includes the need to feel confident (B). Self-actualization (D) is the highest point of Maslow's pyramid, representing achievement of one's full potential.

56. **(C)** (C) is correct. An *internal locus of control* is defined by an individual's belief of his ability to affect the outcomes of his job and career. Individuals with a high internal locus of control believe that they can positively affect their level of success both in life and on the job.

    The question doesn't speak to opinion (A) nor does being the master of one's destiny necessarily correlate to a high degree of confidence (B). *Context* (D) is a term used to describe cultures, not individuals.

57. **(C)** The correct answer is (C). *Pay compression* occurs when a company's existing pay rates don't keep pace with the market.

    (A) and (B) are forms of discrimination based on protected class characteristics. (D) is a pay strategy used to group like jobs into ranges.

58. **(A)** The correct answer is (A). *Perquisites* are generally noncash items that aren't taxed as income.

    They include cars, housing, executive memberships, and other status items, not just transportation (C). (B) is tricky because it could also be correct, but perks are more characterized as noncash items than being taxable. Perks (D) aren't a form of deferred compensation.

59. **(B)** The correct answer is (B). The Lilly Ledbetter Act, also known as the Fair Pay Act, established that the 180-day statute of limitations for filing a charge of pay discrimination resets every time an employee is paid.

60. **(C)** The correct answer is (C). Several factors will help HR professionals determine if a worker is an independent contractor or employee. The easiest way is to think of a plumber. To find a plumber, you'll probably look for his advertisement. When you call, the plumber will tell you when he will arrive. The plumber will have a license number, set his own schedule, and be allowed to work for multiple customers at once. These factors all indicate the worker is a legitimate independent contractor.

    Exempt (A) and non-exempt employees (B) are pay classification categories for employees that generally don't work for others, similar to a business owner (D).

61. **(C)** A *cafeteria plan* allows employees to select and therefore customize a benefits package that suits their needs. Older workers may be more interested in prescription coverage, whereas a family with young children may desire a lower deductible.

    Therefore, (C) best serves a broad range of needs based on employee demographics. Any option that focuses on price (A) instead of scope may not be broad enough to meet the needs of the employees (B). A cash incentive (D) doesn't meet the benefits needs of the workers.

62. **(A)** The correct answer is (A). Transparency and clear expectations are critical to successful pay-for-performance systems. In an environment with narrowly focused attendance problems, such as high absenteeism on Mondays or Fridays, the issues are best addressed through direct and honest action.

    Discipline as a form of training isn't a pay strategy, making (B) incorrect. Reducing team-based incentives (C) and eliminating gainsharing (D) payments for individual infractions will be perceived as unfair and doesn't address the individual issue.

63. **(B)** The correct answer is (B). The Fair Labor Standards Act (FLSA) was passed to accomplish three things: discourage the use of child labor, discourage the use of overtime, and establish a minimum wage.

64. **(C)** *Pay openness* refers to the degree of transparency employers have as it relates to employee pay rates, making (C) the right answer. Other elements of pay openness include communicating pay policies and having procedures on how pay rates are decided.

    Confidentiality in pay isn't an ethical issue (A). *Pay equity* (B) refers to the perceived or real fairness of pay between employees. *Pay honesty* (D) is an answer distractor, and not a legitimate term.

65. **(D)** The correct answer is (D). A *golden parachute* is used in executive contracts to offset risks inherent to higher level positions. These risks include the availability of similar high paying job and the termination due to a company acquisition.

    There is no such thing as the golden boot (A). A retirement proposal (B) isn't a type of severance benefit. Golden handcuffs (C) keep executives via payment of bonuses, not offer wage replacement upon separation.

66. **(A)** The correct answer is (A). Employee stock options grant employees ownership shares of publicly traded companies. Because they now own shares in the company, it's a form of equity compensation.

    Annual bonuses (B), performance incentives (C), and perks (D) aren't equity rewards.

67. **(B)** (B) is correct. Retirement benefits such as IRAs and pensions are offered at the discretion of the employer and not required by federal or state law. After the plans are offered, however, the government regulates these plans.

68. **(A)** The correct answer is (A). Giving employees a lump-sum increase at the end of each year rather than a wage can hold down costs related to hourly pay, including overtime and pension payment calculations.

    LSIs don't accelerate base pay growth (B), nor are they necessarily easier to track (C). An increase in pension payments (D) isn't an advantage for employers.

69. **(A)** The correct answer is (A). These tests are able to focus on detecting a broad panel of drug use without unintentionally revealing genetic information or other irrelevant information.

    Hair screening (B) can't be used to test for alcohol, and breath testing (C) is most commonly used to determine alcohol impairment. The use of blood tests (D) is more invasive and therefore more likely to result in privacy issues than the other types of testing.

70. **(B)** In risk management, the best solution is the one that eliminates the choice, making (B) the correct answer.

    A chief privacy officer (A) isn't the most realistic solution for many companies. Both (C) and (D) are viable options in protecting privacy, but they are behavior-based, which makes them less reliable as a safeguard than removing the risk altogether.

71. **(D)** An *implied employment contract* can be created when an employee has longevity with a company, if a supervisor promises continued employment as long as she does her job well, or if she receives favorable performance reviews, making (D) the correct answer.

    The *public policy exception* (A) to employment at-will protects workers from being fired for complying with the law. The *duty of good faith and fair dealing* (B) is the concept that parties to a contract must deal honestly with each other. *Statutory rights* (C) are rights granted by law, such as the right to vote.

72. **(D)** The correct answer is (D). Both the employer and the union are required to bargain in good faith during negotiations of an agreement, which includes coming prepared to the meetings and sending participants who have the authority to act on behalf of the company and union members.

73. **(A)** The correct answer is (A). Known as *Weingarten rights,* union members have the right to representation if they're asked to participate in a meeting that they reasonably believe may lead to discipline.

74. **(B)** The correct answer is (B). The TIPS doctrine is an acronym used to describe unfair labor practices. *Interfering* with an employee's right to engage in union organizing is an unfair labor practice.

    Interference includes prohibiting the employee from discussing the union on work time if they're allowed to talk about other non-work related subjects. Employers also may not *threaten* (A) employees with termination or shop closing, *spy* (C) on employees to gain information, or *promise* (D) workers more pay or benefits in exchange for keeping the union out.

75. **(D)** The correct answer is (D). In *EEOC vs. Swissotel Employment Services, LLC,* the EEOC ordered Swissotel to pay $90,000 to a disabled worker who was discriminated against under the ADA and wrongfully terminated.

76. **(B)** The correct answer is (B). A *reference guide* is a tool used to communicate concentrated, highly relevant information for employees to do their jobs.

    Standard operating procedures (A) are used to document and train on formal processes. A *policy* (C) is used to communicate employee and employer rights and responsibilities and often include work rules (D), such as employee codes of conduct.

77. **(C)** The correct answer is (C). The organizational climate is easily described as the temperature of the workplace. Surveys, focus groups, and staff meetings are all ways HR can best gather input from employees and measure how well or how poorly the company is doing.

    Hiring the most qualified workers (A) is a sound business practice to ensure employee fit and product quality. Surveying employees to gain input (B) is an important activity to measure the organizational climate. Executive coaching activities (D) may not always be necessary or appropriate, and they're often used as an intervention rather than prevention strategy.

78. **(C)** The correct answer is (C). *De minimus* violations are those that are technically out of compliance with OSHA standards but not a direct threat to employee safety or health.

    Serious violations (A) are those that are likely to cause employee injury, and willful violations (B) are those in which the employer knew of a threat to employee safety, but didn't take steps to correct it. Other than serious (D) are violations of standards that aren't likely to cause death or serious injury but still a hazard to employees.

79. **(D)** The correct answer is (D). Claims of negligent hiring arise when an employer hasn't taken due diligence to screen potential hires.

    Background checks (A), reference checking (B), and verification of education credentials (C) all help minimize claims of negligent hiring.

80. **(C)** The correct answer is (C). Employers with ten or fewer employees are partially exempt from maintaining injury and illness records. However, any fatality or illness requiring hospitalization of three or more employees must be reported.

81. **(C)** The correct answer is (C). An HR manager is generally responsible for more than one HR function.

    There are many types of safety specialists, including technicians (A), injury and other types of leave coordinators (B), and safety trainers (D).

82. **(A)** The correct answer is (A). Hofstede described the degree to which an employee identifies with her organization as characterized by feeling connected with a company's values, products, services, and clients.

    The *degree of acceptance* (B) is focused on leadership styles. *Employee versus work orientation* (C) is a management perspective that is focused on the completion of tasks, and the dimension of *local versus professional orientation* (D) refers to the degree to which an employee identifies with her business unit or location rather than the company as a whole.

83. **(D)** The correct answer is (D). Jobs that require specific licensing or certifications may have impact on the rate of economic recovery because not enough qualified workers meet the requirements (A). It can be argued, however, that qualifying the workforce through licensees and certifications better controls the type of recovery that occurs.

    Regulations also may make it more difficult for those without licenses or certifications to find work (B) and require higher pay rates (C) to recruit qualified talent, which makes (D) the best answer.

84. **(A)** The correct answer is (A). A *regression analysis* makes a comparison of past relationships to other components. In this example, the analysis would compare number of employees to gross sales.

    Staffing ratios (B) are used to identify labor support needs, such as the number of sales reps per customer. *Simulation models* (C) attempt to mimic a situation in order to anticipate outcomes, and *productivity ratios* (D) calculate output per employee.

85. **(D)** The correct answer is (D). A *center of excellence* is a team of experts brought together to achieve a specific business objective.

    Lean (A) refers to a quality program that focuses on the elimination of process waste. *Community of experts* (B) refers to a group of cross-functional subject matter experts on a broad topic such as organizational development. *Community of practice* (C) is a group of people that share a profession, grouped together inside or outside of the organization.

86. **(A)** The correct answer is (A). In valuating items, an individual choice or preference will drive the value. High preferences of one item over another will increase the value.

    The *market value of a nontangible item* (B) is the attempt to measure the worth of a non-physical item, such as holding a patent. *Supply and demand* (C) refers to the availability of a good or service (supply) compared to the desire for that good or service in the market (demand). *Cost to build* (D) is a tangible financial measure that calculates the cost to build a product (raw material, labor ancillary expenses).

87. **(C)** The correct answer is (C). The Global Sullivan Principles were enacted to promote economic, social, and political justice by companies that do business globally.

    Nondiscriminatory treatment practices (A) are required by Title VII (B) as efforts of compliance with American labor law. A *greenfield operation* (D) refers to the start-up of a new operation at another location.

88. **(C)** The correct answer is (C). Neither the Family Medical Leave Act (FMLA) nor the Americans with Disabilities Act (ADA) prohibit discrimination on the basis of race or ethnicity. Both FMLA and the ADA require covered employers to grant medical leave to an employee under certain circumstances. (A) is incorrect because the ADA applies to employers with 15 or more employees, and the FMLA applies to employers with 50 or more workers. The ADA doesn't cover pregnant workers because pregnancy by nature is a temporary state (B). The FMLA is unpaid leave, making (D) an incorrect answer.

89. **(B)** The best answer is (B). Under the Family Medical Leave Act, *interference* occurs when an employer restrains, denies, or retaliates against an employee who exercises his rights under the law.

    Retaliation (A) occurs when an employer punishes an employer for exercising his rights under a law. *Discrimination* (C) happens when an employment decision is based on a protected class condition. Harassment (D) is hostile behavior on the part of an employee or co-worker in the workplace.

90. **(C)** The correct answer is (C). Discrimination prohibitions of Title VII, the Americans with Disabilities Act, and the Age Discrimination in Employment Act may be different for business operating in foreign countries.

    In general, companies aren't required to comply with these laws if doing so would violate the laws of another country, making (A) incorrect. Some labor laws do apply in other countries, so (B) is incorrect. (D) is an unlikely and unrealistic outcome in today's global society.

91. **(D)** In *Harris vs. Quinn,* the Supreme Court found that partial public workers may opt out of joining a union and not be required to pay union fees, making (D) the correct answer.

92. **(C)** (C) is correct. An *ombudsman* is a neutral employee who serves as an impartial problem-solver within organizations.

    An employee *advocate* (A) can be anybody within the company, including an HR professional. A *union steward* (B) is both an employee of the company and a union official representing union members. An *arbitrator* (D) is a neutral individual used in alternative dispute resolution proceedings.

93. **(A)** (A) is the first response.

    Protecting a company's financial assets allows the company to continue business operations, which will frame its responses to the media (B), communicate status to the stakeholders (C), and help to provide thorough information to regulatory agencies (D).

94. **(A)** The correct answer is (A). Establishing company credit policies and objectives can help to reduce expenses by looking at loan or credit fees and establish credit use rules.

    Providing oversight of department expenses (B) and managing the company budget (D) are overreaching examples of HR's authority. An employee code of conduct (C) isn't primarily a risk-management activity.

95. **(D)** The correct answer is (D). A general diagnosis isn't considered an unlawful medical inquiry under the ADA, provided that it's consistently applied and only requests information about the nature of the illness.

    Inquiring about current meds (A) or medical history (B) may be an unlawful inquiry, and the FMLA limits the amount of information that an employer can request in a medical certification (C).

96. **(B)** The correct answer is (B). Warren Bennis believed that visionary leaders have a passion for their work, are able to embrace mistakes, and are willing to take risks, making (B) the least important piece of visionary leadership.

97. **(C)** The correct answer is (C). A *collaborative work force* is characterized by the idea that all workers are knowledge workers, regardless of their production capacity.

    Organizations that segment employees by thinkers and doers (A) and a downward flow of direction from management (B) are characteristics of a less collaborative workplace. Restriction to confidential information (D) isn't a characteristic of a collaborative work environment.

98. **(C)** The correct answer is (C). Mintzberg classified management into three categories. *Informational* leaders are tasked with the processing of information, both inbound and outbound.

    Interpersonal (A) leaders are focused on the relationships between people, and *decisional* (B) leaders use the information and relationships to make decisions. (D) isn't one of Mintzberg's management roles.

99. **(A)** The correct answer is (A). The presence of a strategic plan, especially when entering a new competitive market, is the best option to contribute to the company's success.

    Executive competencies (B) impact a company's success, but without a strategic plan that includes company performance metrics, it may be difficult to measure. The strategic planning process is often where the mission, vision, and values are developed (C) and where the external market is scanned for potential threats and opportunities. From this plan, policies may be developed and operationally, SOPs established to meet the goals of the strategic plan (D).

100. **(C)** Schein best describes shared basic assumptions as beliefs and behaviors that are deeply embedded into organizational culture, making (C) the best answer.

     Tribal knowledge (A) exists when most work is done from the intelligence of the workers, not from written procedures. A *brain drain* (B) is said to occur when talent leaves a company or a country, particularly on a regional scale. *Shared responsibilities* (D) is the obligation of two or more employees to complete a task or duty, often present in a team environment.

101. **(B)** The correct answer is (B). A *learning organization* is characterized by a culture of problem solving by subject matter experts, which includes learning and growing from the mistakes.

     It takes a whole system view of the work, including the existence of quality management program (A) and a strong management team to support these objectives (C). Employee intelligence (D) isn't a factor in developing a culture of problem solving and learning.

102. **(A)** Although having succession plans in place is important for all businesses, the best answer is (A).

     Larger companies (B) and (C) and joint ventures (D) are more likely to have talented individuals in place should death or disability occurs in the top ranks. This may not be the case for small, family-owned businesses.

103. **(D)** The correct answer is (D). Organizational development (OD) is about making changes through people, process, or companywide interventions. A successful OD program is built on a foundation of respect and inclusion.

     Financial realities (A) may not support OD actions even though they may be necessary. (B) and (C) will be part of an overall OD strategy, but they aren't necessarily the foundation of OD efforts.

104. **(C)** The best answer is (C). An *extinction burst* occurs when an employee increases the frequency and force of the older, undesirable behavior because she has been conditioned to expect certain outcomes using that behavior. Think of a soda machine as an example. When you drop in your coins and push the button, you expect a soda.

     If the soda isn't delivered, you may push the button several more times and with more force. Some employees actually welcome change, making (A) incorrect. Although communication (B) and hiring right (D) are keys to successful change management, employees will still need time to embrace the new behaviors.

105. **(A)** The correct answer is (A). *Negative reinforcement* is the process of removing something when an employee behaves in a certain way. It also occurs when a behavior prevents something from occurring, as in the example.

     Positive reinforcement (B) occurs when an employee is rewarded by the addition of a desirable incentive for the correct behavior. *Conditioning* (C) is the overall theory of motivation under which positive and negative reinforcement are components and isn't the best answer for this question. *Safety reinforcement* (D) isn't part of the theory of operant conditioning.

106. **(A)** The correct answer is (A). *Utility* is a term that can mean useful or satisfactory. It's this description that makes a utility or *usefulness* analysis the appropriate tool when measuring the amount of movement an intervention affected in employee performance.

     A *cost-benefit analysis* (B) measures the value of inputs when compared to outputs, as does *return on investment* (C). An *economic value add* (D) refers to the economic model used to calculate profit when compared to the cost of capital.

107. **(C)** The correct answer is (C). A *balanced scorecard* helps a company look at nonfinancial measurements. It can be designed to report on many factors, such as customer service, employee training, and development and process efficiencies.

     Reports that are on a timed scheduled, such as quarterly (A), annual (B), and end-of-year P & L (D), generally report on financial criteria to measure success.

108. **(C)** The correct answer is 36 percent. You calculate it by dividing the total operating expenses by the total pay and benefits cost.

109. **(C)** *Strategic business units (SBU)* are specialized divisions of an organization that make their own decisions about their products, services, and finances, which makes (C) the correct answer. Although still responsible to top management, the company has a higher degree of control over most business elements. It often has an independent mission statement and strategic plan.

     A decentralized structure isn't directly linked to foreign subsidiaries (A) or the existence of a board of directors (D). A *flat-line structure* (B) is another way to organize leadership and can exist in both centralized and decentralized structures.

110. **(C)** The correct answer is (C). The *Delphi technique* involves creating a series of questionnaires that are circulated among experts.

     In a traditional approach to this system, the experts don't meet so you won't need to directly interview individuals (A) or facilitate meetings (B).

111. **(C)** *Due diligence* is best described as an investigation to collect information, making (C) correct.

     Due diligence will satisfy legal (A) and often ethical (B) or financial disclosure requirements (D) as well.

112. **(B)** The correct answer is (B). A *foreign subsidiary* is defined as a company that is more than 50 percent owned or controlled by a parent company in another country.

113. **(A)** The correct answer is (A). A *needs assessment*, also referred to as a *gap analysis,* is used to compare the current state to a desired future state. It may be used to review a company's core competencies (B) as part of the strategic planning (D) process. Training needs (C) are identified through a training needs assessment.

114. **(B)** The correct answer is (B). A *monopsony* exists when there is a large buyer of goods and services, whereas a *monopoly* (A) exists when there is a single seller. Discrimination (D) isn't occurring, and an unfair business practice (C) is dependent on multiple factors.

115. **(C)** The correct answer is (C). When the needs of stakeholders such as customers, vendors, and the communities from which companies operate are considered, value — including profit — is created.

     American labor law (A) doesn't require specific efforts toward social responsibility per se, but rather offers guidance in areas, such as global (D) practices in the area of wages and working conditions as part of compliance efforts. No direct correlation exists between ethical leadership and profits (B).

116. **(B)** Unlike company strategies, a corporate mission statement communicates the purpose of the organization and is unlikely to change often, making (B) the correct answer.

     Fluidity (A) and evolving (D) imply movement rather than a stable guide. The term in answer (C) is irrelevant, because it's neither stable nor moving.

117. **(D)** This HR manager is most likely conducting a training needs assessment, so the correct answer is (D).

     Top-down communication (A) occurs when information flows from upper management down through the ranks. An *occupational assessment* (B) screens for required job competencies, and *cultural intelligence* (C) refers to a person's ability to function in culturally diverse situations.

118. **(A)** The correct answer is (A). The need for virtual team members to be highly independent is in the very nature of their work. A virtual team can be spread out among different time zones, and there is very little day-to-day direction, which means team members must be able to work independently and manage their own goals and outcomes.

     Technical proficiency (B), being aware of costs (C), and existing in the same time zone (D) are all important, but less likely to influence positive performance than an ability to work independently.

119. **(C)** The correct answer is (C). An *assessment center* is less of a place and more of a series of activities designed to measure a candidate's job related competencies through tests and simulations.

     Staffing agencies (A) and professional employer organizations (PEO) (B) are employers of record and most likely to process new hire paperwork than they are to assess for proficiencies. An occupational clinic (D) is used at the pre-hire stage to conduct employee physicals and drug screens.

120. **(A)** The correct answer is (A). The EEOC found that the school board's decision was based on the underlying conduct, not the fact of the arrest (C) or his national origin (D), and concluded that no discrimination had occurred.

     Disparate impact occurs when a seemingly neutral employment decision results in a discriminatory outcome against a protected class group, not individual, so (B) is incorrect.

121. **(C)** The correct answer is (C). *Outplacement services* are a strategy that HR uses to help exiting employees make the transition into job seekers. Activities include allowing unemployment departments or other organizations to come in and interview skilled workers and help them build their résumés.

     Outplacement assistance is less a factor of compassionate leadership (A) or a function of recruiting (D). The Worker Adjustment and Retraining Notification Act (B) doesn't require outplacement assistance when laying off workers.

122. **(B)** The correct answer is (B). *Ad hoc* meetings or solutions aren't planned and are generally in response to a specific issue or event. A helpful way to remember this is that the term *ad hoc* means *for this*.

     Rapid response (A), emergency response (B), and disaster recovery (D) are all terms that refer to action plans in light of an emergency.

123. **(C)** The correct answer is (C). Civil law differs from criminal law in the level of proof that must be present. In civil law, if there is a dispute between parties to an employment contract, the case is decided based upon the balance of probabilities; if it's more likely than not that the accused caused the harm, the court can uphold a civil claim.

124. **(D)** The correct answer is (D). The EEOC has interpreted Title VII of the Civil Rights Act of 1964 to include protections for lesbian, gay, bisexual, and transgender workers.

125. **(A)** The correct answer is (A). In this scenario, the EEOC found that adverse impact against women had occurred as the result of a pre-employment test that, although job-related, were significantly more difficult than the job itself. On a side note, (A) is the only answer to which the question gave you enough information to decide.

126. **(C)** The correct answer is (C). The EEOC found that the retail store violated Laura's rights under the Americans with Disabilities Act for failing to reasonably accommodate an otherwise qualified applicant's needs.

     She wasn't eligible for protection under the FMLA (A) because she had not worked for the employer for 1,250 hours in the previous 12 months, nor do you know if she was a member of a different protected class to know if (B) is correct. (D) isn't a true statement.

127. **(C)** The best defense against a defamation lawsuit is the truth, making (C) the correct answer. Employers can avoid defamation lawsuits by keeping accurate records and providing objective information when giving an employment reference on a past employee.

     Although many lawyers would say (A) is the best way to handle these calls, doing so isn't always realistic, especially if it conflicts with required reference information such as background checks for childcare workers or substance abuse records for commercial drivers. (B) and (D) aren't bad strategies, but (C) is the best answer.

128. **(C)** (C) is correct. The goal of orders of back pay to remedy past discrimination is to make the affected employee *whole,* which may include awarding interest, benefits, lost overtime, or hourly pay rates. The Office of Federal Contract Compliance (OFCCP) is one such group under the Department of Labor that may use back pay to remedy discriminatory pay practices.

129. **(A)** The correct answer is (A). When more than one person interview a candidate and everyone agrees or shares similar opinions about the qualifications of the candidate, a strong *inter-rater reliability* is said to exist.

    It isn't shown if one interviewer feels the same way after multiple interviews (B), nor is it related to the actual test reliability as in (C). The interview is considered valid if the person hired has successful performance on the job (D).

130. **(C)** The correct answer is (C). In a true professional employer organization (PEO) relationship that is primarily administrative in scope, the PEO remains the employer of record.

    Joint employment (D) may become a reality if the businesses share employees to get work done or the PEO has the right to hire, terminate, or manage the actions of the employee. Where the work is done (A) isn't the primary factor of determining the employer of record. Independent contractors (B) are self-employed.

131. **(A)** The correct answer is (A). *Auditory learners* learn best by hearing the information.

    Although graphs and charts (B) and hands-on training (C) are useful tools, this employee would best be served by a recording. *On-the-job training* (D) is more of a tactile and visual learning method.

132. **(B)** The correct answer is (B). *Mentorships* are useful for a company that has a depth of talent from which to draw. A formal internal or external program can help develop high potential employees and serve a corporate succession plan.

    Technical training (A) may be more necessary for business start-ups and companies in growth mode. *Lifelong learning* (C) is a state of existence that can occur at any business life cycle stage, as is the need for *work-life balance* (D), which is the ability of workers to find harmony between their work and off duty time.

133. **(C)** The correct answer is (C). Having natural talent isn't enough of a reason to identify and develop high potential employees (HiPo). A strong work ethic, level of motivation, presence of a support team, and other factors must be considered when selecting high potential employees to invest in.

    HiPo can actually get bored and move on if not properly managed and developed (A). They can exist anywhere in the organization, not necessarily by department (B) or in the ranks of management (D).

134. **(C)** The correct answer is (C). BPOs are becoming a more popular option for outsourcing back office functions such as HR and accounting. Some professional organizations serve as a BPO, and companies simply expand upon their current offerings, such as insurance providers and IT groups.

    A *preferred provider* (A) is a medical group that is within an insurance company's network. A *professional employer organization* (B) is a form of employee outsourcing by using a third-party employer of record. An *enterprise risk manager* (D) isn't a term used to describe general management positions.

135. **(A)** The correct answer is (A). Individuals who have reached a career plateau have a decision to make: Should I stay or should I go? Often, finding a way to re-energize and motivate seasoned workers who still have more to give is best, so transferring the employee into another department re-enforces the organizational commitment on both sides and most benefits the company.

    Without a win-win strategy, the employee may choose to find work in another field (B), and the talent will exit. He may also go back to school to improve his education, which may or may not benefit the organization (C). Taking a sabbatical leave (D) isn't the best choice from the company's perspective, because it leaves a temporary void to be filled.

136. **(B)** (B) is correct. The best answer in this scenario is to provide coaching to the supervisor's manager. All employees learn from behavior modeling to some extent, so providing coaching to those in leadership positions is a quality investment for overall employee behavior.

   Discipline or demotion (A) shouldn't be the first step because the employee may be trainable. Assigning the employee another mentor (C) doesn't support a long-term outcome of developing both the employee and manager. (D) eventually may be necessary, but it's best to use the situation as an opportunity to develop and enhance the relationship between the worker and his manager.

137. **(B)** The correct answer is (B). A *construct* is a psychological concept that can't be traditionally measured, such as in pounds or inches. An example is employee motivation. Because psychological tests regularly measure what they say they're going to measure, they have high construct validity.

   Content validity (A) differs in that it doesn't review the outcome of a psychological test, but rather that the tool is comprehensive enough to capture all angles of a concept. *Reliability* (C) is said to be high when the test — over a period of time — consistently measures what it says it's going to measure. *Predictive value* (D) is the degree to which a positive or negative test correlates to the predicted future behavior.

138. **(A)** The correct answer is (A). A *360-degree review* gathers data from the multiple stakeholders dependent on job performance. It allows for an accurate and relevant view from those most affected by employee behavior.

   Because multiple raters are involved in giving a 360-degree review, the decision shouldn't be dependent upon an employee's ability to judge his own performance (B). Any review format should be able to adequately respond to employee performance deficiencies (C), and supervisor bias should be addressed with the supervisor, not by changing methods (D).

139. **(C)** Traditional *classroom-style* seating (C) is best used for lecture training in which minimal participation is required.

   Modular set-up (A) encourages small group discussion, and the *circular set-up* (B) invites face-to-face participation, similar to the conference room setting (D).

140. **(B)** The correct answer is (B). Training on the line can result in an overproduction of inventory, causing cash flow and other production issues. *Vestibule training* occurs in a simulated environment, independent of real-time production. Vestibule training isn't characterized by space (A), time (C) or trainer issues (D).

141. **(D)** *Forced distribution* is a ranking tool that evaluates employees within a department against each other. It's generally represented as a bell curve. Often, supervisors must discipline or eliminate the bottom 10 percent of employees who are at the needs improvement level of performance.

142. **(A)** The correct answer is (A). Knowing what each job entails and the subsequent identification of the roles and responsibilities is an important first step to designing an accurate, relevant, and meaningful feedback system.

   Alignment to the mission (B) of the organization is a secondary priority of a feedback system, after it's patterned off the job requirements. Creating performance measurables (C) would be difficult until the job analysis is complete. (D) is a method that can be used to complete the job analysis.

143. **(C)** The correct answer is (C). Employees must accept the methodology of the performance-feedback process. If it lacks relevance or meaning to their day-to-day job, they will be more reluctant to fully engage in the process.

   (A), (B), and (D) aren't related to the assessment, making them incorrect.

144. **(B)** The correct answer is (B).

    Job enlargement differentiates itself from job enrichment (A) in that it's driven by the quantity of work, not necessarily the quality of work. *Autonomy* (C) is the degree of decision-making authority an employee has. (D) isn't an example of job satisfiers/dis-satisfiers.

145. **(A)** The correct answer is (A). In *job enrichment,* the quality of the work is improved or serves the employee's career development versus the job specific tasks required on a day-to-day basis, as is the case with job enlargement (B).

    Job rotation (C) is when employees are cross-trained in multiple jobs and rotate through them on a regular basis. *Mentoring* (D) is a development activity that involves performance coaching another employee or subordinate.

146. **(C)** (C) is correct. A *high-context culture* is characterized by shared knowledge and outcomes; therefore, behavior modeling on the job is the best answer.

    A focus on productivity (A), standardized procedures (B) or the technical aspects of a job (D) are more closely related to low-context cultures.

147. **(C)** The correct answer is (C). Several different types of behaviors are measured when giving performance feedback. *Results-based feedback* is often focused on quantifiable elements of the job such as productivity. (A), (C), and (D) are measures of people or jobs rather than output.

148. **(C)** The correct answer is (C). SMART goals are specific, measurable, attainable, relevant, and time-based. Although goals may be used to measure performance, in this example multiple factors beyond a single employee's performance will be necessary to achieve this goal. Examples include overtime management and proper workforce planning.

    A performance measure (A) or objective (B) is identified as part of the SMART goal. In this case, the objective is to hit the 11% target. The question doesn't focus on team goals (D).

149. **(B)** The correct answer is (B). Maslow theorized that until an employee's lower needs were met, the employee couldn't be motivated by higher needs, such as safety (D), esteem (C), belonging, or self-actualization. In this scenario, the supervisor's efforts to address the employee's deficiencies addressed the symptom, not a root cause, thereby making the strategy less likely to succeed. Maslow's hierarchy doesn't have a psychological need (A).

150. **(B)** The correct answer is (B). A *low-context culture* is characterized by dependence on standard operating procedures and accomplishing goals.

    This is in contrast to a *high-context culture* (C), where the emphasis is placed on collaboration and the relationships that must exist to get things done. (A) is a style of leadership, and (D) serves as a distractor.

151. **(B)** The best choice is (B). *Cafeteria plans* allow employees to select benefits that best suit their needs.

    Paid time off (PTO) programs (A) and cash-in-lieu of benefits (D) may be valued more by some than by others, so they aren't good answers. Flex spending accounts (C) don't address the diversity component of the question, so it's not a good option.

152. **(A)** The correct answer is (A). Employees spend a lot of time in a pay-for-performance environment trying to actively work the criteria to their advantage or to focus on the job outputs that best serve the incentive. (B), (C), and (D) are not necessarily true statements.

153. **(B)** The correct answer is (B). Employers who regularly survey and respond to market pay rates are less likely to experience an issue of pay compression. Building this in as a regular activity helps to avoid the issue altogether and ensure pay equity when compared to market rates.

    Red-circled employees (A) are paid above the pay grade for positions, but freezing their raises only addresses the immediate issue. Terminating workers who are paid above the grade may result in disparate impact if they're older workers (C). Increasing supervisors without market data or based on performance creates higher overhead without long-term resolution to the issue (D).

154. **(D)** The correct answer is (D). The Sherman Antitrust Act prohibits wage fixing, price fixing, bid fixing, and other types of activities that negatively affect another person such as the consumer or employee. For employers, this means that wage surveys must be strategically designed to avoid inadvertent collusion.

155. **(B)** The correct answer is (B). A *maturity curve* is closely related to seniority; however, it has the advantage of increasing employee pay based on skill development, not length of service. It isn't a true pay-for-performance system because it also rewards years of service through work experience.

156. **(A)** (A) is correct. *Top-hat executive retirement plans* are nonqualified plans that are funded entirely by the employer. They offer retirement benefits above and beyond that of traditional plans such as IRAs or 401(k)s.

157. **(C)** The correct answer is (C). The Omnibus Budget Reconciliation Act of 1993 sought to eliminate the ability of organizations to deduct executive compensation in excess of $1 million unless it was qualified as performance-based.

    Discretionary bonuses (A) aren't tied to performance, and a board isn't necessarily the most neutral body to determine performance criteria (B). (D) is trickier but it's a more subjective answer than (C).

158. **(D)** The correct answer is (D). Variable pay such as bonuses and incentives are part of a total compensation package that is negotiated between an employer and employee. Employers are compelled to pay employees only a minimum wage for work. Minimum wage isn't tied to employee performance, (A), nor is it deliberate (B) or discretionary (C).

159. **(C)** This manager's compa-ratio is 82 percent of the midpoint range for the position. You find the compa-ratio by dividing the employee pay by the midpoint of the range for the position. In this example, you need to convert the annual salary to an hourly rate by dividing it by 2,080 working hours in a year. The formula then becomes $39.42 divided by $47.91 multiplied by 100 to get a percentage.

160. **(C)** Identifying the degree of importance of job factors and assigning relevant weights are activities of the point method of pricing jobs, making (C) the correct answer.

    Ranking (A) is the easiest form of job classification methods, simply requiring ordering the jobs by level of importance. The classification method of *job evaluation* (B) is more difficult, requiring employers to group jobs with similar tasks into job classes for comparison. In benchmarking (D), employers attempt to categorize jobs by similar characteristics.

161. **(B)** (B) is correct. Employers aren't fully restricted from listening to employee phone calls at work with one exception. If the employer is monitoring a call and realizes the call is personal, the employer must immediately stop listening.

162. **(A)** The correct answer is (A). *Confidentiality agreements* are an important step to engaging a peer review panel as an alternative to traditional corporate disciplinary action. These agreements ensure that the data reviewed at the meetings will be treated as confidential information.

    A vote (B) isn't necessary to approve a method for discipline unless it's part of the collective bargaining and ratification process. Additional pay (C) for sitting on a peer review panel isn't required by law so it can be determined at the discretion of the employer. A peer review panel doesn't have to have a neutral arbitrator (D).

163. **(C)** In *distributive justice,* employees have issues with the perceived fairness of the distribution of outcomes, making (C) the correct answer. If the employee believed that the punishment fit the crime, he would have been more likely to respond by modifying his behavior in response to the discipline.

    Favoritism (A) would be the correct answer if the question pointed you in the direction of mistrust of the supervisor. (B) would be correct if the employee felt the procedure used to decide his punishment was the focal point. Unfair treatment based on a protected class status would have to be present in order for (D) to be correct.

164. **(A)** The correct answer is (A). This common law doctrine allows for any parties in employment to terminate the relationship at any time and for any reason. Policies that promise a series of disciplinary actions dilute the employer's ability to terminate at will.

Respondeat superior (B) stands for *let the master answer.* It's a legal principle that holds the employer responsible for the behavior of supervisors. The *duty of good faith and fair dealing* (C) is the doctrine that requires parties to a contract to act in an honest manner with each other. *Rights granted by statute* (D) refers to the definition of a law.

165. **(C)** The correct answer is (C). Purchasing employment practice liability insurance is the only example given that transfers the risk to another agency — in this case, the insurance. The other answers relate to avoiding or mitigating the risk of harassment and other types of adverse employment actions.

166. **(B)** The correct answer is (B). Union members are allowed to dissent with their union and engage in protected activities, such as expressing their view on the activities of union officials. The Labor-Management Reporting and Disclosure (Landrum-Griffith) Act protects these rights.

The National Labor Relations Act (Wagner Act) (A) granted workers the right to organize and have rights established through the collective bargaining process. The Labor-Management Relations Act (Landrum-Griffith) (C) sought to balance the power of unions with employer rights. The Railway Labor Act (D) was a cooperative effort between existing unions of the times and the railroads (eventually adding airlines) to minimize disruptions to transportation caused by striking workers.

167. **(C)** The correct answer is (C). The NLRA was passed to protect an employee's right to organize. This right included protecting the collective bargaining process from companies who would refuse to bargain in good faith.

The Labor Management Reporting and Disclosure Act was designed to safeguard members from union corrupt practices (A) and to identify union unfair labor practices (B). The Labor Management Relations Act sought to regulate union activity (D).

168. **(B)** The correct answer is (B). Having a well-utilized open door policy in which employees are encouraged to talk to management about their concerns is one way to avoid the unionization of the workforce.

Training and development activities (A) aren't directly related to open door policies, nor are productivity improvements (C). Improved job satisfaction (D) is a trickier answer because job satisfaction and unionization are often linked; however, it's a subset of union avoidance, making (B) the best choice.

169. **(D)** The correct answer is (D). Employees join unions because they believe a union can improve their working conditions — pay, benefits, hours, and managers. Therefore, union-avoidance strategies should focus on listening to what employees need and responding accordingly.

Educating workers (A) should focus on why the company wishes to remain union free. (B) and (C) are viable options, but both are efforts linked to the correct answer.

170. **(C)** The correct answer is (C). Although not directly required by a single labor law, a handbook helps employers comply with multiple requirements of having certain policies and communicating said policies to employees.

171. **(A)** The correct answer is (A). Managers have the most effect on organizational climate because they work directly with the human talent. As a result, they're responsible for multiple climate factors including improving employee morale, celebrating successes, and avoiding dysfunctional turnover.

Executives (B) and human resources (D) exist at more of an arm's length from the day-to-day operations of an organization, making them less influential on climate than managers. Employees (C) are the subject of the question, not a direct influencer.

172. **(C)** The correct answer is (C). *Arbitration* is a binding legal proceeding in which both parties agree to engage should a dispute arise.

    Along with nonbinding mediation (A), it's a type of alternative dispute resolution (D). Grievance procedures (B) are nonbinding.

173. **(B)** The best answer is (B). *Employee assistance programs* are used to help employees who are experiencing personal issues.

    Preparing for the discipline process (A) is too soon, because this employee is normally a productive worker. Paying the employee to take time off (C) is unreasonable, and manufacturing a layoff (D) is an unethical solution to this issue.

174. **(B)** The best answer is (B). Even if the suspicions are proven, all employees have the right to have their medical information kept private. The Americans with Disability Act (A) specifically excludes current users of illegal drugs from its protections.

    Time off to seek rehabilitation (C) is the right of the employer to decide, and employees who use illegal substances at work have no job protection requirement under the ADA (D).

175. **(A)** The correct answer is (A). In general, an injury that occurs at work due to employee behavior such as drinking, fighting, or other horseplay may be denied coverage under the employers workers' comp insurance.

    Mental stress claims (B) and car accidents (C) while under the control of the employer are both most likely covered if they're proven to be work related.

Part V
The Part of Tens

If you're one of the millions of people with access to some form of mobile technology, you probably have your smartphone right by you. Refer to www.dummies.com/extras/phrsphrexam for a list of the top smartphone apps to use while getting ready for your exam. From organizational tools to social media, something is out there that can replace the traditional textbook only way to prepare.

In this part . . .

- ✔ Figure out where to go to get started on the application process so you know how long you have to prepare.

- ✔ Identify what you need to gear up to study for the important test and then implement some helpful study tips.

- ✔ Strategize on ways to reach out for support and get your work or family ready for your intense new schedule

- ✔ Enhance your efforts by taking advantage of Internet resources that build on exam-related topics.

Chapter 17

Ten PHR/SPHR Exam Pitfalls and How to Avoid Them

- -

In This Chapter
▶ Identifying common exam snags
▶ Strategizing to avoid common mistakes
▶ Anticipating exam day hurdles

- -

T he exam format can ambush even the best-laid plans. Know that both the PHR and the SPHR exams are designed to test your knowledge and competencies, not to measure whether you're a good test taker or not. Having said that, you should be aware of several exam-specific pitfalls. Note that awareness without action is pointless, so this chapter focuses on a few of the most common snags you should prepare to avoid.

Sitting for the Wrong Exam

If you're planning on taking the SPHR, be aware that you must prepare for *all* of the exam content, with very few exceptions labeled *PHR only* in the exam body of knowledge (BOK). For this reason, take both a PHR and SPHR assessment exam *prior* to applying for your exam. After you take both assessments, you can compare your PHR score to your SPHR, using that information to decide on which exam to take. Keep in mind that your goal in taking these assessment exams is not to *pass* them. Your goal is to identify your current knowledge levels and use that information to decide which exam to take and then to create a study plan and timeline based on the assessment results.

The investment of both your time and dollars can motivate some individuals to leap right into the SPHR exam water, but the resource investment shouldn't be the primary driver of your final exam choice. Think of the certification process as a marathon, not a sprint — a long-term career goal that may take a few years to achieve.

Check out the online cheat sheet at www.dummies.com/cheatsheet/phrsphrexam for more help and information on choosing the right exam to boost the odds in your favor.

Underestimating Exam Preparation Time

Test takers often misjudge how much time they need to prepare for taking the test. Unfortunately, there is no way to pinpoint exactly how much or how little prep time you may need. I can only offer you an educated perspective based on my own exam preparation experience, the reports of other exam survivors, and industry best practices:

- **My own experience:** I sincerely wish that I had my own *For Dummies* resource when I sat for the PHR and the SPHR exams. Understanding the 50,000-foot view would have helped me drill down into the boots-on-the-ground exam prep and better understand what I was up against. Here is a short list of what I did to prepare:

  - The first textbook I used was the *PHR/SPHR Professional in Human Resources Study Guide* by Anne Bogardus (Sybex/John Wiley & Sons, Inc.), mainly because the $30 or so price tag was just about what I had to spend in my prep budget. I had the privilege of updating this same book for the last review period. Bogardus covered many of the main points covered in the exam objectives, and in most cases, she helped illuminate concepts for which I needed more resources.

  - The second textbook resource was *Human Resource Management* by Robert L. Mathis and John H. Jackson (Southwestern Cengage Learning). I credit their work with teaching me about business management and strategy. Here is where I first discovered the life cycle of the employee and Michael Porter's five forces, concepts I use still today in my work as a consultant and author. If you want baseline knowledge similar to what you would find in an MBA course, start here. For those individuals on a budget, consider the previous edition rather than current, but don't go back more than one edition.

  - When I sat for the PHR in the days of the dinosaur, the Internet wasn't the viable resource that it is today. For the SPHR, I accessed government websites and printed fact sheets on labor laws. I researched strategy and the concept of HR as business partners.

  - I reviewed flashcards while eating breakfast. I recorded myself reading exam prep material and listened to it while driving. I made myself worksheets and matching games and worked them while waiting for dinner to cook. In all, I spent between 12 to 14 hours studying per week, but I spent many more hours immersing myself in the subject material. For both exams, I finished well under the time limit and passed on the first try. Regardless of the outcome, I recognized that this accelerated-immersion approach taught me more than I ever thought there was to know about the field of human resources, and I'm a better professional as a result of the dedicated study time.

- **Reports of exam survivors:** Several different online forums are available of people sharing their prep experience. I also have first-hand reports from individuals who have taken my prep classes. Their time commitment varied from the superstars of 20-plus hours to those who came at it when they had a chance. The average seemed to be about 12 to 14 hours per week over a four-to-six-month period. In addition, all of the successful exam takers couldn't emphasize enough the importance of taking practice exam after practice exam. They shared in frustration that *none* of their study materials covered *all* of the material on the exams, which is why practice exams from multiple resources can help increase your chances of seeing familiar material on the tests.

- **Industry practices:** As a general guideline, most exam preparation programs run about 14 weeks. With six functional areas and the core knowledge requirements, it equates to about two weeks per topic. Chapter 2 also gives you pointers on how to build a custom study plan designed around your strengths and weaknesses. In addition, the HR

Certification Institute (HRCI) sells a booklet titled *The Official PHR and SPHR Certification Guide,* which I highly recommend that you put it into your budget. It not only has sample test questions, but it also gives you excellent samples of an eight-, ten-, and 12-week study schedule for both exams.

How much time each week to dedicate to your studies is largely dependent on your comfort level and initial assessment scores. Understanding your time/assessment score data and applying it to your study plan is critical because no single resource is customized to your existing knowledge levels; you must be the captain of your ship. Remember, authors of exam prep material aren't granted special access to exam content. We build the material from years of experience, thought leader interviews, industry best practices, and most importantly, the exam bodies of knowledge.

Unlearning State Specific Applications

Both the PHR and SPHR exams are written to federal law. State laws in similar areas must meet or exceed the federal guidelines, and as an HR practitioner in California, I had to practice setting aside my West Coast ways and relearn some of the HR basics. Differences such as minimum wage, overtime, and safety were very real obstacles to baseline knowledge. Creating a cheat sheet of labor laws in your state that are different from the federal standards is worth your study time. Taking your time navigating these test questions can also help you spot multiple choice answers that are correct in your state, but not at a federal level.

Getting Tripped Up: The Perils of Overthinking

Overthinking both the question stem and the options is a very real threat to a passing score. The answers are intentionally written with *distractors*, which means more than one answer could be correct, and that all answers make sense. When you come up against these issues, keep the following in mind:

- **Don't linger on the answer choices.** If you understand what the question stem is asking, you should be able to quickly narrow down the answers to the two most likely correct options. Spend your minute-or-so-time-per-question strategy noodling through those two choices, rather than trying to interpret and compare all four options.

- **Go back and re-read the question, focusing on the verbs.** Are they asking you to design a solution? Or act on a complaint? Perhaps they want you to diagnose a problem or assess a need? The verbs are your *call to action* and the best answer will usually be the tool to do so.

- **Focus also on the subject of the question stem.** Is it written from the perspective of a boss or an employee? A regulatory agency may even be driving the issue. The expectations of people and agencies you serve in your day-to-day activities are different, depending on the origin of need.

These strategies may work in the scenario-based questions, but they aren't necessarily the best option on the questions that are testing your knowledge. The good news is that these question tend to be easier, because the answers are often objective, right-or-wrong types of choices. Subjective judgment or critical thinking is less important. In this case, your best defense is being prepared, and practice exams are the most effective way to do so. Refer to Chapter 3 for more in-depth strategies for answering different types of questions.

Playing the Guessing Game

As someone who writes test questions, I can tell you that I spend a ridiculous amount of time reviewing my answers to ensure that the proper mix of multiple choice options are presented on the practice exams. Don't listen to the so-called experts that say that option C is the most often correct choice because it's just not true. The only way to successfully guess on these exams is to properly eliminate the obvious incorrect answers first.

If you have narrowed down your answer to the two best choices and still just aren't sure, try using the answer in a sentence. Draw upon the question stem and plug in the answers to see which one fits best. Look for the option that fully addresses what the question is asking.

Your final option is to mark the question for review and hope that as you move through the rest of the exam, your memory will be jogged or, better yet, you'll find the answer in another related question. Whatever you do, don't leave a question blank. Make your best guess, mark it for review, and come back to it later. If you run out of time before you have a chance to review, you lose the opportunity entirely to get the answer correct.

Trusting Your Instinct

Read each question once or twice to ensure that you know what it's asking. Before looking at the multiple choice options, answer the question in your mind. Then review the answers for the one that most closely aligns with your first instinct. If you have scratch paper available, consider writing down your answer before you review the options and work through the question as though it were a puzzle. Why did you answer it the way you did? What logic or criteria did you call upon to find your answer? As with most of these strategies, the first time to practice them should not be on test day. Take a practice exam or chapter review questions while practicing this approach to see if it works for you.

Many test takers report having a gut feeling about which answer is correct. Trust this feeling when you have exhausted the other options that I recommend here. You have spent many hours studying this material and are a seasoned HR professional, so go with your intuition when necessary.

Changing Answers

When you take the PHR or the SPHR, you have the ability to mark questions for review at the end to go back and take a second look. This strategy is extremely valuable when you aren't sure of an answer, but you need to move on. Reviewing questions is also handy if more than one exam question is related to the one on which you're stuck, and you can find the answer somewhere else in the exam. Changing answers works for some, but not for others, so you need to know where you stand with this strategy before your exam date. Here are a few perspectives from both sides.

Speaking from experience, I can't change my answers. I get flummoxed too easily. Although I did pass my exams when I took the PHR and SPHR, I certainly didn't ace them. I was also finished more than an hour before the time limit. For this reason, if I had to do it again,

I would use the mark for review feature more often. You don't want to be in the position of failing this exam by only a few points, and one or two questions may tip the scales in your favor.

On the other hand, a research study that appeared in the *Journal of Personality and Social Psychology* conducted over a 70-year period suggests that exam takers that change their answers go from wrong to right 51 percent of the time, so if you feel compelled to make the switch you should do so.

I also recommend that you read an excellent article about other multiple choice, test-taking tips at www.socialpsychology.org/testtips.htm#taking.

If you do decide that you need to change an answer, be very thoughtful before clicking the radial button and making a change. Try to link the question and options back to the exam objectives and make the argument both for and against the change to be certain that you want to do so.

If you didn't mark the question for review, don't go back and change an answer. You were confident enough in your first pass to not mark it for review, so trust your knowledge and run out the clock on the ones you definitely were sure in your answer.

Focusing Too Much on the Clock

You have a little more than a minute per question, and some questions take longer to answer than others. Many test takers fall victim in watching the clock too closely, which distracts them from answering questions, so you need to figure out how closely you should watch the clock or not.

The best advice is to take at minimum two simulation exams. In one, watch the clock. In the other, don't watch the clock. At the end of both exams, ask yourself the following questions:

- ✔ Did you feel more pressure when you were watching the clock?
- ✔ Did watching the clock make you work faster?
- ✔ Were you more likely to mark an answer for review and move on when watching the clock?
- ✔ How much review time did you have left on both exams?

I'm a huge fan of balance, and this advice will serve you well. A healthy blend of keeping your eye to the hourglass without overthinking it allows you to react quickly if you need to speed up without dominating your thought process. Don't let the clock force you into making riskier choices than are necessary, but also don't linger on questions that stump you.

Be sure and select an answer for every question; don't leave one blank. If you have to make an educated guess, mark it for review later, but take your best guess just in case you run out of time and can't go back. Refer to Chapter 1 for more information about the exam scoring and Chapter 3 for more tips on dealing with the unknown.

Managing Distractions

Part of your studying efforts should be figuring out how to tune out your personal distractors. The first step is to discover what bothers you and figure out ways you can block them out.

For me, my distractors are my phone and hunger. The phone isn't allowed in the exam room, so if your phone is one of your distractors, then you won't have to deal with that distractor while taking the test. If you study or take practice exams with your phone on, you aren't properly applying yourself to exam day conditions. Turn it off, hide it, do whatever you have to do so that you're training yourself to live without it on game day.

Hunger is also solvable. Although your nerves may not allow you to eat a large meal prior to the test, I encourage you to be prepared. Low blood sugar or just a growling stomach can detract you from the total mind focus that these exams demand of you. You can't take food into the exam room, but you can have a healthy snack in the locker.

Room temperature can also be a major distractor because being too hot or too cold is uncomfortable. Plan accordingly and dress in layers on exam day so that you can adapt quickly and easily. Be sure and bring a light sweater that you can take off, and wear pants that are comfortable to sit in for a three-hour stretch.

Plan to take a quick break at the halfway point to eat some raw almonds or choke down a string cheese and bottle of water. Protein is your best choice for a quick brain boost, and the reprieve will allow you a moment to reset your mind and body for the final hour and a half. The clock is still ticking, so don't dilly dally, and be sure *not* to check your phone in case the proctors think that you're cheating. Your phone isn't allowed and could cost you the exam.

Some test takers report the other test takers as distractions. People come and go, coughing, sneezing, and all of the other lovely body sounds of a large group of people in a small room. Part of your training should be figuring out how to concentrate with a lot of movement around you. Plan to take an exam simulation at the public library or at a local coffee shop. Practice using headphones — the noise-cancelling kind, not the ear buds — to see if they help or hinder. On exam day, keep your mind on the task at hand, and be courteous to your other test takers by not becoming a distraction yourself.

Resist the temptation to be distracted by others who finish their exam earlier. They may be taking a different test. If you plan to sit for the exam with a study partner, chat ahead of time about what you'll do if the other finishes early. Don't give up if your partner finishes before you, and use all of the time allotted to maximum effect.

Avoiding Mind Tricks

It's easy to panic, especially if you're hit with difficult or unknown test questions right out the gate. You must train your mind to avoid negative self-talk or self-defeating statements. I have heard from many failed exam takers that they "knew they were going to fail after the first question" and that "halfway through the exam they realized there was no way they could finish all of the questions in time." These types of thoughts can cripple even the most prepared individual, so be on alert for them while you take practice exams and *shut them down* on exam day.

While you're taking practice exams, work on replacing negative thoughts by reminding yourself to take it one question at a time. Mark for review the ones that cause you anxiety, and then move on. Don't worry about what's coming; simply stay focused on the question in front of you. In other words, stay in the present moment.

A failing score doesn't mean that you aren't good at your job. As with most goals people set for themselves, it may take one or two tries to master the beast, but you're well worth it. Successful certification can happen for you, and the credential will result in career highs. Kudos to you for putting yourself out there and adding credibility to your profession that the business you serve and employees that you represent so desperately need. Your employer is counting on you to be the best HR practitioner that you can be, and the studying, application, and commitment is well worth your positive attitude as you go through this career-changing process.

Chapter 18

Ten (or So) Study Tips for the Exam Bodies of Knowledge

In This Chapter

▶ Finding ways to get (and stay) organized

▶ Subscribing to video channels to emphasize HR best practices

▶ Asking for help from subject matter experts

*O*ne of the biggest oversights of people planning to take the PHR or SPHR exams is that they don't properly utilize the roadmap that is the exam body of knowledge (BOK). This document is straight from the horse's mouth — the Human Resource Certification Institute (HRCI). Although many excellent preparation resources are on the market that have successfully prepared exam takers for decades, the exam BOK should be the foundation of all of your efforts. This chapter describes organizational tools and textbook-alternative resources you can create using the exam BOK as your guide. Doing so ensures that you have a well-balanced approach to tackling the exams that goes beyond simply reading a textbook.

There really is no wrong way to study. What works for you may not work for someone else so don't get caught up in form at the expense of content. The only constant for *all* exam takers is the exam BOK. Seek to understand what the roadmap is asking of you by applying the objectives to every facet of your studying efforts. If you can't align a topic with an objective, first work harder and do some research. If you still can't relate it, check out the knowledge requirements and see if you can make sense of it there. If you *still* can't match the topic to the objective, ask a question of an expert. After you have exhausted these options, simply move on.

Being Organized and Planning

Having a plan and then knowing what you need to do with the right materials can be the difference between streamlined studying that produces results or disorganized chaos that is stressful for all involved. The following items share a common thread. They're all tools that you can use to get ready to study:

✔ **Binders:** I'm a binder freak. For exam prep, you need one place to put all of the detritus that will collect during the preparation process. I recommend a binder with seven dividers — one section for core knowledge and the rest for the functional areas. Store fact sheets, notes, and other data related to the exam objectives. Follow this important process before you even first pick up your study guide:

  • **Print out the exam objectives from HRCI.**

  • **Divide it out by exam functional area.**

  • **Insert the documents under the proper functional area.**

Refer to these objectives every time you crack open a book or log in to study. In fact, attempt to match up what you read to the relevant exam objective or knowledge requirement to ensure that you're properly aligning your knowledge with what may be presented on the test.

- **Index cards:** Index cards are useful to breaking down complex pieces of information into manageable concepts. Consider color-coding your index cards with highlighters and using single colors for key exam concepts. Assign one color per exam objective or be more selective and use certain colors for difficult topics. For instance, I had trouble understanding Business Management and Strategy concepts during my exam prep, so all my notes for those exam objectives were in pink: pink paper, text highlighted in pink, and flashcards made on pink index cards. Using the same color adds another dimension of sorting, ordering, and cataloguing the data, making visual connections to eventually piece together.

- **Recordings:** Reading or speaking aloud into a recording device is a valuable technique that allows you to study the same material in different ways, first by reading it aloud and then by listening to it later. A client of mine once told me that a person's favorite word in the whole universe is his own name. Similarly, auditory learners seem to retain information better when they hear content in their own voice. I highly recommend reading aloud into your phone's recording device and playing it back while exercising or driving as a study activity. For non-auditory learners, consider this approach for difficult concepts. This way, when faced with the relevant info on the exam, you can recognize it because you studied it auditorily and you can travel successfully back to retrieve the information upon demand.

- **Peppermint gum:** Peppermint has been shown to be a gentle brain stimulant that increases both recall and memory. Peppermint *gum* has an added benefit for tactile learners. Chewing gum while studying is a physical activity and can help your brain create deep grooves for information recall.

Long-term retention of information occurs over time. You must engage in activities that help you carve out deep pathways to the place where your brain stores information so that you have an indestructible path to travel back to retrieve it on test day. Think of your exam preparation activities as a trail of breadcrumbs, guiding you back when you need it.

Using Outlines

An *outline* is a great way to condition your mind to build frameworks out of complex information. Examples of complex information on these exams include academic theories or processes that have multiple threads that must be followed to successful completion. An outline is a tool that forces you to extract the main point of a theory or process, and then fill in the blanks as you further review the data.

Try to write your outline from the *end* to the *beginning* of a concept rather than from beginning to end. Starting with the end will at first be confusing, but as you work your way up, your mind will be required to pay attention to the items that naturally help you fill in the blanks and make the necessary connections for understanding.

On the other hand, using outlines for whole chapters or exam functions has limited value. Outlining entire chapters/exam areas is a tactile tool to touch information through writing or typing it out. You can get greater value in selecting two or three related exam objectives, bringing in the core knowledge components, and then filling in the blanks with research.

Figure 18-1 is an example of an outline for Workforce Planning and Employment. Create one and go one step further and begin to research the sub-bullets by completing the information as it relates to the specific exam objective. Consider using the who, what, where, when, why, and how approach when researching the laws as they relate to the objective.

As this example shows, first identify the exam objective and knowledge requirement that belong together — in this case, 02 and 11. I then use the outline format to drag and drop other exam objectives that are impacted by 02 or 11. From there, you can do research to fill in relevant information from credible sources, such as the Department of Labor and the Equal Employment Opportunity Commission.

This type of outline is much more valuable than simply transferring information from a textbook or other resource, because it requires you to do the homework, think and synthesize, and then apply what you've studied to finish information related to critical exam objectives.

Challenge yourself to pick one topic per functional area and use the outline format to study. Remember that it's not enough just to transfer data; you need to give yourself a call to action to research, just as you would if the topic came up on the job.

Exam Objective 02-01
Ensure that workforce planning and employment activities are compliant with applicable federal laws and regulations.
Knowledge Requirement 11
Applicable federal laws and regulations related to workforce planning and employment activities; for example, Title VII, ADA, EEOC Uniform Guidelines on Employee Selection Procedures, Immigration Reform and Control Act.
Exam Objective 02-11
Develop and implement selection procedures; for example, applicant tracking, interviewing, reference and background checking.
* Uniform Guidelines on Employee Selection Procedures
* Fair Credit Reporting Act
* Privacy Act
* Laws related to defamation of character
Exam Objective 02-13
Administer post-offer employment activities; for example, execute employment agreements, complete I-9/eVerify process, coordinate relocations, and immigration.
* Title VII Civil Rights Act of 1964
* Immigration Reform and Control Act
* Department of Homeland Security—eVerify
Exam Objective 02-17
Develop and implement the organization exit/offboarding process for both voluntary and involuntary terminations, including planning for reductions in force (RIF).
* Worker Adjustment and Relocation Notification (WARN)
* Laws related to wrongful termination and wrongful discipline
Exam Objective 02-03
Conduct job analyses to create and/or update job descriptions and identify job competencies.
* Americans with Disabilities Act
* Occupational Information Network (Onet Online)

Figure 18-1: An example outline to create when studying.

© John Wiley & Sons, Inc.

Going Online

As I mention repeatedly throughout this book, particularly in Part III, the Internet has tons of resources that you can tap into to drill further into the exam objectives. Be careful because the Internet is full of potential distractions and rabbit holes from which you can fall (such as Facebook, Instagram — the list is endless) and emerge an hour later not having accomplished anything related to studying for the exam.

When you go online to gather more information about a specific topic, I recommend that you stay extremely focused. When creating your study plan, pick two or three exam objectives per functional area, and then plan to use online videos to support your studying.

Two credible YouTube channels that I recommend are

✔ **World at Work TV:** World at Work (www.youtube.com/user/WorldatWorkTV) is a nonprofit organization that studies HR practices from the perspective of total rewards. This free channel regularly posts videos about all things related to compensation and benefits, including sales compensation and other pay-for-performance programs.

✔ **SHRM Official:** SHRM Official (www.youtube.com/user/SHRMofficial) is the YouTube channel of the Society for Human Resource Management. Its video list includes a broad selection of many topics that are identified in the exam BOK, so this site is well worth regular visits as you prepare for the exams.

HRCI (www.hrci.org) has a list of study resources that you should utilize in your study plan. The site includes a list of books and management authors. Click on the tab titled "Exam Preparation" then "How do you Study?" to find the resources.

Interviewing Subject Matter Experts

More than likely, you have contacts in the industry who would be helpful in breaking down information related to the exams. You may even have a few at your place of employment. Taking time to ask these HR professionals about their expertise and about specific scenarios can help you study for the exam.

I personally believe that this tip is the most underutilized form of studying. When you want to interview someone, ask politely, and then be courteous of her time by coming prepared and narrowing your focus to her particular area of expertise. Expecting her to try and address every objective in a particular area is inconsiderate and unprofessional, so focus on the ones that best match her talents. For example, from Compensation and Benefits, take three related functional areas, such as 03, 04, and 07 (refer to Chapter 10 for them).

I assume that you outsource your payroll and are preparing to interview an expert at the vendor. Here are five sample questions related to these exam objectives:

✔ What kind of information needs to be collected and tracked for compliant payroll processing?

✔ What other payroll-related processes can be outsourced, and why should an employer choose to do so?

✔ What types of employee self-service technologies are you seeing emerge, and how can they be adapted?

✔ What are some common misconceptions about payroll outsourcing?

✔ What forms of training do you use for your employees, and would you recommend it to me as I prepare for this exam?

Presenting Unfamiliar Exam Objectives

One technique to master difficult concepts that I like to recommend is what I refer to as *teach-to-learn*. You more than likely have training responsibilities on your job. With the variety of exam objectives in all functions of HR, there is probably a topic in which your employees could use a training class. Pick an item that you aren't extremely familiar with and create a training presentation that forces you to go into research mode. Some examples include preventing harassment, coaching employees, or increasing production through employee motivation techniques.

If you don't have the opportunity in your job to train, look online for a local HR association and volunteer to present at a monthly or quarterly meeting. Preparing for a group of your peers may be just enough pressure to ensure that you master a difficult concept backward and forward, so you'll know it when test day arrives.

If neither of those options are appealing to you, take a difficult concept and try to explain it to your spouse or a friend who is unfamiliar with the topic. Note what questions he or she had and where you were unable to articulate a point. You can then plan to study it more in-depth to ensure that you understand the exam item.

Comparing HR Best Practices to Your Work Experience

Take some time to review the exam objectives for each functional area and compare them to how they apply to your workplace. You may not be surprised to note that you do things a bit differently where you work, which is because these are HR practices that HRCI — through field studies and interviews with subject matter experts (SMEs) — has identified as best in the field. Knowing where your workplace veers off of the exam objectives will raise your awareness on where you may struggle on your exam. For example, your employer may not place a high value on the strategic planning process. By doing this exercise, you can identify that you need to do some extra legwork to understand why the strategic planning process is a valuable tool for employers.

If you work in the type of environment where it's acceptable, take this strategy a step further and educate your bosses on why they should be doing things a different way. Practice building a *business case* (data-driven justification for a work activity) and use it to sway your employer to the best business practice of the exam objective(s).

Discerning Action Objectives from Knowledge Objectives

Closely look at each exam objective to spot action words such as *design, implement,* and *measure,* which is in contrast to the knowledge components that use phrasing such as *techniques, methods,* and *types.* Understanding *what* the exam objectives are asking of you will define the *how,* as in how you need to study the concepts and the *what,* as in what should be studied (techniques, methods, types).

Establishing both context and form is important. Understanding that you need to know how to develop (action) and test (action) business continuity plans (exam objective) is different from the knowledge of data storage and back up.

Work to spot these links and differentiate between what is actionable versus knowledge based. Doing so can help you interpret what the exam items are asking of you when you face them on the test.

Space Practicing for Success

Spaced practice is the studying of material over a longer period of time, which is the opposite of *massed practice,* which is more commonly referred to as cramming. Giving yourself 12 or 14 weeks to study allows your brain to absorb not only pieces of information, but also how the information applies as a whole. On a smaller scale, consider using spaced practice on a weekly basis.

For example, if you have ten hours per week to study, space that practice over five two-hour sessions rather than two five-hour sessions. Everyone has what I refer to as the *saturation point* when studying, and after about two hours your ability to absorb (and thereby retain for future recall) more information begins to diminish.

Knowing Where to Focus When Studying Labor Laws

These exams do have a few studying techniques that work better than others, particularly in the area of going over the labor laws. Concentrate on the following when studying labor laws:

- **Labor law names:** Particularly with the union labor laws, studying both the formal act name and the author names is necessary. These laws include the National Labor Relations Act (Wagner Act), Labor Management Relations Act (Taft-Hartley Act), and the Labor Management Reporting and Disclosure Act (Landrum-Griffith Act). Use the acronym WTL (standing for Wagner, Taft-Hartley, and Landrum-Griffith), which refers to the authors' names in the chronological order the acts were passed.

- **Dates when laws passed:** Instead of memorizing the dates, shape your knowledge in context. Focus on when laws passed, such as in the 1960s, 1970s, 1980s, and so on. Align the decades with social cues, and you're more likely to critically apply it on the exams.

✔ **The numbers:** You need to know the number of employee threshold that triggers labor law compliance, and be sure to review the number of months that activates certain activities, such as the Consolidate Omnibus Budget Reconciliation Act (COBRA) coverage and union elections.

Refer to the appendix for a more complete listing of the various labor laws you should understand for both exams.

Appendix

Federal Employment Law

*W*ith the exception of Business Management and Strategy (refer to Chapter 7), each functional area of the exam bodies of knowledge (BOK) starts with some version of "ensure that these activities are compliant with applicable federal laws and regulations." Hence, make sure that you're prepared for the PHR or SPHR exam and know these laws. Rote memorization isn't sufficient though. Become close friends with the information in this appendix. Focus on:

- ✔ **The number of employees that triggers coverage:** Regardless of the size of the employer you work for, a labor law applies. Some of the test questions attempt to distract you with incorrect information based on the number of employees required to trigger protection.

  Make yourself a table that has a few columns, as shown in Table A-1. Head each of the columns with a number and fill in the blanks with the labor laws that are triggered by that number of employees.

  You need to do the legwork here. The practice of doing the research to find the numbers takes you deep into the material, a sure way to reinforce the concept for recall on the exam.

- ✔ **Who the law is designed to protect:** Some of these laws protect the worker, some grant the employer certain rights, and a few others protect a union. Know who the law is protecting so you can interpret exam questions more effectively.

- ✔ **Why the law was passed in the first place:** Adult learners tend to retain information best when they understand *why* something is relevant. If this describes you, pay attention to a bit of the history surrounding the law or court case to improve your ability to recall the details on test day.

- ✔ **The employment context:** Many of these laws apply to more than one legal domain. Be sure and focus your studying on how the law defines the employment context.

Most of these labor laws in Table A-2 have some form of a frequently asked question (FAQ) document online. Take the time to access these documents (use credible sources such as the Department of Labor or the Equal Employment Opportunity Commission), and then use the FAQs to create digital flashcards or quizzes on free websites such as www.examtime.com. Other credential seekers may have already done some of this for you, so check it out.

Table A-1		Test Preparations	
1	**15**	**20**	**50**
Workers compensation laws	Americans with Disabilities Act	Age Discrimination in Employment Act	Executive order 11246
Fair Labor Standards Act	Title VII of the Civil Rights Act of 1964		Family Medical Leave Act

Table A-2		Important Employment Laws and Bureaus
Name	*Year*	*Description*
Payne vs. The Western & Atlantic Railroad Company	1884	Defined employment at-will.
Bureau of Labor Statistics (BLS)	1869	Established to study industrial accidents and maintain accident records.
Sherman Antitrust Act	1890	Controlled business monopolies; allowed court injunctions to prevent restraint of trade. Used to restrict unionization efforts.
Clayton Act	1914	Limited the use of injunctions to break strikes; exempted unions from the Sherman Antitrust Act.
Federal Employees Compensation Act (FECA)	1916	Provided benefits similar to workers' compensation for federal employees injured on the job.
Longshore and Harbor Workers' Compensation Act	1927	Provided workers' compensation benefits for maritime workers injured on navigable waters of the United States or on piers, docks, and terminals.
Railway Labor Act	1926	Protected unionization rights; allowed for a 90-day cooling-off period to prevent strikes in national emergencies. Covers railroads and unions.
Norris-La Guardia Act	1932	Protected the right to organize; outlawed yellow-dog contracts.
National Labor Relations Act (NLRA); also referred to as the Wagner Act	1935	Protected the right of workers to organize and bargain collectively; identified unfair labor practices; established the National Labor Relations Board (NLRB).
Federal Insurance Contributions Act (FICA)/ Social Security Act	1935	Required employers and employees to pay Social Security taxes.
Federal Unemployment Tax Act (FUTA)	1936	Required employers to contribute a percentage of payroll to an unemployment insurance fund.
Public Contracts Act (PCA); also referred to as the Walsh-Healey Act	1936	Required contractors to pay prevailing wage rates.
Fair Labor Standards Act (FLSA)	1938	Defined exempt and nonexempt employees; required and set the minimum wage to be paid to nonexempt workers; required time-and-a-half to be paid for nonexempt overtime hours; limited hours and type of work for children; established record-keeping requirements.
Labor-Management Relations Act (LMRA); also referred to as the Taft-Hartley Act	1947	Prohibited closed shops; restricted union shops; allowed states to pass "right to work" laws; prohibited jurisdictional strikes and secondary boycotts; allowed employers to permanently replace economic strikers; established the Federal Mediation and Conciliation Service; allowed an 80-day cooling-off period for national emergency strikes.

Name	Year	Description
Portal-to-Portal Act	1947	Clarified the definition of "hours worked" for the FLSA.
Patent Act	1952	Established the U.S. Patent and Trademark Office.
Labor-Management Reporting and Disclosure Act (LMRDA); also referred to as the Landrum-Griffin Act	1959	Controlled internal union operations; provided a bill of rights for union members; required a majority vote of members to increase dues; allowed members to sue the union; set term limits for union leaders.
Equal Pay Act	1963	Required that employees performing substantially similar or identical work be paid the same wage or salary rate.
Title VII of the Civil Rights Act	1964	Established the Equal Employment Opportunity Commission (EEOC); prohibited employment discrimination on the basis of race, color, religion, national origin, or sex.
Executive Order (EO) 11246	1965	Prohibited employment discrimination on the basis of race, creed, color, or national origin; required affirmative steps for all terms and conditions of employment; required a written Affirmative Action Plan (AAP) for contractors with 50 employees.
Immigration and Nationality Act (INA)	1965	Eliminated national origin, race, and ancestry as bars to immigration; set immigration goals for reunifying families and preference for specialized skills.
Service Contract Act	1965	Required government contractors to pay prevailing wages and benefits.
Age Discrimination in Employment Act (ADEA)	1967	Prohibited discrimination against persons 40 years of age or older; established conditions for bona fide occupational qualification (BFOQ) exceptions.
EO 11375	1967	Added sex to the protected classes in EO 11246.
Consumer Credit Protection Act (CCPA)	1968	Limited garnishment amounts on employee wages; prohibited discharge of employees for a single garnishment order.
EO 11478	1969	Included disabled individuals and those 40 years of age or older in the protected classes established by EO 11246.
Black Lung Benefits Act (BLBA)	1969	Provided benefits for coal miners suffering from pneumoconiosis due to mine work.
Occupational Safety and Health Act (OSH Act)	1970	Required employers to provide a safe workplace and comply with safety and health standards; established the Occupational Safety and Health Administration (OSHA) to enforce safety regulations; established the National Institute for Occupational Safety and Health (NIOSH) to research, evaluate, and recommend hazard reduction measures.

continued

Table A-2 *(continued)*

Name	Year	Description
Fair Credit Reporting Act (FCRA)	1970	Required employers to notify candidates that credit reports may be obtained; required written authorization by the candidate and that the employer provides a copy of the report to the candidate before taking an adverse action.
Griggs vs. Duke Power	1971	USSC: Required employers to show that job requirements are related to the job; established that lack of intention to discriminate isn't a defense against claims of discrimination.
Equal Employment Opportunity Act (EEOA)	1972	Established that complainants have the burden of proof for disparate impact; provided litigation authority for the EEOC; extended the time to file complaints.
Rehabilitation Act (RA)	1973	Expanded opportunities for individuals with physical or mental disabilities; provided remedies for victims of discrimination.
Privacy Act	1974	Prohibited federal agencies from sharing information collected about individuals.
Vietnam Era Veterans Readjustment Assistance Act (VEVRAA)	1974	Provided equal opportunity and affirmative action for Vietnam veterans.
Employee Retirement Income Security Act (ERISA)	1974	Established requirements for pension, retirement, and welfare benefit plans including medical, hospital, accidental death and dismemberment (AD&D), and unemployment benefits.
Albemarle Paper vs. Moody	1975	USSC: Required that employment tests be validated; subjective supervisor rankings aren't sufficient validation; criteria must be tied to job requirements.
NLRB vs. J. Weingarten, Inc.	1975	USSC: Established that union employees have the right to request union representation during any investigatory interview that could result in disciplinary action.
Washington vs. Davis	1976	USSC: Established that employment-selection tools that adversely impact protected classes are lawful if they have been validated to show future success on the job.
Copyright Act	1976	Defined fair use of copyrighted work; set the term of copyright effectiveness.
Mine Safety and Health Act (MSHA)	1977	Established mandatory mine safety and health standards and created the Mine Safety and Health Administration (MSHA).
Automobile Workers vs. Johnson Controls, Inc.	1977	USSC: "Decisions about the welfare of the next generation must be left to the parents who conceive, bear, support, and raise them, rather than to the employers who hire those parents."

Name	Year	Description
Uniform Guidelines on Employee Selection Procedures (UGESP)	1978	Established guidelines to ensure that selection procedures are both job related and valid predictors of job success.
Pregnancy Discrimination Act (PDA)	1978	Required that pregnancy be treated the same as any other short-term disability.
Civil Service Reform Act	1978	Created the Senior Executive Service, the Merit Systems Protection Board (MSPB), the Office of Personnel Management (OPM), and the Federal Labor Relations Authority (FLRA).
Revenue Act	1978	Established Section 125 and 401(k) plans for employees.
EO 12138	1979	Created the National Women's Business Enterprise Policy; required affirmative steps to promote and support women's business enterprises.
Guidelines on Sexual Harassment	1980	Assisted employers to develop antiharassment policies, establish complaint procedures, and investigate complaints promptly and impartially.
Retirement Equity Act	1984	Lowered the age limits on participation and vesting in pension benefits; required written spousal consent to not provide survivor benefits; restricted conditions placed on survivor benefits.
Consolidated Omnibus Budget Reconciliation Act (COBRA)	1986	Consolidated Omnibus Provided continuation of group health coverage upon a qualifying event.
Tax Reform Act	1986	Reduced income tax rates and brackets.
Immigration Reform and Control Act (IRCA)	1986	Prohibited employment of individuals who aren't legally authorized to work in the United States; required I-9s for all employees.
Drug-Free Workplace Act	1988	Required federal contractors to develop and implement drug-free workplace policies.
Employee Polygraph Protection Act (EPPA)	1988	Prohibited the use of lie-detector tests except under limited circumstances.
Worker Adjustment and Retraining Notification Act (WARN Act)	1988	Required 60 days' notice for mass layoffs or plant closings; defined mass layoffs and plant closings; identified exceptions to the requirements.
Americans with Disabilities Act (ADA)	1990	Required reasonable accommodation for qualified individuals with disabilities.
Older Worker Benefit Protection Act (OWBPA)	1990	Amended ADEA to prevent discrimination in benefits for workers 40 years of age and older; added requirements for waivers.
Immigration Act	1990	Required the prevailing wage for holders of H1(b) visas; set H1(b) quotas.
Civil Rights Act (CRA)	1991	Allowed compensatory and punitive damages; provided for jury trials; established defenses to disparate impact claims.

continued

Table A-2 *(continued)*

Name	Year	Description
Glass Ceiling Act	1991	Established a commission to determine whether a glass ceiling exists and identify barriers for women and minorities. As a result, the Office of Federal Contract Compliance Programs (OFCCP) conducts audits of the representation of women and minorities at all corporate levels.
Unemployment Compensation Amendments	1992	Reduced rollover rules for lump-sum distributions of qualified retirement plans; required 20 percent withholding for some distributions.
Energy Policy Act of 1992	1992	Allowed employers to provide a nontaxable fringe benefit to employees engaged in qualified commuter activities such as bicycling and mass transit.
Family and Medical Leave Act (FMLA)	1993	Required qualifying employers to provide 12 weeks of unpaid leave to eligible employees for the birth or adoption of a child or to provide care for defined relatives with serious health conditions or to employees unable to perform job duties due to a serious health condition.
Taxman vs. Board of Education of Piscataway	1993	Found that in the absence of past discrimination or underrepresentation of protected classes, preference may not be given to protected classes in making layoff decisions.
Harris vs. Forklift Systems	1993	USSC: Defined an actionable hostile work environment as that which falls between merely offensive and that which results in tangible psychological injury.
Omnibus Budget Reconciliation Act (OBRA)	1993	Revised rules for employee benefits; set the maximum deduction for executive pay at $1 million; mandated some benefits for medical plans.
Uniformed Services Employment and Reemployment Rights Act (USERRA)	1994	Protected the reemployment and benefit rights of reservists called to active duty.
Congressional Accountability Act (CAA)	1995	Required all federal employment legislation passed by Congress to apply to congressional employees.
Illegal Immigration Reform and Immigrant Responsibility Act (IIRIRA)	1996	Reduced the number and types of acceptable documents used to prove identity and employment eligibility, and launched the eVerify pilot programs.
Mental Health Parity Act (MHPA)	1996	Required insurers to provide the same limits for mental health benefits that are provided for other types of health benefits.
Health Insurance Portability and Accountability Act (HIPAA)	1996	Prohibited discrimination based on health status; limited health insurance restrictions for preexisting conditions; required a Certificate of Group Health Plan Coverage upon plan termination.

Name	Year	Description
Personal Responsibility and Work Opportunity Reconciliation Act	1996	Required employers to provide information about all new or rehired employees to state agencies to enforce child-support orders.
Small Business Job Protection Act	1996	Redefined highly compensated individuals; detailed minimum participation requirements; simplified 401(k) tests; corrected qualified plan and disclosure requirements.
Small Business Regulatory Enforcement Fairness Act (SBREFA)	1996	Provided that a Small Business Administration (SBA) ombudsman act as an advocate for small business owners in the regulatory process.
EO 13087	1998	Expanded coverage of protected classes in EO 11246 to include sexual orientation.
Burlington Industries vs. Ellerth	1998	USSC: Established that employers have vicarious liability for employees victimized by supervisors with immediate or higher authority over them who create an actionable hostile work environment.
Faragher vs. City of Boca Raton	1998	USSC: Established that employers are responsible for employee actions and have a responsibility to control them.
Oncale vs. Sundowner Offshore Services, Inc.	1998	USSC: Extended the definition of sexual harassment to include same-sex harassment.
NLRB: Epilepsy Foundation of Northeast Ohio	2000	Extended Weingarten rights to nonunion employees by allowing employees to request a co-worker be present during an investigatory interview that could result in disciplinary action.
NLRB: M. B. Sturgis, Inc.	2000	Established that temporary employees may be included in the client company's bargaining unit and that consent of the employer and temp agency aren't required to bargain jointly.
Needlestick Safety and Prevention Act	2000	Mandated recordkeeping for all needlestick and sharps injuries; required employee involvement in developing safer devices.
Energy Employees Occupational Illness Compensation Program Act (EEOICPA)	2000	Provided compensation for employees and contractors subjected to excessive radiation during production and testing of nuclear weapons.
EO 13152	2000	Added "status as a parent" to protected classes in EO 11246.
Circuit City Stores vs. Adams	2001	USSC: Arbitration clauses in employment agreements are enforceable for employers engaged in interstate commerce except for transportation workers.
EO 13201	2001	Applies to federal contractors and subcontractors.

continued

Table A-2 *(continued)*

Name	Year	Description
Sarbanes-Oxley Act (SOX)	2002	Mandated improved quality and transparency in financial reporting and increased corporate responsibility and the usefulness of corporate financial disclosure; required companies to establish and maintain an adequate internal control structure and procedures for financial reporting.
Pharakhone vs. Nissan North America, Inc.	2003	Established that employees who violate company rules while on FMLA leave may be terminated.
NLRB: IBM Corp.	2004	NLRB reversed its 2000 decision in Epilepsy, withdrawing Weingarten rights from nonunion employees.
Jespersen vs. Harrah's Operating Co.	2004	Established that a dress code requiring women to wear makeup doesn't constitute unlawful sex discrimination under Title VII.
Smith vs. City of Jackson, Mississippi	2005	USSC: Established that ADEA permits disparate impact claims for age discrimination comparable to those permitted for discrimination based on sex and race.
Pension Protection Act (PPA)	2006	Amended ERISA financial obligations for multi-employer pension plans; changed plan administration for deferred-contribution plans.
Burlington Northern Santa Fe Railway Co. vs. White	2006	USSC: Established that all retaliation against employees who file discrimination claims is unlawful under Title VII, even if no economic damage results.
Sista vs. CDC Ixis North America, Inc.	2006	Established that employees on FMLA may be legally terminated for legitimate, nondiscriminatory reasons, including violations of company policy if the reason is unrelated to the exercise of FMLA rights.
Bates vs. United Parcel	2006	Established that when employers apply an unlawful standard that bars employees protected by the ADA from an application process, the employees don't need to prove they were otherwise qualified to perform essential job functions. The employer must prove the standard is necessary to business operations.
Taylor vs. Progress Energy, Inc.	2007	Established that the waiver of FMLA rights in a severance agreement is invalid. FMLA clearly states that "employees cannot waive, nor may employers induce employees to waive, any rights under the FMLA."
Repa vs. Roadway Express, Inc.	2007	Established that when an employee on FMLA leave is receiving employer-provided disability payments, he may not be required to use accrued sick or vacation leave during the FMLA absence.

Name	Year	Description
Phason vs. Meridian Rail Corp.	2007	Established that when an employer is close to closing a deal to sell a company, WARN Act notice requirements are triggered by the number of employees actually employed and the number laid off on the date of the layoff, even if the purchasing company hires some of the employees shortly after the layoff.
Davis vs. O'Melveny & Myers	2007	Established that arbitration clauses in employment agreements won't be enforced if they're significantly favorable to the employer and the employee doesn't have a meaningful opportunity to reject the agreement.
Velazquez-Garcia vs. Horizon Lines of Puerto Rico, Inc.	2007	Established that the burden of proof that a termination wasn't related to military service is on an employer when an employee protected by USERRA is laid off.
Genetic Information Nondiscrimination Act (GINA)	2008	Prohibits employment discrimination on the basis of genetic information. Prohibits employers from requesting, requiring, or purchasing genetic information, and describes exceptions.
Patient Protection and Affordable Health Care Act	2010	Created new requirements for employer-sponsored healthcare plans. Amended the FLSA to require large employers to provide lactation breaks and facilities for employees who are breast-feeding.

Index

About the Author

Sandra M. Reed is a leading expert in the certification of HR professionals. She is the co-author of the 4th edition of the *PHR / SPHR: Professional in Human Resources Certification Study Guide.* Reed is also the author of case studies and learning modules for the Society of Human Resource Management, teaching and writing content geared toward undergraduate studies at both public and private universities.

Reed is a sought-after, engaging facilitator of human resources and management principles, with a strong focus on management development and exam preparation. She is currently the owner of EpocHResource Group (www.epochresources.com), a management and consulting company based in California. She holds her Adult Vocational Teaching Credential from California State University, San Bernardino, and she is both PHR and SPHR certified through the Human Resource Certification Institute.

Dedication

This book is dedicated to my children, Calvin and Clara, who inspire (and require) me to be present every single day. And to Chris, my champion, whose own hard work and dedication gives me the freedom to explore. I am thankful.

Author's Acknowledgments

Writing a book feels like a highly personal experience, when in reality it requires a community of experts. In fact, the overriding theme of this text is that you need multiple resources to prepare for these exams; nowhere does that principle apply better than when publishing a book.

Many thanks to Michelle Hacker, project manager extraordinaire, whose cool head and calm nudges kept me on task, especially when I was panicking about things like gerunds. Also thanks to Erin Calligan Mooney, for believing in my talent. Thanks to Dr. Ed Hernandez, my technical editor; when he signed on to edit I breathed a huge sigh of relief, knowing that he was right there to challenge and expand on what the reader needs to know to successfully pass these exams. Also thanks to Chad Sievers, development editor, whose professionalism kept the work flowing properly while challenging me to be bigger, faster, better, stronger. When did a double space at the end of a sentence stop being a thing?

Finally, thanks so much to the best clients in the world (MVF, TGS, VWC, RFC, LQSLC, UOP) for writing me a hall pass for an intense few months without giving me permission to disappear entirely. The candidness, transparency, and boots-on-the-ground feedback became critical resources to call upon for real-world examples of HR in the trenches.

Publisher's Acknowledgments

Executive Editor: Lindsay Lefevere, Erin Calligan Mooney

Project Manager: Michelle Hacker

Development Editor: Chad R. Sievers

Copy Editor: Chad R. Sievers

Technical Editor: Ed Hernandez, PhD

Art Coordinator: Alicia B. South

Production Editor: Shaik Siddique

Cover Photos: © iStockphoto.com/Mark Stay

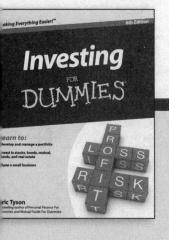
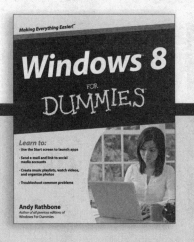

Anatomy and Physiology For Dummies,
2nd Edition
978-0-470-92326-9

Astronomy For Dummies, 3rd Edition
978-1-118-37697-3

Biology For Dummies, 2nd Edition
978-0-470-59875-7

Chemistry For Dummies, 2nd Edition
978-1-118-00730-3

1001 Algebra II Practice Problems
For Dummies
978-1-118-44662-1

Microsoft Office

Excel 2013 For Dummies
978-1-118-51012-4

Office 2013 All-in-One For Dummies
978-1-118-51636-2

PowerPoint 2013 For Dummies
978-1-118-50253-2

Word 2013 For Dummies
978-1-118-49123-2

Music

Blues Harmonica For Dummies
978-1-118-25269-7

Guitar For Dummies, 3rd Edition
978-1-118-11554-1

iPod & iTunes For Dummies, 10th Edition
978-1-118-50864-0

Programming

Beginning Programming with C
For Dummies
978-1-118-73763-7

Excel VBA Programming For Dummies,
3rd Edition
978-1-118-49037-2

Java For Dummies, 6th Edition
978-1-118-40780-6

Religion & Inspiration

The Bible For Dummies
978-0-7645-5296-0

Buddhism For Dummies, 2nd Edition
978-1-118-02379-2

Catholicism For Dummies, 2nd Edition
978-1-118-07778-8

Self-Help & Relationships

Beating Sugar Addiction For Dummies
978-1-118-54645-1

Meditation For Dummies, 3rd Edition
978-1-118-29144-3

Seniors

Laptops For Seniors For Dummies,
3rd Edition
978-1-118-71105-7

Computers For Seniors For Dummies,
3rd Edition
978-1-118-11553-4

iPad For Seniors For Dummies,
6th Edition
978-1-118-72826-0

Social Security For Dummies
978-1-118-20573-0

Smartphones & Tablets

Android Phones For Dummies,
2nd Edition
978-1-118-72030-1

Nexus Tablets For Dummies
978-1-118-77243-0

Samsung Galaxy S 4 For Dummies
978-1-118-64222-1

Samsung Galaxy Tabs For Dummies
978-1-118-77294-2

Test Prep

ACT For Dummies, 5th Edition
978-1-118-01259-8

ASVAB For Dummies, 3rd Edition
978-0-470-63760-9

GRE For Dummies, 7th Edition
978-0-470-88921-3

Officer Candidate Tests For Dummies
978-0-470-59876-4

Physician's Assistant Exam For Dummie
978-1-118-11556-5

Series 7 Exam For Dummies
978-0-470-09932-2

Windows 8

Windows 8.1 All-in-One For Dummies
978-1-118-82087-2

Windows 8.1 For Dummies
978-1-118-82121-3

Windows 8.1 For Dummies, Book + DV
Bundle
978-1-118-82107-7

e **Available in print and e-book formats.**

Available wherever books are sold. **For more information or to order direct visit www.dummies.com**

Take Dummies with you everywhere you go!

Whether you are excited about e-books, want more from the web, must have your mobile apps, or are swept up in social media, Dummies makes everything easier.

Leverage the Power

For Dummies is the global leader in the reference category and one of the most trusted and highly regarded brands in the world. No longer just focused on books, customers now have access to the For Dummies content they need in the format they want. Let us help you develop a solution that will fit your brand and help you connect with your customers.

Advertising & Sponsorships

Connect with an engaged audience on a powerful multimedia site, and position your message alongside expert how-to content.

Targeted ads • Video • Email marketing • Microsites • Sweepstakes sponsorship

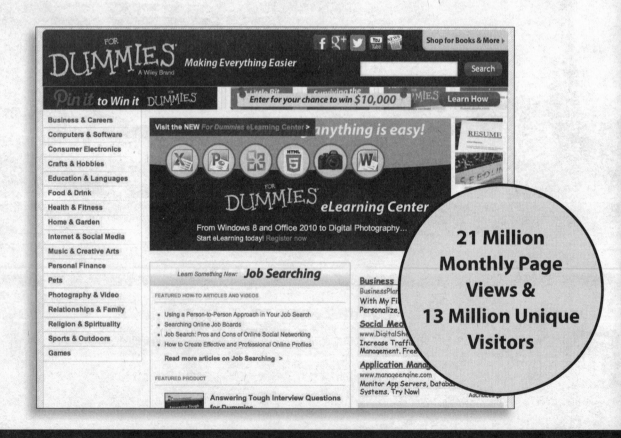

21 Million Monthly Page Views & 13 Million Unique Visitors

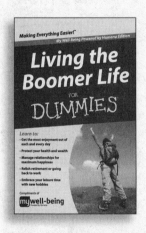

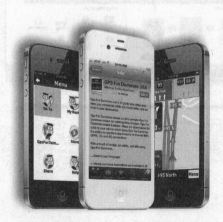